Theology without Deception

THEOLOGY WITHOUT DECEPTION

God, the Poor, and Reality in El Salvador

Jon Sobrino

Conversations with Charo Mármol

ORBIS BOOKS
Maryknoll, New York 10545

Founded in 1970, Orbis Books endeavors to publish works that enlighten the mind, nourish the spirit, and challenge the conscience. The publishing arm of the Maryknoll Fathers and Brothers, Orbis seeks to explore the global dimensions of the Christian faith and mission, to invite dialogue with diverse cultures and religious traditions, and to serve the cause of reconciliation and peace. The books published reflect the views of their authors and do not represent the official position of the Maryknoll Society. To learn more about Maryknoll and Orbis Books, please visit our website at www.orbisbooks.com.

Library of Congress Cataloging-in-Publication Data

Names: Sobrino, Jon, Interviewee. | Marmól, Charo, Interviewer.
Title: Theology without deception : God, the poor, and reality in El Salvador / Jon Sobrino ; conversations with Charo Mármol.
Other titles: Conversaciones con Jon Sobrino. English
Description: Maryknoll, NY : Orbis Books, [2023] | Translation of: Conversaciones con Jon Sobrino. | Includes bibliographical references and index. | Summary: "A theological memoir by Jesuit liberation theologian Jon Sobrino"—Provided by publisher.
Identifiers: LCCN 2022051241 (print) | LCCN 2022051242 (ebook) | ISBN 9781626985216 (trade paperback) | ISBN 9781608339839 (epub)
Subjects: LCSH: Sobrino, Jon—Interviews. | Jesuits—El Salvador—Interviews. | Liberation theology. | Church and social problems—El Salvador.
Classification: LCC BX4705.S66385 .A5 2023 (print) | LCC BX4705.S66385 (ebook) | DDC 230.2097284—dc23/eng/20230126
LC record available at https://lccn.loc.gov/2022051241
LC ebook record available at https://lccn.loc.gov/2022051242

To my parents, Juan and Rosario.

And to my sisters, Txaro and Mari Loli.

They have already walked with God until the end.

Contents

Prologue

When this book sees the light it will be just five years since I was asked by the PPC publishing house to conduct and write a long interview with Jon Sobrino. The idea was to frame it within the framework of the 50th anniversary of the Second Vatican Council and to talk about what this had meant for a theologian of Sobrino's stature and figure. Without thinking too much about it, and without foreseeing what I was embarking on, I accepted the proposal,

But since then a lot has happened. I met Jon on several occasions, three times in the first two years. On those occasions we met at various times and chatted at length. As a product of those meetings and conversations, in March 2015 I sent the publisher a manuscript that, although printed, never made it to bookstores.

I think that Sobrino must have considered that simple work too slight for all that he had to say, and so he began to work on a project that has continued throughout these years, interrupted by various vicissitudes: illnesses, the beatification of Monseñor Romero, and a thousand other demands he has attended to throughout this time.

We have kept in touch, always through email, with me encouraging Jon to write and he encouraging me to be patient about a work that seemed to have no end in sight. But that end has finally arrived, and it has made all the waiting worthwhile.

The final result is a work in which we can meet the son, the brother, the theologian, the companion, the student. . . . Through these pages I believe we can approach the most intimate parts of the person, where he speaks not only about the poor, but of how he has lived his relationship with the poor; where he speaks not only of theology, but about his path in doing that theology. He speaks of God and his relationship with God. And, of course, he speaks about the people who have been important and have marked his history.

I remember an occasion when I had to prepare a prayer with a group for the end of the year. I thought about offering a prayer of thanksgiving. I cut out drawings of a footprint and distributed them around the chapel. I invited the people who were with me to be silent, to pray, and to think of those who had left a footprint in their lives. They collected the footprints and wrote on each of them the names of the people who had marked their lives.

I believe that the first version of this book, simple as it was, was the template of the footprint from which Jon has written and remembered all those who have been companions along the way: Karl Rahner, Pedro Arrupe ("he helped me to think about theology and above all for God to appear"), Rutilio Grande ("on March 12, 1977, Rutilio Grande was assassinated along with two peasants. . . . That day I encountered Christianity"), Monseñor Oscar Romero, Ignacio Ellacuría. The references to Romero and Ellacuría are a transversal axis throughout the book. "With Monseñor Romero, God passed through El Salvador," Ellacuría said. "With Romero and Ellacuría, with the Salvadoran people," I dare say, "God passed through Jon's life."

> In St. Louis, the *problem* of God "arose" for me, unexpectedly and unthinkingly, as the greatest of all problems, and with it there burst in an experience of suspicion, doubt, bewilderment, and a kind of bottomless sadness. God was fading away. . . .
>
> In El Salvador, it was the poor—and the impoverished—who "burst in," *not the problem* of the poor, but *their factual reality,* and with it a clear word addressed to us, the non-poor, that I was unable to silence. And unlike what happened in Saint Louis, the reality of the poor was imposed on me naturally and peacefully, and my primary reaction was one of gratitude. Something good had happened to me.

In these conversations with Sobrino his sincerity is striking, especially as he traces his journey from the beginning as a European theologian who discusses and thinks about God to the theologian who discovers in the poor, in the crucified people, the God of life:

> My insertion, in the sense of direct contact with the poor, has been minimal. I did try to go periodically to places of the poor

in the suburbs of San Salvador, and in times of war, especially to the shelters. . . . Whatever the reason for my lack of insertion, as we awoke from our sleep, I discovered that the poor were human beings whom the sin of the world had turned into human waste and scrap. And, without looking for it, what came to my mind is that *sin is what gives death.* . . . And without looking for it, what also came to my mind is that *God is the God of life.*

Of course, he speaks of the martyrs and the mark they have left on him. I end by underlining one of Jon's paragraphs which I think is particularly relevant:

> In Jesus, the poor are the recipients of the kingdom of God, and that God, and no other, was the ultimate reality that I was thinking about. It is the God who expressed himself in the words, "I have heard the cry of my people and have come down to set them free." In the words of Micah: "Listen once and for all to what is good and what I desire of you: that you practice justice, that you love tenderly, and that, in history, you walk humbly with your God."

I don't want to delay you any longer from immersing yourselves in the work you hold in your hands. But I want to thank Jon for the effort he has made over the years to write this book. There have been many difficulties along the way, but we have succeeded. Thank you.

—Charo Mármol

1

In the First World

Training and Studies, the Problem of God, Karl Rahner

✧ *The first thing that struck me when I dive into your biography is that I find a Basque born in Barcelona. How did this happen?*

My family was mostly Basque, both grandmothers and my maternal grandfather. My parents, Juan and Rosario, lived in a town called Barrika, about twelve miles from Bilbao, and my older sister, Txaro, was born there. In 1937, Franco entered Bilbao. My grandfather was deported to a prison in Cadiz, and two aunts, my mother's sisters, who were eighteen or twenty years old, also spent a few months in prison near Barrika.

My father was a sailor, and with my mother they must have decided to go to live in Barcelona, still a Republican zone, where many Basque families were already living. I was born there in 1938, and my sister Mari Loli in 1940. In 1950 we returned to Bilbao. As children, we were not told about these things at home. Later I started to learn about them.

✧ *Where did your vocation to the priesthood come from? What influence did your family have on your decision?*

In Barcelona I studied at the Jesuit school in Sarriá, and when we returned to Bilbao, I continued at the Jesuit school. After graduating in 1956, I entered the Jesuit novitiate in Orduña.

Vocation? I will say it simply. My family, my mother certainly, were very good people and Catholics of ethical integrity. They did not belong to any specific parish group or to any of the movements that abound nowadays. They lived the Catholic religion with conviction, naturalness, and generosity. From them—I believe—I received the fundamentals of how to be human and Catholic.

In my last year of high school it came naturally to me that God wanted me to "join the Jesuits." That's all. My parents never spoke to me about it or pushed me into it. Nor did they oppose it in any way. I think they experienced it as naturally as I have mentioned, although they obviously had a hard time with me leaving. When I told my father I was going to be a Jesuit, he accepted it with a little sadness and with greater peace. My mother, I think with peace, and even with normal Christian pride.

In the last few months I did find it hard to give up the normal dreams of youth. If you ask me why and for what reason I entered, I can only answer that something important was imposed on me, without my having any clear idea of what my life was going to be like. In later years I formulated it as a kind of "imperative," neither Kantian nor agonizing. It was a natural imperative that I believe was wrapped in the environment of goodness in which I was raised.

I did not feel it as a personal call, as if I had been chosen by God among many others. I have never thought like that. I did not understand this as a vocation "to be a priest" or "to be a saint," nor did I feel any special "apostolic" desires, whether to preach Christ or to save souls. Nor was I moved by the possibility of deep studies, and certainly it was not from fear of the pains of hell, a frequent argument in those days for deciding on religious matters.

My spiritual director at the school for the last four years, of whom I have fond memories, was convinced that I would "enter as a Jesuit." But he never spoke to me about vocation, nor did he move me toward it.

That must have been more or less the "imperative" during my first years. If you prefer the words of Saint Ignatius of Loyola, I entered "without hesitation or the ability to hesitate," and without knowing where I was going. And what strikes me most as I write these lines is that it did not even occur to me at the time that my parents would object. It was a good thing.

✧ *How did you end up in Latin America?*

I entered the novitiate in Orduña, in the province that was then called Castilla Occidental. It had previously been part of the territory of the province of Loyola and would later become so again. Very soon, during the month of *Exercises* that we began shortly after entering the novitiate, we were told that we could volunteer to be sent to Central America, more specifically to the novitiate of El Salvador. I volunteered, again for no special reason and in ignorance of what my future would be. I also did it "without hesitation or the ability to hesitate." Although now I think that, along with the imperative previously mentioned, a kind of invitation was also present. My family reacted as they had before. They accepted it without fuss and went to Madrid to see me off.

I think that for them the call of God and his demands were clearer than what I have conceptualized as an imperative and an invitation. And when speaking of these things we should remember that, in those years, ten, fifteen, or twenty years could pass without us returning to Spain, that is, without seeing our families again.

Why did I go to El Salvador in particular? In Latin America, at that time, there were few Jesuits and few vocations, with the exception of Mexico and Colombia, while in Spain there were many. The General Curia in Rome asked each of the provinces of Spain to support a specific region of Latin America and also to send novices, since the common language made it easier. My province was asked to send young novices to Central America, and so it happened. In 1949, Father Elizondo, together with seven novices, scholastics, and coadjutors who were doing their novitiate in Loyola, arrived in El Salvador and the novitiate was founded. Some of them, including the martyr Ignacio Ellacuría, became very well known.

✧ *How was your first encounter with Latin America?*

In El Salvador I encountered a very different world. I was struck by the poverty and religiosity, without understanding them. In that first encounter in 1957, and seeing that reality for the first time, I did not get to know what it really was. I understood almost nothing of the causes of poverty, nor was it explained to us. What to do was clear: to make of these people good Catholics, like us Castilians and Basques. The metaphysical presupposition, if I may put it this way, was that "we were the real thing."

To know its truth and to understand what I had to do, I had to wait until the early 1970s, when I returned to the country to stay. To say it from the beginning, *the fundamental change* in those later years was that the "imperative" that I was supposed to give something of my own to the Salvadorans no longer had priority. The priority, said without any piousness, but with total seriousness, was *grace.* I received something in El Salvador, without merit on my part, better than what I had given.

In October 1958 I took my vows at the Santa Tecla novitiate. And since there were no institutions in Central America to do the normal Jesuit studies—for that we had to wait until the UCA [the Universidad Centroamerica José Simeon Cañas]—was opened in 1965, I was sent to Havana to study literature, Latin and Greek, writing and rhetoric—in other words, the humanities.

On January 1, 1959, Fidel Castro triumphantly came down from the mountains with Camilo Cienfuegos and Che Guevara. . . . I think all of us Jesuits were happy, because the dictator Batista had had to leave the country. Together with Trujillo in Santo Domingo and the Somozas in Nicaragua, they were dictators, oppressors, criminals, and at the same time friends and lackeys of the United States. That was clear enough to me, but we did not have the capacity to analyze socially and politically what was happening, whether it was good or bad, why one thing or the other. At that time we did not even consider the specific goodness or badness of the Marxism brought by Fidel, who, as is well known, had been a student at the Jesuit school.

I was in Havana until June 1960. Personally, it was not an easy time. In terms of the atmosphere the arrival of Fidel produced strong upheavals in many social circles, as well as in the community life of the Jesuits. Several of the young Jesuits were Cubans. They were generally from well-to-do families, and with the arrival of Fidel they saw serious danger of having their families' property seized. They were understandably nervous and uneasy. Among the older Jesuits some were in favor of Fidel and others against. For us young Jesuits, such public discord among the older fathers was novel, disconcerting, and even scandalous.

I had already experienced new processes and novelties in Bilbao, Orduña, and Santa Tecla, but I had perceived them within a fundamental continuity. In Cuba, the experience was very different: the reality was not thinkable beforehand. Years later, and in the midst of very hard and explosive situations, I formulated the decisive importance of maintaining "honesty with the real," especially when reality shows itself unexpectedly and in a way contrary to what came before. That is, I think, what was beginning to impose itself on me, even without being able to formulate it, in those two years of my juniorate.

In the novitiate they had spoken to us about the unconditional openness we should have to "what God wants of me" in a context of social isolation. In Havana the context was very different. And it was not just a personal matter but a collective one. They were *real* realities, not just *possible* realities imagined in prayer with the intention of making us more like Jesus. And they were *greater* realities, surpassing what had gone before. And much greater novelties were soon to come.

✧ *And after Cuba?*

In 1960 I was sent to the United States, to Saint Louis University in St. Louis, Missouri. I found a world totally different from that of El Salvador and Cuba. And also coming from Franco's Spain, many things caught my attention, especially in the sense of freedom: freedom of expression, free elections, democracy. . . . I arrived when John F. Kennedy was competing against Richard Nixon in the presidential election, and I was also able to discover the world of television, since we were allowed to watch the televised debates. Everything was new and interesting to me, although I was also struck by the sometimes notorious ignorance of Americans when it came to geography and history.

As for my studies, for five years, from 1960 to 1965, I studied philosophy and engineering. The first three years I studied the normal philosophy course for the Jesuits, although already in those years I took some engineering courses. The last two years I devoted myself to engineering full time. I got a master's degree in engineering mechanics with the following thesis: *A Study of the Non-Harmonic Solution of the Harmonic Equation in Complex Variables.*

These were five important years for thought, very different from the intellectually more anodyne years in Havana. But they turned out to be complicated and painful because of two things I am going to dwell on. One was that the issue of *obedience* burst in. The other, more fundamental, was that the *problem of the existence of God* burst in. I am going to explain this at some length.

As far as obedience is concerned, I liked mathematics, and I had a knack for it. But I had no inclination toward engineering and never had much ability for it. But in those years in Central America the Jesuits were opening universities in Nicaragua, Guatemala, and El Salvador. And engineering was important. The superiors were looking for future Jesuit engineers.

In addition to my detachment from the study of engineering, I was soon strongly attracted to philosophy, which made it psychologically more and more difficult for me to study engineering. And I was frightened by the idea, at the age of twenty-two, that engineering would be my future in the Society, and perhaps for my whole life. My superiors, however, insisted, and I obeyed. It was the most costly obedience—I think the only really serious one—that I ever faced in the Society. The imperative that I have already mentioned was imposed on me, but in a very different way. This time it was without "the environment of goodness" to surround it, but hanging by a thread, by a duty that I assumed when I took the vows. And I felt nothing of invitation. While I was dealing with that, in my third year of philosophy I wrote a text entitled *The Virtue of Obedience in the Thought of Saint Thomas*. It was an attempt to find something reasonable in the essence of obedience and something reassuring in my personal situation.

So I studied both things, philosophy with passion and engineering with the *agere contra* [to act against] of which Saint Ignatius speaks. But fortunately, Father George Klubertanz, SJ, the prefect of studies at the philosophate, who was very intelligent and a great friend, grasped the situation very well. He proposed to my Central American provincial to make an exchange, that is, that a Jesuit from the Missouri province be assigned to the Central American province[1] to support engineering in the universities, and that I stay in the Missouri province to teach philosophy. He came up with the idea that in 1964 I should teach a short course on ancient philosophy and the next year another on the texts of Saint Thomas.

Seen from today, the most important thing I can say about the issue of obedience is that "it happened."

---

[1] I speak of the *province* throughout, although Central America was early on a vice-province; it formally became a province in 1976.

✧ *What about the problem of the existence of God?*

It began with the study of philosophy, a study that attracted me from the beginning. I was attracted to ancient philosophy, that of the Greeks, perhaps because it was the first thing they taught us. With pleasure I read Plato and his writings on Socrates. Aristotle was more difficult for me. And even with a mediocre memory I have never forgotten Epicurus for his sharpness and wit. Undeterred, he said that in the face of worry about death it is enough to accept the reality: "If you are not dead, you have nothing to worry about, and, if you are dead, you cannot worry." Later I also liked Saint Thomas, especially with the kind of rereadings of Thomism that were being made at that time.

The most important thing about the encounter with the philosophers, however, more than the content, was to find myself thinking and trying to understand things, sometimes with others, but in the end, alone, sometimes helpless, unable to accept without further ado the truth of my previous knowledge, however obvious it might seem and however venerable its origins. And I began to suspect that in what had previously seemed obvious to me there might be truth or falsehood, reality or unreality.

In my case, suspicion had its peak in the existence of God. That is what I would encounter directly in the study of the philosophers of modernity, the so-called masters of suspicion. But some pre-Socratics had already made that impact on me. One of them, Xenophanes of Colophon, said that "the Ethiopians affirm that their gods are flat nosed and black, and the Thracians have them with blue eyes and red hair." With that he did not deny the existence of the gods. He even affirmed that "there is only one god, the greatest among gods and humans, not similar in his form nor in his thoughts to men." But he pointed out that human beings create much, if not all, of the content of what we believe to be God. Years later I would read Feuerbach: The human being can engage in self-projection. God would become that self-projection of man. And in this way he not only affirmed that there is no God, but also explained why an idea of God could exist without a counterpart in reality. And, evidently, "God" resembled the human.

I also read other philosophers. Some of them impressed me: Albert Camus, with his existentialism, accompanied by an endearing flavor;

not so with Sartre. I was attracted to Gabriel Marcel and his hope, and Henri Bergson's *The Two Sources of Morality and Religion*. From all of them I think I got some benefit, especially from Bergson.

❖ *I see you read a lot of thinkers. Did you encounter any theologians?*

Yes, I did. In the library I used to browse through the books that came in, and although most of them were on philosophy, others were on theology or a mixture of both. The theological authors were unknown to me, but I began to read them with curiosity and eagerness, in case they would calm my bewilderment about God. They were in English. I read books by Hans Urs von Balthasar, Jean Daniélou, and especially Henri de Lubac. I really liked his books on the church and Christianity, brilliant, full of the wisdom of the fathers of the church. And I also came across his book *The Drama of Atheist Humanism,* which fit my concerns like a glove. I also came across *On the Theology of Death* by Karl Rahner, about whom I will speak at length later. And I came across some books by Miguel de Unamuno.

In the library of the philosophate, Unamuno's works were kept in a special place, together with forbidden works, either because they were listed on the *Index of Forbidden Books* or because they were considered dangerous for students. I think this place was called "el infiernillo" (the little hellhole). From what I had heard about Unamuno, I felt attracted to read him, a novelist, a poet, and above all for me, a thinker who was concerned about faith and religion. I asked permission to take his books out of the little hellhole, and Father Klubertanz gave them to me.

Unamuno lived a tormented faith, anxiously searching for God. In the epitaph he wrote for his tomb, he said it endearingly:

> Put me, eternal Father, in your bosom, mysterious home.
>   I will sleep there, for I have come back
>   disheveled from the hard work.

I have read it when I have had to preside at funeral masses of tragic deaths, those that usually leave the human being—and God—out in the open.

The readings I have mentioned can explain the confusion I experienced before the existence or nonexistence of God. And the reading of

Unamuno coincided precisely with an event that had a great impact on me. In the summer of 1963 I was taking a course in hydraulics at Marquette University when a famous Jesuit and mathematician of mature age committed suicide by throwing himself from the sixth floor of a building. How was that possible for a man who believed in God? Does God exist? Does anything make sense?

With the Second Vatican Council a previously unthinkable atmosphere of freedom had been generated, and so I could see that other Jesuit companions were also asking similar questions. Some of them came to talk to me about it, and it seemed, paradoxically, that when I spoke honestly about my experience, they found it helpful. I, for my part, spoke with two older, capable, understanding, and loving Jesuits. Their words somewhat alleviated my situation but did not entirely remove the darkness and bewilderment. In short, in the 1960s, faith, including the existence of God, was a real and central issue for many of us, one that was arduous and painful.

A few years later, in 1969, Ignacio Ellacuría, eight years older than me, used to talk about similar problems. He told a group of young Central Americans in Madrid that "Rahner bears his doubts about faith with great elegance." And I thought to myself that this was also the case with Ellacuría himself.

This is not the moment to enter into the subject of the existence of God, nor do I believe I have a special capacity to approach it conceptually. Now I just want to state how in those years in St. Louis the topic of God was deeply important to me. And, seen from now, I also believe that if "God" was the distressing problem for me, and not other serious problems of humanity, such as oppression and injustice, it was because the fundamental problem for me in those years was *myself*. In any case, I believe that the dark years of St. Louis left me with something positive.

Since then, whether in times of darkness or light, God has always been an unavoidable reference point. And it has certainly never occurred to me to *trivialize* the problem of God, in one direction or another, whether by dismissing it simplistically as a "sin of youth" or clinging to it with "the faith of the charcoal burner," which horrified Unamuno.

And I have to say that, even in theology, no other theological theme—the Trinity, the church, grace, sacraments, virtues and sins, the Second Vatican Council, or any other ecclesial event, including the beatification of Monseñor Romero—has interested me independently of the theme "God."

✧ *You have spoken at length about your time at Saint Louis University. Then you went to Germany to study theology. What place does Germany have in your formation as a theologian? Who were your European teachers?*

From St. Louis I returned to El Salvador and stayed there for a year, from June 1965 to June 1966. I gave introductory classes in mathematics and philosophy, but my dream was to study theology, specifically in Germany. And so it happened.

At the Theologische Hochschule Sankt Georgen in Frankfurt I pursued the four-year theology course. I had good professors who had been at the Second Vatican Council, although in my course they did not tell us much about it. The contact with exegesis was novel and also painful. I went through a crisis about the truth of the story told in the biblical texts. Modernism and especially the work of Bultmann made us suspect how little we knew about the reality of Jesus of Nazareth. And if we did, it would not be of much use, for the Christ who saves is the Christ of faith. He is accessed in faith, and faith saves because it consists in living a decentered life, with authenticity, according to Heidegger's existentialism. Demythologization was imposed, which in many purely factual matters seemed to me sensible and good. But in others it meant calling into question what had always seemed assured: the historical reality of Jesus and the content of his life and resurrection.

The jolt that the latter gave me was not as radical as the one in St. Louis, but psychologically it was not small either. Years later, in 1991, James M. Wall and David Heim, responsible for a series *How My Mind Has Changed,* asked me to write about my experience. In my response I expressed several of the things I have already said in these conversations. And when I came to the subject of the historical Jesus, I wrote, if I remember correctly, that, having to change many things in the face of the evidence of historical criticism, I sometimes felt as if my skin were being peeled off bit by bit. What was left of Jesus?

But the years in Sankt Georgen were not all about exegetical frights, and dogmatic theology did not pose the same worries. Understanding the need to know as well as possible the historical reality of the word of revelation helped me a lot in understanding its content. Whatever its factual reality, it was very positive to understand the depth and radicality of what it affirmed. I believe that this predisposed me existentially to accept, rather than discard, the reality of which the word speaks. At least to reasonably bet on it.

In Sankt Georgen I spent another three years to get my doctorate; my thesis was *The Resurrection of Jesus in Pannenberg and Moltmann.* Pannenberg enlightened me on some important things: the decisive importance of the kingdom of God for understanding Jesus; the proleptic, anticipatory character; the collective implication of his resurrection; and the necessity of historical, *kerygmatic* statements in order to be able to formulate meaningful transcendent, *doxological* statements. I felt that Pannenberg was a thinker of great depth, but he did not communicate to me the encouragement to put into practice what he taught.

Jürgen Moltmann was something else. Like many others in those years I was struck by his book *The Theology of Hope,* and it introduced me a little into the thought of Ernst Bloch. Personally, I was more impressed by his later work, *The Crucified God,* and the reason was not that I already had experience of the *crucified people,* which would only happen years later. But to seriously bring God and the cross together in a way that I had not seen before was a jolt, and it remains so to this day. I don't know if I understood his conceptual argumentation well, but I think I understood his personal and existential logic. Without the cross it is not possible to understand Jesus, of course, but neither is it possible to know about God.

And even in the context of hope, it has stuck with me that hope is possible not only with the resurrection, but also with the cross. Moreover, the cross offers hope a specific dimension that need not be offered by the resurrection alone, so that without the cross the hope expressed in the resurrection can be trivialized. This is not a common reflection, since hope is usually attributed *to*—and is usually based *on*—the resurrection of Christ, and moreover, in a dialectical way, as surpassing the cross. Moltmann, however, had the lucidity and audacity to write: "Not every life is an occasion for hope, but the life of Jesus, who, out of love, took upon himself the cross, is." In El Salvador I have often quoted these words to encourage victims and the oppressed when I have nothing left to say and I try not to slip into purely pious considerations.

Over the years I remember the impact of the theology of hope and have made use of it. Theology is *intellectus spei*—understanding hope—and hope seeks to be understood, *spes quaerens intellectum*. These are great and novel truths that I learned from Moltmann. But, personally, what I remember most about him is the real occasion of hope: a life of one who, out of love, bears the cross. Years later I rephrased theology as *intellectus amoris*—understanding love—and love too seeks to be understood— *amor quaerens intellectum*. Moltmann was fine with this reformulation as a fitting way to describe liberation theology.

I have had some personal contact with Moltmann. After the assassination of the UCA Jesuits in the garden, the soldiers dragged the corpse of Juan Ramón Moreno to my room, which was empty because I was in Thailand. And in the commotion a book fell from one of my shelves. It was Moltmann's *The Crucified God*. It was soaked with Juan Ramón's blood. Later we put that book in the Martyrs' Hall at the UCA. I took a photo and sent it to Moltmann. Years later he came to visit me, and he prayed at length in the garden where the Jesuits were murdered.

Returning to my thesis, I have nothing important to say. Due to lack of encouragement I spent a long time, too long, without writing much of anything. The final text was nothing special.

✧ *Seven years in Frankfurt is a long time. Can you say something you miss about it?*

For me it was good and profitable to encounter the tradition of German theology, and I do not regret having studied in Frankfurt. But it was a limitation not to encounter other theological traditions—French, American, Spanish—let alone the beginnings of theologies in the Third World. I want to dwell now on some limitations of another kind, although I only became aware of them years later.

The most important limitation consisted in *what we were not told* about realities of great historical, ecclesial, and theological importance of those years, although from the beginning I want to make a clarification so as not to be unfair. Some students had a different or more nuanced experience than mine. I had to wait until I returned to the Third World to learn about these new developments and their importance.

The first has to do with 1968. In Europe there were social upheavals, and something was also happening in Sankt Georgen. But around the same time, also in Latin America, social and other deeply Christian and theological developments were breaking out. However, I do not think that Medellín,[2] the new theology of Gustavo Gutiérrez, or the base communities were important news. Out of elementary honesty, I would like to remind you that I had no special interest in those topics, since I was still personally in love with God. But neither did the teachers arouse my interest in subjects outside the classroom.

There was a second, more serious limitation, which I only became aware of in 1977, when Rutilio Grande[3] was assassinated. Rutilio was not the first priest murdered in El Salvador. Father Nicolás Rodríguez had already been assassinated on November 28, 1970, but that was not widely known. With Rutilio began a stream of assassinations, hundreds of civilians and lay Christians, priests, and nuns. These murders, especially those of our Jesuit companions, would have a deep impact on us. And we reacted to them with the best we had. We spontaneously called them and all the others *martyrs*. They became central to us, as human beings, Christians, Jesuits, and theologians.

In this context, one day something came to my mind that made me uneasy. I realized that in the seven years that I was in Sankt Georgen, from 1966 to 1973, I do not remember anyone speaking to us about current martyrs, even though there were plenty of them in Germany during the Nazi era. From the awareness of the martyrdom that later burst forth in El Salvador, that silence seems inconceivable to me. The martyrs under the Nazis neither attracted nor bothered us. They did not exist.

I do remember hearing that Alfred Delp, a Jesuit, signed his last vows in the Society of Jesus while he was in prison, with his hands bound. He had been an outstanding example of a faithful Jesuit. But I don't

---

[2] The second meeting of CELAM, the Latin American Bishops' Conference, in Medellín, Colombia, in 1968, was a watershed event in the history of the Latin American church. Applying the teachings of Vatican II to Latin American reality, the bishops analyzed the prevailing structures of poverty and injustice, and strongly advocated for a prophetic pastoral mission on the side of the poor.

[3] Rutilio Grande, SJ (1928–77), was assassinated on March 12, 1977, along with two peasants in his car, an old man and a teenaged boy. As Sobrino discusses at length in this book, his death was a turning point for the church in El Salvador, particularly for its impact on Oscar Romero, the newly installed Archbishop of San Salvador. Grande and his companions were beatified in 2022.

remember hearing that he was arrested and put in prison for belonging to a group of anti-Nazi Jesuits who were meeting to see what to do
with Germany after the war was over. He was arrested and executed on
February 2, 1945. In any case, I do not remember Father Delp being
presented as a Jesuit martyr for justice, as we would call him today.

And in El Salvador I also became aware of a remarkable paradox related
to what we have just said. In Sankt Georgen, in courses and seminars,
Dietrich Bonhoeffer was frequently mentioned. The context was secularization, as a cultural and social reality, and its roots, real or possible,
in the biblical and Christian tradition. Given this context, it was normal
that the words of Bonhoeffer that I heard most often quoted in class
were that one must live *etsi Deus non daretur* (even if God did *not* exist),
which the professors tried to explain with varying degrees of success.

But, as far as I remember, they did not speak of the Bonhoeffer who
wrote the poem of the men who go to God and find him nailed to a
cross: "Christians remain with God in the passion."

And, above all, I did not hear them talk about the fact that Bonhoeffer had belonged to a group that wanted to eliminate Hitler. The Nazis
discovered him, and he was arrested and executed. They didn't talk about
it, or not much, and when I did hear about it, I was very surprised.

What I have just said about the silence of the martyrs in Sankt Georgen
may not be accurate. It could be that I was not particularly interested in
finding out more, preoccupied as I was with other problems. And in any
case it was understandable that Jesuits who had lived through the war,
some of them both wars, did not want to open very painful wounds.

✧*Anything else about your years in Germany that was important for your
future theological work?*

The most important thing was reading Karl Rahner. I already said
that, by pure chance, at Saint Louis University I read his book *On the
Theology of Death*. I did not know the author, nor was I particularly interested in the subject of death. But the book and the author attracted
my attention, and that led me to read any text I could find by Rahner. I
didn't understand everything I read, of course, but, unlike the way other
authors affected me, I was struck from the beginning by the fact that
Rahner always ended up touching "thick" subjects of faith, and that he
touched them as "real" things.

To begin with, I was very struck by what Rahner says about what theology *ultimately says*. With audacity and lucidity, he writes that, despite its many dogmas and moral assertions, Catholic theology says only one thing: "The mystery remains eternal mystery." There is no definition here, but there is a clarification beyond which I do not think it is possible to go to know what theology ultimately *says*. Rahner put into solemn words what I think I somehow perceived in the reading of his texts.

Regarding Rahner's understanding of *mystery*, the first thing that struck me is that he distanced himself dialectically from the understanding of *mystery* in use in his time. *Mystery* is not the *provisional*, but the *permanent*. It is not a characteristic of *a statement*, but the ultimate substratum of *reality*. It is not arbitrarily diversified into *a plurality* of statements, but *is the one reality* of God. That one mystery unfolds: *ad intra*, in the trinitarian reality, and *ad extra*, in Christ by nature and in us by grace. "God is the holy mystery," Rahner concludes. He is *mystery* because he is incomprehensible and unattainable. He is *holy* because he subtracts himself from us even in his very presence. And he is salvation. These statements of Rahner's on mystery have been very important for me.

As for the *content* of mystery in Rahner, I perceived it above all in how he conceives the incarnation; that is, when God decided to be not only God, he became flesh and took on the history of all human flesh. And he assumes it forever; the mysterious God never dissociates himself from Jesus. Already in 1953 Rahner had written about the "eternal significance of the humanity of Jesus for our relationship with God."

With Rahner, something important changed for me. I realized that Jesus is the story of the mystery of God. There is something in Jesus that makes God present. And there is something in God that does not allow him to be God without expressing himself in Jesus. This changed my theoretical thinking about God or not-God. And also, I think, my personal experience.

✧ *So far you have told us about the impact of the classical Rahner, an exceptional dogmatist and profound expositor of the spirit. Do you want to add something else about Rahner?*

In his last ten years I noticed a novelty in Rahner, not because he was disregarding what he had written or because he was replacing it with another way of thinking. But I believe that in his theological thinking and in his public behavior as a theologian he took more into account the social-historical dimension of reality.

Rahner had written in depth on the *humanity* of Christ, as is well known. Nevertheless, in 1972, without disavowing what he had said, he published the text of a course on Christology given in Münster together with the exegete Wilhelm Thüssing. His text was entitled *Fundamental Lines of a Systematic Christology*. What I found new in this text was his interest not only in the humanity of Christ, but also in the concrete man Jesus of Nazareth, which included a new interest in the kingdom of God and in the historical understanding of the meaning of the death of Jesus. I picked this up in my Christology books.

In 1971 Rahner published *Structural Change in the Church*. In it he made concrete three fundamental questions: *Where are we? What do we have to do? How ought we imagine the church of the future?* If I remember correctly, Rahner responded by addressing very concrete problems in the church, for example, whether a German Catholic could vote for the SPD, the socialist party. Today this may not seem important, but at that time it *was* important. When I read these things, Rahner seemed to me to be an *advanced person* in the church. And as far as his own past was concerned, he seemed to me to be a courageous theologian, not a stagnant one.

Also at the beginning of the 1970s, I remember my surprise when reading the manuscript of his great work *Foundations of Christian Faith* (which I had received in mimeograph prior to its publication), I saw that in the midst of his profound reflections he mentioned and analyzed the reality of *the banana plantations in Honduras*. What he had heard led him to rethink the social dimension of a reality full of injustice and to rethink the reality of the unjustly treated Honduran peasants. If I may be allowed the irony and humor, it made Rahner think a lot—and now with added interest—about *what a banana is* and *what sinfulness is*, expressed in the banana that the Germans were eating in peace.

In the early 1980s I had the opportunity to talk to him when we met at the Frankfurt Book Fair. Johann Baptist Metz had organized the day dedicated to religion. He brought together, if I remember correctly, four theologians—Rahner, Ernst Käsemann, and Leonardo Boff and myself as young liberation theologians. In a pause I went to greet Rahner and thanked him for his support of the persecuted Christians and churches in Latin America. "What less could I do?" he replied.

In the evening we met in Sankt Georgen and were able to talk more casually. Rahner was very interested in what happened at the meeting of the Latin American bishops in Puebla,[4] what the influence of John Paul II would be, and how the bishops reacted to the martyrs. It is known that Rahner had analyzed theologically and in depth the sinfulness of the church *as a church,* and not only in its members. The novelty is that Rahner was now seen to be interested and affected also by the real, actual, and concrete sins of the church, whose historical consequences he perceived. He was also interested in the positive aspects of Puebla.

I also remember that in those years he wrote a public letter in defense of the theology of Gustavo Gutiérrez. And I remember his public protest when the Archbishop of Munich, who was then Joseph Ratzinger, vetoed the appointment of Metz—the obvious candidate—to the chair of fundamental theology at the University of Munich. A large photo of Rahner appeared in a newspaper, raising his hand with an angry face and saying: "Ich protestiere" (I protest).

I cannot forget what this Rahner—of advanced age and very conscious of the historical reality that accompanies theological problems—wrote in 1983, a year before his death. It was a four-page article in the journal *Concilium* entitled "Dimensions of Martyrdom." His purpose was to "advocate a certain broadening of the traditional concept of martyrdom." For this he used his knowledge of church history and theology, and the sharpness of his intelligence. But in this article, in order to make his argument, he also made use of the realities of current history. And in the end, it was the best argument he had to offer about a new model of martyrdom: "Why should not Monseñor Romero, for example, be considered a martyr, fallen in the struggle for justice in society, in a struggle that he carried out from his deepest Christian convictions?" Thus Rahner argued to broaden the concept of martyrdom.

I believe that Rahner, though always rigorous and profound, was still growing, as a theologian, in historical maturity. His great friend Metz used to say to him with loyal friendship, but also in complaint: "Karl, how is it possible that you can do theology without taking Auschwitz

---

[4] The third meeting of CELAM in Puebla, Mexico, in 1979, was strongly contested between bishops who wanted to advance the directions set at Medellín and those who wanted to pull back. The final document is remembered for articulating the church's "preferential option for the poor."

into account?" My opinion is that, in his last fifteen years, the Christian and theologian Rahner was greatly affected, not just as a human being, but also as a thinking theologian by the immense suffering of human beings and that he was shaken by the responsibility to eliminate it.

In my work in El Salvador I feel I have been complementing Rahner. And the big surprise is that this happened in a world very different from the world in which I first encountered him.

2

Back to El Salvador

*The Irruption of the Poor and the Martyrs,
Awakening from Sleep, Glimpses of God*

✧*So far you have spoken at length about your formative years in Havana,
St. Louis, and Frankfurt. I think what you have said is very useful to know
how you thought before you began to teach, write, and publish theology on
a regular basis. As you have spoken, at the center of it all I think has been
God. But you have been suggesting that later things would change in important ways. And that change occurred upon your return to El Salvador
in the early 1970s.*

I stumbled upon something that would change my way of living
and thinking. Taken together, an "irruption" occurred. Unexpectedly,
new realities appeared with the strength to make themselves felt and to
impose themselves as *real things*. Living amid them, I believe that my
way of doing theology began to take shape.

When I returned in the 1970s, I found a different Savior. He let himself be seen, so to speak, in his truth, with strong demands and with the
capacity to offer salvation. The demands were not an imperative in the
sense I have spoken of before, but rather they were above all an invitation. We had to bear this reality that was bursting in, but it also bore us.

For me, that irruption was a good thing. I don't know if it came from
above, grace, or if it came from below because of some merit of our own.
It never occurred to me to wonder. Grace, merit, or both, the important
thing is that it happened.

Radically new things irrupted at two different times, although both
were related to each other, which was already a novelty. The poor *irrupted*

and the martyrs *irrupted*. And among the poor and the martyrs, God *appeared*. In speaking of God, I do not use the language of irruption, but the more modest language of *peeking in*, with the advantage, I think, that it is more mystagogic.

For me, first and foremost *the poor*—men and women for whom living is their greatest task and dying amid hardship is always a near destiny—irrupted. This is how I formulated it many years ago. Now I usually say that *the poor are those who cannot take life—health, education, rest, being appreciated—for granted.*

A conviction was also imposed on me. Poverty in El Salvador was not due to the limitations of nature but to the inhumanity of groups of individuals. They seemed to disregard the poor, but in reality they needed them in order to live in abundance. In the service of this macabre need, primordial injustice burst in. I call it so because it produced the poor. The poor were those impoverished by others in a thousand ways. And the rich were the impoverishers, in a thousand ways, of others.

This macabre relationship configured what Ellacuría later called the *civilization of wealth*. In this civilization, the engine of history is the accumulation of capital. Its meaning is the enjoyment of what has been accumulated. And, going ahead, let us say that this civilization can only be redeemed by the civilization of poverty. Thus, both injustice and the absolute necessity of justice had burst in.

The impoverished could be impoverished by the rich without provoking a particularly bad conscience in the rich because such a world seemed to them to be normal. Sometimes they even thought of themselves as benefactors of the poor. And when, in order to maintain their abundance, it was necessary to add repression to oppression, they did not hesitate to do so. They produced—I am talking about what I discovered when I returned to El Salvador—mistreatment, violence, murder, small massacres. And the violation of the Ten Commandments of God's Law irrupted, as if in cascade. In more primordial language, it was the violation of any human reality that should be at the basis of the organization of society, of the international community, of democracy.

The impoverishers were individuals with specific names. But, by supporting one another in various ways, they formed a large social group. They could be recognized by specific names. In El Salvador, one spoke of "the fourteen families." The untouchable social superiority of a minority of human beings over immense majorities burst in.

These minorities controlled and could manipulate practically all areas of reality. They shaped politics and the economy. They had at their service the armed forces and the police; other social forces such as law, commerce, and education; and also very often the ecclesiastical ones. They acted with autonomy and with greater or lesser shamelessness. They were clear signs that reality was structured in groups or classes. And these groups shaped the country in an iniquitous way. For me, social classes burst in.

It took me a while to grasp the structural nature of oppression. We did grasp that the evils were not the product of individuals alone. At the origin of "the poor" there was a force greater than individuals. It was the structures. We did not see these structures at first, and we spoke of them timidly, with dissimulation, so that the words would not sound Marxist. But the structural dimension of poverty soon became evident.

Capturing social reality in this way was a radical change we went through in those years. Here I am only mentioning it without analyzing it. What I want to insist on is that these structures irrupted as a whole as being really evil, that is to say, as doing evil, and as really pernicious, that is to say, as doing harm. They are of long duration, occurring both in times of war and peace. And their power is often greater than that of the new ways of shaping society.

The most tragic thing is that already in those years repression against the poor and against those who defended them was also irrupting, whenever it was necessary to maintain power and, more specifically, to maintain the accumulated capital. Repression became savage and ruthless.

In short, when I returned to El Salvador in the 1970s, I found that a world had irrupted, of which I had been unaware when I made my novitiate in 1957, and even when I became a teacher in 1965. It was there, but for me it had not existed. And as a counterpart, a greater novelty gradually appeared: the realization that salvation comes from the poor. Of this, I will speak later.

✧ *Don't you think that there is now greater awareness, and that it is no longer as necessary to insist on an irruption of the poor?*

Yes and no. Certainly, there is not nearly enough awareness of the reality of poverty and not enough determination to take decisive action to eradicate it. And it upsets me to hear that today the issue of poverty is already taken for granted. It brings to mind an anecdote from college.

A student in class told a professor to stop talking so much about Kant, saying, "Kant is already outdated." The professor responded, "Kant is not outmoded. The fact is that he is ignored." It bothers me that the irruption of the poor is not taken as an *explosion* but merely as a news item. And it bothers me when the authorities mention some undeniable aspects of that irruption but are silent about its essential roots. What began to break through for me was that the rich produce the poor and that the poor produce the rich. Then, gradually, I realized that there was a more unexpected irruption: the poor bring salvation.

Before I continue, I would like to mention the most important encounter I have had with the poor in El Salvador. Father Rogelio Ponseele, a Belgian, worked for many years in Morazán during the war. We Jesuits of the UCA knew him well. He spent six weeks in hiding in our house.

Once he sent me an invitation to visit Morazán, and especially to talk to Rufina Amaya. I went.

Rufina Amaya lost her husband and four children when troops fighting leftist rebels ravaged the village of El Mozote and other nearby towns in the department of Morazán in a three-day massacre that began on December 11, 1981.

The elite soldiers were from a US-trained battalion and they killed approximately eight hundred people. Señora Rufina Amaya miraculously escaped death by hiding behind a tree. She was thirty-eight years old at the time.

Rufina spoke to me with great serenity while showing me the different places where men, women, and children were separated and killed. She was the only survivor of the El Mozote massacre. Years later I have read how Rufina Amaya explained what happened:

> At five o'clock in the afternoon they started with us. They lined us up in rows of five; I was in the last one. They took the children away from us; they pulled the youngest one practically from my chest. They locked them in a house and began to kill the women. Two from my own row burst into tears and hysteria. I knelt down remembering my four children, threw myself to one side, and got behind a tree. In the confusion the soldiers did not see me, and I stayed there.

The military commanders always denied the massacre, while the US authorities tried to play down the news of the massacre, of which Rufina Amaya was a key witness before the whole world.

> My husband was one of the first to be killed because he wanted to get out of the line. I saw how they shot him and then hit him with a machete. We could see everything through the windows. By noon they had finished killing them all.

Rufina Amaya died of a stroke in a state hospital in the city of San Miguel at the age of sixty-three. Her body was transferred to a peasant community named after the Jesuit martyr Segundo Montes, which was built in Morazán after the end of the war, in January 1992.

✧ *You also spoke of a second irruption?*

The second irruption was that of the *martyrs*. It was the greatest irruption: human beings who struggled to defend justice and truth, with dedication, fortitude, and fidelity. All of this was to defend the poor we have just mentioned. For me, it was a great novelty. I was able to see human beings with a greater love. Only three years after my return to El Salvador, on March 12, 1977, Father Rutilio Grande, a Jesuit priest and companion, was assassinated. The impact was immense. Rutilio's assassination, along with Señor Manuel and the boy, Nelson, who accompanied him, brought about an important change. I think it made it practically impossible to turn back.

In the martyrs a reality more real than anything I had experienced burst through. Much more is said about these martyrs today than during my first stay in El Salvador, but much less is said than should be said. "The world has no ears to hear this rumble," Saint Ignatius of Loyola supposedly said when it was made public that a Borgia, viceroy of Catalonia and Grandee Spain, was to enter the Society of Jesus in the sixteenth century. Nor does the world of today have ears to hear the sound of the martyrs.

I have used the term *martyrs*. And I have done so quite naturally. I am not referring to Christians devoured by lions in the Colosseum in Rome, or to Christians murdered in the sixteenth century for belonging to one church or another, or to the priests and religious murdered in Spain during the Civil War.

The term *martyr* that emerged in El Salvador forty years ago, if we look at the external circumstances, had little to do with what we have just spoken of: murders at the hands of powerful empires, quasi-imperial monarchical churches, sacralized dictatorships, and so on.

Nor did the term *martyr* begin to be used simply because those who were killed publicly professed the Christian faith or other beliefs. In El Salvador people have been called martyrs, usually of Christian faith, who have been killed unjustly, innocently, and defenselessly, because they stood in the way and defended the poor and oppressed. This means that they are not called martyrs for the explicit proclamation of beliefs, not even of Christian faith. Rather, these martyrs are those who, some more and some less, lived and died like Jesus of Nazareth. In this sense Leonardo Boff calls Jesus the first Christian martyr.

Seeing the ways and reasons why many Salvadorans have been killed, I have no doubt that in life and in death they have resembled Jesus. For me, that realization is what irrupted.

✧ *Was there no third irruption?*

Properly speaking, it was not an irruption, but for me something new did happen: God showed up. He did not burst in with dazzling clarity in moments of darkness, nor did he overwhelm my freedom so that I no longer had to make decisions with fear and trembling. I was still circling "around God," but in a different way. God was coming out, and he was beginning to be different from the one around whom I had circled so many times.

The mystery was still a mystery, but of a different kind. It was a mystery of life, and unexpectedly, of the life of the poor. And it was a mystery against the death of human beings, and certainly against the death of the poor. It was a mystery grasped—or at least better grasped—among the poor and martyrs. God could not be *grasped,* as we used to say in philosophy, but God let himself be *glimpsed.*

The expression was suggested to me by Ellacuría at the end of his life. A few months before his assassination he wrote a long programmatic article entitled "Utopia and Prophecy in Latin America."[1] It was his last

---

[1] Ignacio Ellacuría, "Utopia and Prophecy in Latin America," in *Mysterium Liberationis: Fundamental Concepts of Liberation Theology*, ed. Ignacio Ellacuría, SJ, and Jon Sobrino, SJ, 289–328 (Maryknoll, NY: Orbis Books, 1993).

theological article, and it ended with these words: "Beyond the successive historical futures the saving God, the liberating God, *is in sight.*"

In conclusion, for me the irruption of the early 1970s was to a certain paradoxical extent blessed. Above all, that irruption has settled me in reality. And thinking of the poor and of the martyrs, and of the God who appears in them, I have come to write that "the poor bring salvation." More directly, "Outside the poor there is no salvation." Or even more directly, "In the poor and in the martyrs we see salvation."

❖ *I have the impression that you have summarized thoughtfully and densely what happened to you in the first years of your return to El Salvador. But let's go step by step. Is it after Germany that the most important stage of your life begins?*

Yes, I have explained what happened inside me, which may shed some light on how I was going to do theology. Now I am going to explain what was happening in Central America upon my return.

In 1974 I returned to El Salvador, although I had already spent brief periods there in the summers of 1970–73 to teach a theology course. In those first visits, without yet speaking of irruption, what struck me most was the *change* that had taken place in my Jesuit companions who had already been there for some years after returning to Central America. They spoke and thought very differently from the way I thought in Germany and from the way almost all of us thought in the 1960s. Then, I think we tended to think of ourselves with European superiority, hopefully without becoming absurdly arrogant.

I have already said that we went to Central America to bring salvation, to teach the Catholic religion without superstitions, and to demand moral conduct with the rigidity that, theoretically, the church in Europe then demanded. For example, there was the issue that many couples, especially in the countryside, were living together without getting married in the church. By the way, I was surprised when I learned that an important reason, sometimes the main one, for not getting married, and for not getting married in the church, was that the couple did not have the money to pay the priest or to celebrate a modest feast in the village. That embarrassed them. However, they were not surprised—as I was in those years—that a priest might have a wife and family, as long as he took good care of them, thereby fulfilling the fourth commandment.

More specifically, according to a long tradition, we Jesuits felt called to teach others, to help overcome ignorance. Many of the things I saw in El Salvador seemed right to me, some of them good. But it never occurred to me that I had anything important to learn from these Salvadoran Christians. Everything important for life and for being a Jesuit, I thought, I brought from Europe. Consciously or unconsciously, I think that we understood ourselves as *missionaries,* although that expression was not used, because that was the name given at that time to those who went to distant non-Christian lands. Without grasping the depth that the term connoted, we were missionaries because we were sent by others, and only years later did I understand what had never crossed my mind: being a missionary could be dangerous. It all depended on *by whom, for what,* and *against what* we were being sent. We were not bad, but we saw ourselves as superior outsiders. Evidently, this was more or less the case among the dozens of Jesuits who came from Spain. Each one can tell his own experience.

When I returned to El Salvador to stay, in 1974, my colleagues already spoke of the poor in a different way, along the lines of what I have mentioned: the poor were the impoverished. And above all they spoke critically of those who impoverished them, some of them former students of ours. Some more and some less, they began to put into words the inevitable questions: what had we Jesuits done in Central America in favor of the impoverished, and what, if anything, had we done so that the impoverished would cease to be impoverished? And a minimum of honesty with our past led to a new question that became the decisive one: what were we going to do to prevent others from continuing to be impoverished?

The impoverished poor became for me the real thing; I often consciously speak redundantly of the *most real of the real.* Certain books helped me to see it that way: *The Open Veins of Latin America* by Eduardo Galeano (1971), for example. But it helped, above all, as the scales fell from my eyes, that the impoverished poor revealed an indisputable fact: they were oppressed, they were a multitude, a majority. Coming from Germany, I could still have doubts about many things in heaven and earth, but not about the existence and fate of the impoverished poor and the impoverishing powerful.

❖ *You speak of a radical irruption upon your return to El Salvador. There was also an irruption in St. Louis, so you experienced two irruptions?*

For me it is important to answer this question not only to satisfy the reader's curiosity, but also to get to the bottom of many issues.

In St. Louis the *problem* of God arose for me, unexpectedly and un-thinkingly, as the greatest of all problems, and with it there irrupted an experience of suspicion, doubt, bewilderment, and a kind of bottomless sadness. God was fading away, and that burst into my psychology, of which I have already spoken sufficiently.

In El Salvador it was the poor—and the impoverished—who irrupted, *not the problem* of the poor, but *their factual reality,* and with it a clear word addressed to us, the non-poor, that I was unable to silence. And unlike what happened in St. Louis, the reality of the poor was imposed on me naturally and peacefully, and my primary reaction was one of gratitude. Something good had happened to me.

Then I asked myself what is this *irruption?*—a term that I now use naturally. And moved by the obvious dynamics of thought, I asked myself what the new irruption in El Salvador meant and what similarities and differences there were between St. Louis and El Salvador. Irruption goes along the lines of powerful and unexpected appearance. Later I related it to the demand to *awaken from a dream.* Well, that is what irrupted, with its own nuances, in St. Louis and in Germany. In both cases I was required to *wake up from a dream.* And the demand was radical: I had to wake up *in order to be human.*

In St. Louis, without being aware of it then, my awakening referred to Kant: "One must awaken from the dogmatic sleep," without delegating to others the personal and nontransferable responsibility of thinking on one's own account. "Have the courage to think for yourself," I read in Kant's famous essay, "What Is Enlightenment?"

In El Salvador I was referred to the Dominican friar Antonio Montesinos,[2] of whom I had no previous knowledge, and who in the

---

[2] Antonio Montesinos, OP (d. 1540), a Spanish Dominican on the island of Hispaniola, was the first European to denounce publicly the enslavement and op-pression of the indigenous peoples in the New World. His prophetic sermons had an enormous impact on Bartolomé de las Casas, inspiring his own prophetic witness.

First World (still today) was much less known than Kant. I am going to expand on the second awakening, since it has a humanizing potential that the Western world does not offer, not even when its democracies are going through the best moments of enlightened awakening. Let us listen to Montesinos: "You are all in mortal sin and in it you live and die, for the cruelty and tyranny that you use with these innocent people." Thus began his famous sermon before the encomenderos in Hispaniola in December 1511, a sermon prepared communally by the Dominicans, who chose Montesinos for the preaching because of his gifts as an orator.

Montesinos goes on to enumerate the horrors that the encomenderos committed against the Indians. He accuses them with irrefutable logic and corners them with the force of his eloquence so that they could not slip away:

> Tell me, by what right and by what justice do you hold these Indians in such cruel and horrible servitude? By what authority have you waged such detestable wars against these people who were in their meek and peaceful lands, where you have consumed so many of them, with deaths and ravages never heard of? How have you kept them so oppressed and fatigued, without feeding them or curing them of their diseases, that from the excessive labor you give them, they incur and die, or rather you kill them, to get and acquire gold every day? And what care have you for those who teach them and make them know their God and creator, be baptized, hear mass, keep the feasts and Sundays?

He continues: "These, are they not men? Have they not rational souls? Are you not obliged to love them as yourselves? This do you not under-stand, this do you not feel?" And he concludes, "How are you in such lethargic slumber asleep?"

This dream is not the dogmatic Kantian dream from which we must wake up. It is another dream against which Montesinos rebels without escape. It is to be asleep in a dream of cruel and unjust inhumanity. I remember to this day the impact Montesinos's words had on me, certainly for my personal life, but also for my theological thinking. In this sense Montesinos's words were also an irruption for me.

✧ *What did Montesinos's words make you think when you started doing theology?*

The fundamental thing, I believe, has been that "being asleep" and "not knowing" not only hinder or prevent thinking, and thinking correctly, which is obvious. More fundamental has been the realization that both make it easier to be responsible for *ethical and dehumanizing evils.* Then it occurred to me to think about *what kind and what degree of evil* there is or can be in being asleep and in not knowing. In order to grasp it, I tried to place them among other more commonly accepted evils. And I made the following reflection.

Normally there is an intrinsic relationship between violations of the fifth commandment, that is, causing death in any of its forms (taking life, torturing, malicious wounding), and violations of the seventh commandment, that is, stealing in any of its forms (plundering, accumulating, keeping what has been plundered and accumulated). And to facilitate both things we resort to violations of the eighth commandment, that is, lying in any of its forms (concealment, deception, dissimulation, maintained ignorance). Then, with a certain naivety, I began to think about the order in which the commandments are violated. And given the scope of each one of them, I thought that the order is as follows: the seventh, the fifth, and the eighth.

Beyond the fickleness of asking myself why we violate the commandments, Montesinos's text helped me to appreciate in the New Testament theological and anthropological issues of the first magnitude and scope that I had not sufficiently noticed.

It helped me to appreciate the clear statement in John's Gospel: "The Evil One is a murderer and a liar" (Jn 8:44). As a commentary, I usually add: "And in that order." And the sharp statement of the Letter to the Romans: "The wrath of God has been revealed against those who imprison the truth in unrighteousness." Imprisoning the truth unleashes the wrath of God, but it also generates many other very serious evils, as the words that follow in the text of Romans affirm or insinuate; that is, to settle in unreality, not to find God in things, because they no longer reveal him. Anthropologically and ethically, imprisoning the truth produces profound dehumanization, and the human being is given over to all kinds of passions. Imprisoned truth dehumanizes in its totality.

In what I have just said there is no exegetical precision, certainly, but on the other hand, I believe that there is no arbitrary or "wild exegesis" aimed at defending liberationist theses, such as we are often accused of including. If there is one thing I want to defend, it is the absolute importance of truth.

In any case, for now I just want to insist on the good that Antonio Montesinos did me and also for doing theology. That was above all evident in his words: "Wake up. Before the horrors of our world do not remain in lethargic slumber asleep." The time of my return to El Salvador—and of beginning to do theology on my own—coincided with a time of awakening. And it did me a great good, for which I am grateful.

❖ *And do you think that this awakening occurred in El Salvador?*

As far as I know, I believe that, not only in El Salvador in the 1970s, but in different times and places, there have been Jesuits who have awakened. In my case, even with the painful, let's say Kantian, awakening in St. Louis, I think I was still in a lethargic slumber. For me, the world was still the First World. Man was still modern man. The church was still the [European] church of the council. Theology was still German theology. And the historical utopia was still that the countries of the South would become a little bit more like those of the North.

❖ *Do you think that this irruption upon your return to El Salvador fell from the sky, without any previous preparation to capture it?*

I do not believe that things fall from the sky, but some burst in with more force than others. Personally, more or less consciously, I suppose that some novelties of the time were already at work in me and in others: John XXIII's new relationship with the world, not only with the church; the hope and freedom that he transmitted; his special closeness to the poor.

I suppose that other things that had to do more directly with the poor had also made an impact on me, for example what I had heard about the worker priests in France. And, now that you ask, I think that the poor that we visited in the shantytowns of Bilbao in the 1950s, a typical activity in the religious schools, had remained in the back of my conscience. It was not a big deal, but I think the visits to those shantytowns had a greater impact on me than other experiences that were offered to us in the school, and even some during the novitiate. They affected me more than the devotion to the Sacred Heart, for example. However, rather than *preparing the irruption*, I would speak of *offering a distant attunement*. I did have some knowledge of the reality of the poor; of the martyrs for justice, none.

And still on a personal level, it made it much easier for me to begin to grasp the irruption when I joined my natural group of Jesuit companions of the Central American province. In Havana, St. Louis, and Frankfurt I was not close to them but rather to Jesuits from other provinces. When I returned to El Salvador, many of them had already changed, and I think that helped me to change myself.

✧ *You have spoken of the steps that you and others took. But, going to the heart of the matter, do you think that something special happened in the Central American province that made it easier to grasp the irruption you have talked about? In fact, those years made Central America known as an advanced, unconventional province. What was happening?*

A very important change took place. If we put symbolic dates, the beginning of the change took place in the provincial *Exercises* of 1969. It was during that great first epoch of change that Rutilio Grande was assassinated, on March 12, 1977. The end of that era was November 16, 1989, with the assassination of six Jesuits, five of whom worked at the UCA, at the university, and one at Fe y Alegría.

The change was epochal. With some audacity I compare it to what happened in the first generations of Christians. And if I dare to speak this way it is because both in the New Testament and in Central America—especially in El Salvador—blood flowed abundantly, preceded by persecution, defamation, slander, and harassment of Jesuits and close collaborators. And although time passes, reflection on this change is fundamental. It cannot be allowed to fall into oblivion.

Now I am going to answer your question more concretely and as well as possible. I did not join the province until 1974, so I did not know everything that was happening. Sometimes I knew only by hearsay or secondhand.

Anyway, learning about what was happening in the province, there came a time when I began to wonder more about what was going on inside. On the whole, the outward change didn't faze me, but that didn't eliminate questions: What did the province think of itself? What did it want to change, if anything? Why and what for? What criteria guided its desires and decisions? What difficulties did it foresee? Who did it consider its friends and who its adversaries? What friendships did it need to make and which abandon? What did it have to risk and fight for in earnest, if necessary?

There were many questions, and they did not arise at the same time. For me, perhaps the most important early on was whether the province recognized its *real* reality, failures, and even sins, whatever they were, and the need to be otherwise. Did it feel encouragement and joy in embarking in another direction? Since my years in Germany were weak in terms of thinking about the province, I sometimes wondered how things should be, if and how the province should be governed by the events of the Second Vatican Council (about which I did not have many ideas) and by Medellín (which was something even more unknown). And if there was to be a radical change, I did not think much about whether the province was ethically and conceptually prepared for it. But by 1974 I was already convinced that what I called irruption was a very real thing.

I will soon answer the question of whether there was something prior to the irruption, but first I would like to make a reflection so as not to lose sight of the purpose of these conversations; that is, *how I have been doing theology*. I have already said, and I will insist, that what has moved me to think, including theologically, has been reality, things, people, real events. Certainly the poor and the martyrs are important realities. But there are also other more conjunctural realities, the ones you are asking me about now. Not to offer a mini-history of the Central American province, but for this reason I am going to dwell on some issues of the province, big, normal, or small, that have also been shaping my theology. We can continue.

✧ *What was the province of Central America like that made the irruption understandable?*

In Latin America, Medellín demanded and encouraged a serious change in the way of being Christian. And it also demanded a serious change in being a Jesuit. As far as I remember, in the late 1960s that change was noticeable in the Jesuits of Venezuela and Bolivia, and certainly in Central America. Other provinces remained more conservative.

In Central America the change occurred radically. In the 1960s, a group of students studying in the universities of Europe, under the leadership of César Jerez, who became provincial in 1976, and especially Ignacio Ellacuría, who in the early 1970s was responsible for the students of the province, moved things along.

In June 1969 there was a meeting of all the students in Madrid, which I remember well (I was present), where the central theme (in my own words of today) was this: *What is reality asking of us?* To put it in the language of the Second Vatican Council, what did the signs of the times that characterized historical reality demand (cf. *Gaudium et Spes,* no. 4)? I then called them *signs of the times in their historical version* in order to differentiate them from the "true signs of the presence or plans of God" (cf. *GS*, no. 11). These I have called *signs of the times in their theological version.* For me, who had just arrived from Frankfurt, all this was a great novelty. The need for renewal of the province was in the air.

From that meeting of students in Madrid came the idea that the province, as a whole, would make the *Spiritual Exercises* for the year; this took place a few months later. The *Exercises* were given by Father Elizondo and Father Ellacuría. I did not take part in them, because I had to return to Frankfurt to continue my doctorate. But I can speak of their importance for the province. In fact, those *Exercises* were an environmental preparation for capturing the irruption. The newness that occurred made it possible to capture in the province in a generalized way, not only individually, an irruption. And with them also began what I am going to call "the Ellacuría cycle, 1969–89."

✧ *In what ways was this novelty so powerful?*

In two ways. The first was very important, because it was (to be redundant) *absolutely* novel; it was the first time in the history of the province that this had occurred. As a matter of principle, and not just by chance, the Central American province would make the *Exercises* as a province. All the Jesuits were invited, and almost all those in Central America attended. The organizers viewed them as *Exercises* of the province; they were made by the province as such, not as a sum of individuals, but as a collective, as a social body.

The second is that the province was not simply invited to make the *Exercises* for the year but was to approach the *Exercises* from a certain perspective, carefully chosen by Father Ellacuría. That perspective was *honesty* with the Latin American reality. Ellacuría wisely proposed a Latin American reading of the *Exercises*. The *Exercises* of Saint Ignatius had seemed for centuries almost untouchable, as if they were self-explanatory, without any major problems. To reread them from a new perspective, as Ellacuría did, seemed to me really great and fruitful. And the most important thing is that the new perspective was based *on the poor and victims, on the suffering servant Jesus of Yahweh,* who must be contemplated upon the cross. They were based neither in Rome nor in Loyola, but in the Third World, among the suffering and unjustly oppressed.

❖*It is clear that, for you, these* Exercises *were a founding moment of the province. That is why I would like you to explain to us the importance of each of the novelties you mentioned. First of all, what it meant that the* Exercises *were made by an entire province.*

Putting a province, or a majority part of it, under the discipline of the *Exercises* meant several things. It involved the examination of conscience, including the sins, the resolutions of amendment, questions of what to do, what not to do, who to work with and who not to work with, who we Jesuits had to help and who we had to distance ourselves from, who we had to criticize and denounce, what cross we had to carry, and how we had to bring down from the cross the crucified peoples of Central America. It involved reflecting on how God is hidden and present in those peoples and many other questions. All these things were not only matters of concern for an individual Jesuit but essential matters for a whole province with a concrete history.

At this level, the *Exercises* of Saint Ignatius helped in some very important ways that are typically considered. They helped us to awaken to the need to take seriously that the province itself can be, or is, sinful, and yet must follow Jesus and work for the kingdom. I think it was the first time that the province, as a province, had taken these issues seriously.

This did not mean ignoring the personal or individual dimension of the *Exercises*, and I know that these provincial *Exercises* helped many Jesuits personally. Nor did it mean ignoring something essential in the *Exercises* of Saint Ignatius: the possibility of *God communicating directly with the soul* of the retreatant. Although now it was necessary to think of this possibility in analogy, as self-communication also to a collective, which by its nature must take on different forms. By insisting on this communication of God, it was also easier to overcome any kind of legalism, as if God were subject to norms. The signs of the times were deepened in what I have called their theological dimension: "to grasp the presence of God or of his will in the events of our time" (*GS*, no. 11).

While maintaining the important possibility of God communicating with the individual, many experienced the great advantage of making the *Exercises* for the whole province with a provincial consciousness. Without this awareness that we are a body, there is always the danger of a deforming individualism. In the case of a religious order it is the danger of focusing so much on the trees that one can end up not seeing the forest: what the congregation is and what it does, or what it has dissimulated or manipulated. The provincial dimension of the 1969 *Exercises* made it more difficult to hide what we were, what we were doing, and what we were not doing. It brought new problems and very difficult situations, as we will see in a moment, but it made it easier to know our truth. And it facilitated a conversion of greater apostolic effectiveness.

✧*And what did the new perspective mean?*

It was the most important thing: to read the *Spiritual Exercises* of Saint Ignatius from a certain perspective. In the *Exercises* of 1969, Ellacuría sought to reread them from Latin America. In doing so, he wanted to reread them from the Third World. This is how he presented the text. That perspective was the *reality* of the Third World. Ellacuría's ability and genius were to know how to face reality, what to do with it. In words that have become famous, Ellacuría demanded "to take charge of reality," "to be in charge of reality," and "to bear reality"—to which years later I added my own phrase, "to let oneself be burdened by reality." These questions in the face of the suffering reality of Central America produced the right perspective to reread and put the *Exercises* into practice.

Ellacuría did not start from zero in his rereading of the *Exercises* from the reality of the Third World. For the Christian historical rereading he was able to base himself to some extent on the work of the bishops gathered in Medellín in 1968. This I consider important, because Medellín also offers a group perspective (from the bishops of Latin America), which helped with the ideas of giving the *Exercises* to a province, a group.

The bishops at Medellín published *Conclusions*, which recounted what they had reflected and prayed about, and what they proposed. The perspective was clearly the reality of the Third World. In the introduction to the *Conclusions* they affirm the hope of liberation from real evils and of real personal and collective humanization: "We are on the threshold of a new historical epoch of our continent, filled with a yearning for total emancipation, liberation, from all servitude, personal maturation and collective integration."

As I read it, I think they formulated the first document, *Justice,* with even greater conviction. They begin by denouncing the crudest of realities: "There are many studies on the situation of Latin American. All of them describe the misery that marginalizes large human groups. This misery, as a collective fact, is an injustice that cries out to heaven" (no. 1).

The text has always caught my attention. By placing it at the beginning of *Conclusions,* the bishops confess what is in their minds and hearts. And it is striking that, being a text written by bishops, believers in God, followers of Jesus Christ, and servants in the Church, their first words are not religious, biblical, or dogmatic words. They are words about the reality of this world, more specifically about its misery, its social sin, its injustice. The bishops mention those who suffer this sin, and by implication, those who commit it. The greatest sin is injustice. The words "that cries out to heaven" can be understood as in Exodus 3:9, when Yahweh says, "The cry of the children of Israel has now come to me."

I believe that the acceptance and understanding of Medellín was a good support for the provincial *Exercises.*

✧ *You give the provincial* Exercises *a lot of importance. What did they produce?*

Although I did not participate in them, as I said, I soon got to know what happened, and then I was able to see for myself the many things they produced. Now I just want to look at the fundamentals.

Tensions arose that were at the root of the most important change for the Jesuits in Central America. A good number of Jesuits, especially the young, newly ordained Jesuits, were drawn to the theme of faith and justice. Other Jesuits, fewer in number and older in age, felt that the work they had done for years was being criticized or belittled. Some even feared that the orthodoxy of the church was being jeopardized.

Thus, the *Exercises* produced a certain amount of conflict and division. And as I have been repeating, both things were also important in my incipient theological thinking. And although I am moving events forward, because of their decisive importance I would like to recall something fundamental. What overcame the division and transformed the conflict into reconciliation between brothers was not any action of the superiors, who did try to intervene, not even that of Father Arrupe,[3] but the assassination-martyrdom of Father Rutilio Grande on March 12, 1977. The overcoming of the conflicts was produced by something very real and very Christian, and evidently it was also important for my incipient theology. Those years gave me much food for thought.

Those *Exercises* were a beginning and a foundation, a base on which to stand. They set many real things in motion with lucidity and energy. For me, it was a push to a praxis that others had begun before me. More concretely, it was a push to do theology, not only or mainly to increase knowledge or to give classes, but to help build another country, another church, and another Society of Jesus.

✧ *Can you explain how the 1969* Exercises *affected the spirit of the province?*

I have already hinted at this, and I was able to grasp it from my own experience a few years later. Making the *Exercises* in this way helped the *province to wake up*. It helped it to understand and be in tune with the major institutional event that was coming: General Congregation XXXII, which took place in 1975 under the intuition and leadership of Father Arrupe. I take it up now, because in that congregation the Jesuits asked themselves seriously, as I think we have rarely done, what are we as Jesuits, what is our identity, what is our mission? I believe that the Society has not spoken more lucid and daring words since then.

---

[3] Father Pedro Arrupe, SJ (1907–91), a Spanish Basque Jesuit, served as the twenty-eighth superior general of the Society of Jesus. His term (1965–83) was extremely consequential, so much so that he is often called a "second founder" of the Society. Among other things, he convened the landmark General Congregation XXXII (1975), which emphasized the importance of "faith that does justice." As Sobrino notes, this had radical implications for the Society generally and for the Jesuits in El Salvador in particular.

Decree 2 of the General Congregation XXXII states:

> What is it to be a Jesuit? It is to know that one is a sinner, yet called to be a companion of Jesus. . . . What is it to be a companion of Jesus today? It is to engage, under the standard of the Cross, in *the crucial struggle of our time: the struggle for faith and that struggle for justice which it includes.*

Today, more than forty years later, some may think that this is already known, and that what is important and urgent is not to repeat those words, but to update them. In short, some would say that General Congregation XXXII is now the *orthodoxy* of the Society and there is thus no need to give it any more thought. I am not given to easily accept that something has already become flesh and blood, in this case of the Society. Put in the form of a thesis, an orthodox formulation may have formal validity but not much real effectiveness. It often fails to generate or transform history. And it costs a lot to maintain its edges.

I will return to the crucial struggle of the "faith-justice" commitment, but first I would like to dwell on no. 46 of Decree 4, which splendidly formulates what follows from the commitment. It is the price to be paid: "We will not, in fact, work for the promotion of justice *without paying a price.* But this work will make our proclamation of the Gospel more meaningful and its acceptance easier."

With these words the congregation was not making any prophecy in the strict sense, for it was stating the obvious. It was, however, expressing a certain conviction. In the thirty years between 1975, the date of General Congregation XXXII, and 2006, forty-seven Jesuits had been killed for the sake of justice. Since then, the number has grown.

Faith-justice and *the price to be paid* are central affirmations of the congregation, and this is what I wanted to insist on. But I would also like to add that, in addition to a heavy price to be paid by the Society, these martyrs have been a blessing for the Society of Jesus and for the church. And most especially for the poor of this world, who have mourned these murdered Jesuits like no one else. And they keep them alive with gratitude and joy. The martyrs, in this case Jesuits, have come to their defense and have loved them.

❖*Let's go back to 1971.*

I had come from Frankfurt to work for a couple of months in the province. I participated in the *Exercises* of 1971, which Ellacuría organized for all the young Jesuits of the province, and from that I was able to learn many things about the *Exercises* of 1969, but above all I was able to see for myself the impact of the *Exercises* as they were given by Ellacuría. The perspective was that of the Third World, and that changed everything. And I also began to grasp conceptually what I have called the irruption of the poor and the glimpse of God. Making the *Exercises* as a group, with Jesuits from thirty to forty years of age, I found myself *awakening from the dream* with joy and gratitude. And with a communitarian dimension unknown to me. Something deep and true was present, something that did not come from on high and distant, but from below, with its own authority, not borrowed.

Thinking about it later, I realized that I did not have to ignore any of the best of the biblical and Christian tradition that I had received. But the irruption of the poor in a community context, and in tune with the *Exercises* of Saint Ignatius, made everything current and relevant. And Ellacuría's *Exercises* helped me to understand him as a Jesuit and as a theologian, which was very important for me from 1974 when we began to work together.

❖*And what struck you most about the contents of the* Exercises, *as Ellacuría commented on them?*

As far as the content of the *Exercises* is concerned, I was particularly struck by sin, its massiveness and its horror. The text of the *Exercises* speaks of the eternal death produced by sin and, sadly, it was not difficult to think of the historical death of so many human beings in Central America, the product of horrifying injustices, of established structures, and of what we Jesuits had done or had not done. Ellacuría referred naturally, without artifice, to the real world.

In the *Exercises* we speak of sorrow for my sins, but it was not difficult to feel the immense sorrow and personal suffering of the poor Central Americans, product of the many historical sins.

And what I found most brilliant in Ellacuría—although, to be honest, I do not know if I heard it for the first time in the *Exercises* or later—was the historicization of the three questions that Saint Ignatius calls us to ask ourselves before Christ on the cross: "What have I done, what am I doing, and what am I going to do for Christ?" With a genius that I have not found in other thinkers, he asked us to question ourselves before the crucified people: "What we have done to crucify him, what we are doing to take him down from the cross, what we are going to do to raise him up?"

✧ *Let me go back to something that struck me: "the price to be paid." Why don't we talk much about that price today?*

To understand why, I think it helps to make a fundamental distinction between who pays the price and what price they pay. I believe that today those who pay the price are remembered more than before: the martyrs. Those who "push the cart of history," as Ellacuría used to say, and "fall under its weight" are remembered more. Their number is more and more undeniable, and some of them are spoken of with respect, admiration, even affection.

Then there is the price to be paid. Much less is said about this, and it is absolutely understandable. Sometimes it remains in the air that there must have been such a price, but rarely is there an analysis of what price has been paid.

The reason is that the price is onerous, sometimes very cruel. Those who have paid the price can be praised and those who have demanded it can be condemned. But it is difficult to delve into the price to be paid. Perhaps the main reason we don't talk so much about the price to be paid is the fear of honestly facing ourselves and asking ourselves if we are paying that price or not.

Having entered into a crucial struggle, we must examine whether we have paid any price. In simple words, we must examine ourselves to determine whether we have suffered persecution by the powerful. If so, then with humility we can think that we have understood what God's will was in the face of injustice. If there has been no such persecution—and worse, if there has been warm or moderate applause—we must seriously question whether there has been a struggle for justice and whether our discernment has been lucid.

✧*Let us continue with the price to be paid, because it seems to me a very enlightening topic. The most notorious prices paid by the Jesuits and also the names of the most famous of those persecuted are well known. But I would like you to tell us what prices the Jesuits paid in the years immediately after the* Exercises *of 1969 and why they paid them.*

What price did the Jesuits pay after the *Exercises* of 1969? From half a century away, it is not easy to believe. The *Exercises* of Saint Ignatius were by no means harmless. And practically all the works of the Society in every country endured persecution. The persecutions, in all the works and for the same fundamental reasons, gave me a lot to think about as a Jesuit.

From 1972 on, the Externado [a secondary school run by the Jesuits] suffered serious attacks from the government and the right wing. The whole school suffered persecution. In religion classes the texts of Medellín, themes of injustice, and the need for justice were being taught. In sociology rudiments of Marxism were taught. The older students, in their out-of-class exercises, had to learn what the farmworkers earned on the farms of their parents and friends. The parents were furious, felt betrayed by the Jesuits, used the power they had, and organized to put a stop to it. The government officially denounced the school and threatened to expel the non-Salvadoran Jesuits from the country.

The Jesuits responded publicly and with absolute clarity. They published in the newspapers six paid double-page spreads entitled "The Externado thinks like this." They were accurate, scientific, easy to read, and difficult to refute. They were valuable and courageous. Jesuits from various communities, especially from the UCA, collaborated in thinking them up and writing them.

They analyzed the social reality of the country, poverty, and injustice. They argued with reason and, above all, with the gospel and the fathers of the church. In this way the whole country could learn that working for justice belonged to the essence of the Christian faith. In plain words: one cannot be a Christian in El Salvador without fighting for justice.

Many of the parents and newspaper readers felt this as a personal attack and offense. The Jesuits, with some exceptions, were undaunted and moved on. They were consistent and willing to take risks. This caused a commotion in the country.

For years the Externado was vilified, watched, persecuted, and raided. On one occasion armed groups entered the building and took away a group of Salvadorans belonging to leftist political groups that had gathered at the school. Shortly thereafter, their bodies were found dumped on the road.

As for the UCA: defamation, raids, bombs, assassinations. For about twenty years after the 1960s insults and threats were unleashed against the UCA in newspapers, radios, and leaflets. On June 20, 1976, the threat was extended to all Jesuits in the country; they would be killed if they did not leave the country within a month.

The UCA was at the center of the persecution for a long time. There were raids on the campus and in the residences of professors, especially Jesuits: machine gunning, bombings. I remember the first of them, on January 6, 1976, in the office of the magazine *ECA*. Altogether, up to November 1989, about twenty-five bombs exploded. Several Jesuits appeared on lists of people to be killed, almost always headed by Father Ellacuría. And not only Jesuits. Before 1989 several professors and students of the UCA were assassinated.

The UCA was a symbol of Jesuits who had converted to Medellín and to the gospel. The UCA understood itself as a place of teaching and research, but it was innovatively and dangerously defined as an institution of social projection for a radical change in the country. *And it made social projection the main function of the UCA.*

In the country a slogan appeared on many walls: "Be a patriot; kill a priest."

❖ *Ellacuría was very important at the UCA. What else can you tell us about what he did in the early days?*

Now I am going to concentrate on just one thing that, in my opinion, was decisive for the country: the total and decisive support of the UCA from 1977 to 1980, under Ignacio Ellacuría, for Monseñor Romero. Very deep understanding and friendship were established between the two. And Ellacuría saw in Monseñor Romero the deepest inspiration for the UCA. To this day, certainly for those of us who lived in the UCA during those years, the friendship and affection between Monseñor and Father Ellacuría were, if one must say so, part of the glory of the UCA.

Speaking of the tasks that the church had to do, and we within it, Ellacuría used to say that "Monseñor has already gone ahead of us." On March 22, 1985, five years after Monseñor's martyrdom, the UCA awarded Monseñor a posthumous honorary doctorate in theology. On this occasion Ellacuría gave an important speech about Monseñor. He wanted to answer the accusations that the UCA had manipulated Monseñor Romero, and above all he wanted to confess publicly the importance of Monseñor for the UCA and the superiority of Monseñor Romero for the being and doing of the UCA.

It has been maliciously said that Monseñor Romero was manipulated by our university. It is time to say publicly and solemnly that this was not the case. Certainly, Monseñor Romero asked for our collaboration on many occasions, and this represents and will represent for us a great honor, because of who asked us and the cause for which he asked us, . . . but in all those collaborations there is no doubt who was the teacher and who was the assistant, who was the pastor who set the guidelines and who was the executor, who was the prophet who unraveled the mystery and who was the follower, who was the animator and who was the animated, who was the voice and who was the echo.

Ellacuría humbly confessed the debt of the UCA to Monseñor Romero. And for those of us who knew him well, these words also resonated as a personal recognition of his own debt to Monseñor Romero from the depths of his person. Ellacuría and Romero could understand each other as colleagues in their work and struggle in the fields of justice, prophecy, mercy, utopia, freedom, peace. But when it came to Monseñor's faith, or the mystery of God, Ellacuría never considered himself Monseñor's colleague. Even on this personal level, "Monseñor has gone ahead of us." Ellacuría perceived it well. He felt the joy of being a "little brother," and the desire that Monseñor would carry him in his faith.

✧ *Let's go back to the persecution of the Jesuits in those years.*

Certainly, something very important is missing: Aguilares. From 1973 to 1977 the Jesuits were in Aguilares. Father Rutilio Grande with a team of four Jesuits took the Jesuits out of the city and into the countryside, the world of the peasants. This was the beginning of the popular liberating pastoral work. Evangelization was centered on Jesus of Nazareth and the building of communities, not on individual religiosity. A new Christianity grew along the lines of Medellín.

On March 12, 1977, Rutilio Grande was assassinated, a key day in the modern history of El Salvador. On that day the conversion of Monseñor Romero took place, "the miracle of Rutilio," as people used to say. For the Jesuits it was the culmination of the process that began in the *Exercises* of 1969 (in 1989 we would live through another more exacting culmination). In May 1977 the three Jesuits who were working with Rutilio were expelled from the country. Aguilares remained under siege until June 19. On that day Monseñor Romero went to Aguilares to console, denounce, and demand. He began his homily with these words, which I was able to hear live: "It is my turn to pick up corpses." And he denounced "those who have turned a town into a prison."

More than anything else, words like these of Monseñor have enlightened and helped me to understand ecclesial ministry in a Christian way, beyond the traditional sources of theology. And other words of his enlightened and helped me to understand the church of Jesus. On July 15, 1979, he said in a homily in the cathedral: "I rejoice, my brothers, that our church is persecuted precisely because of her preferential option for the poor and for trying to incarnate herself in the interests of the poor." A month earlier, in a sermon on June 30, he had said: "In a country where so many people are being murdered so horribly, it would be sad if we found no priests also among the victims. They are the testimony of a church incarnated in the problems of her people."

Returning to the question that has interested you so much, "the price to pay," years ago, when studying the subject of the persecution of the church, I came across these words of Saint Augustine: "The church goes on pilgrimage between the persecutions of the world and the consolations of God." Beautiful and venerable words. But the words of Monseñor Romero that we have just heard, supported by many—and I say this with modesty, by the Jesuits of those years—are something else. Personally, they have enlightened me to walk through the twists and turns of theology. And in them I have enjoyed a glimpse of God.

✧ *You have spoken at length about persecutions, because they were many and long. Were there not also persecutions within the church and the Society of Jesus?*

The truth is yes, and at very different levels. I do not like to address the subject, because it is known that I was personally involved. Let us say, then, that we have had to pay the price of attacks and misunderstandings, some of them serious, the most important coming from the Vatican Curia. As early as 1976, Cardinal Garrone, prefect of Catholic Education, asked me to answer a series of questions about my publications on Christology. I did so. A few years later, Cardinal Seper, prefect of the Congregation for the Doctrine of the Faith, wrote to say that my answers to the Congregation for Catholic Education were not satisfactory. He rephrased new questions, and I answered. Later, with Cardinal Ratzinger already in the Congregation for the Doctrine of the Faith, there were many years, about twenty, of criticisms directed at liberation theology and my writings, some of them with my name on them. In 2007, the Congregation for the Doctrine of the Faith published a Notification on some dangers and errors in my books on Christology, which became known.

I do not usually speak in detail about such things, nor will I do so now. Those interested in the matter can read a long private letter to Father Kolvenbach in which I give my opinion on what happened.[4] To my surprise and chagrin, although I suppose there was no ill will involved, the letter was leaked and published in many places. I don't see that it is now necessary to repeat what I wrote in it. And I also think that others have already written enough on the matter of the Notification.

Personally, I think that so many years under the harsh, unfriendly gaze of Rome have not affected me excessively. Nor, especially at the beginning, have I ignored the criticisms and how much truth they may

---

[4] In November 2006, the Congregation for the Doctrine of the Faith issued a Notification warning of "certain imprecisions and errors" in Jon Sobrino's work on Christology. He refers here to his response, "Letter to Fr. Kolvenbach, SJ, Explaining Nonadherence to 'Notification' from the Congregation for the Doctrine of the Faith." See Robert Lassalle-Klein, ed., *Jon Sobrino: Spiritual Writings* (Maryknoll, NY: Orbis Books, 2018), 80–194.

or may not have had. At important moments I have discussed it with capable theologians and friends to take into account their opinions and correct mine when necessary.

For me, more serious and sadder than the warnings against me, very often with little foundation, has been the atmosphere generated in several bishops of Latin America and Spain against any theology of liberation; against religious dedicated to the poor; against the reading of the Bible from, for, and with the people. In principle, it seems to me that this has been one of the prices Latin American theology has had to pay for defending the liberation of the oppressed. And the most onerous price has been paid by the people, as is almost always the case, when they are deprived of important aid.

In November 2015 I was with Martin Mayer at Pope Francis's private mass. At the end I greeted him: "My name is Jon Sobrino. I am a Jesuit from El Salvador, from the community of the Jesuits who were killed. I want to express my gratitude and my support." I gave him an envelope with a letter that a secretary had written to him with pictures of his two little children for his blessing. Francis, with simplicity and solemnity, blessed the letter. A minute and a half had passed, and Martin and I said goodbye. Francis gave me a fraternal embrace, and said: "Write, write."

So much for my wanderings among curias and hierarchs. By the way, one of the journalists who followed our steps asked me if, "after the meeting with Francis, I felt rehabilitated." I answered that "I had never felt disqualified." And, as I understood the context of his question, I told him simply: "If you see Benedict XVI, you greet him for me. And thank him for his decision to resign and for the way he did it."

✧ *You have been talking about many things since your return to El Salvador. I think the central thing is the importance you give to the irruption of the poor and the martyrs for what will be your theology. But it strikes me that you have not mentioned your contact with the reality of the poor. In familiar words, insertion. Is it possible to do theology without this contact?*

The question is important, and my answer may surprise and even disappoint. Unlike what happened to other colleagues, capturing the irruption of the poor for me had little to do with physical insertion among them or working with them on a seasonal basis, or even living in the countryside or in peripheral areas. The fundamental reason, I believe, was my fragile health, even then. A month after arriving in the country, in March 1974, I wanted to go to celebrate Holy Week in a canton, a poor place in the countryside, but Father Francisco Estrada, provincial and veteran in these matters, told me twenty-four hours later: "This is not for you. You can't stand it." And I went back home.

My insertion, in the sense of direct contact with the poor, has been minimal. I did try to go periodically to places of the poor in the suburbs of San Salvador, and in times of war, especially to the shelters. When I began to publish writings on Christology, some people commented on how I could write about Jesus and the poor if I had no personal experience of real poor people. And they were somewhat surprised that my Christology texts did not turn out so badly. They used to say similar things about Ellacuría. Above all, at the beginning they would say, in a critical spirit, that he did theology at a desk. And Ellacuría would reply: "I do theology *at* a desk, but not *from* a desk." Now I simply mention it. And I have to add that, when his name appeared on the lists of those threatened with death, this type of comment about Ellacuría ceased.

Whatever the reason for my lack of insertion, as we awoke from our sleep, I discovered that the poor were human beings whom the sin of the world had turned into human waste and scrap. And, without looking for it, what came to my mind was that *sin is what gives death*. When I was giving the *Exercises* to the Sisters of the Assumption in 1976, what also came to my mind was that *God is the God of life*. I was thinking about the reality around me, and, without intending to do so, I was also thinking about them theologically. In this way, I believe that I was appropriating reality and conceptualizing it.

Returning to insertion, over the years I have noticed its lack. It is not that I feel any particular remorse, but I do realize that it has made it difficult for me to deepen my understanding of the reality of the poor, especially what the poor give us and what we receive from them. It is true that I have written a small book[5] in which I advance, conceptually, on the *extra Ecclesiam nulla salus* of the tradition and on the *extra mundum nulla salus* of Schillebeeckx, and I did it with conviction. But I already say in the prologue of the book that to speak in this way about the poor, knowing what many of the real poor are like and what my

---

[5] Jon Sobrino, *No Salvation outside the Poor: Prophetic-Utopian Essays* (Maryknoll, NY: Orbis Books, 2008).

distance is, makes me uneasy. But I add that not speaking in this way makes me even more uneasy. God knows why. What I do believe is that with greater insertion I would feel more desire to work with refugees and Indigenous peoples.

And if I may make a personal confession in closing, the shame of writing about the poor without much direct experience and with little physical proximity is not entirely overcome by seeing that what I wrote helped. What made the shame more bearable was the real persecution in which we lived. With all the analogies of the case, it could somehow bring us closer to their fate.

✧ *I think we are finishing this long first part of our conversations about the fundamental assumptions of how you started doing theology, in St. Louis, Germany, and El Salvador. Can you summarize the basics of what happened in the first years of your return?*

What was certainly fundamental was *the irruption of the poor*. I came to know the reality of the poor who were impoverished and at the same time bearers of salvation, often brimming with grace and truth, who organized themselves to promote justice. I became convinced that the gospel is right: the good news is for the poor. But I think we also get it right when we realize that the poor *are* good news. The poor are—can be—gospel. I thought about this when I was close to Ellacuría. They were steps on the path of doing theology.

The second and more fundamental thing was that Christians—men and women who looked like Jesus and acted like Jesus—were being murdered. It happened in El Salvador in a remarkable way and, as far as I know, more than in other places, even though there were already grassroots movements and liberation theology groups there. In El Salvador the martyrs irrupted. Rutilio Grande and Monseñor Romero, and between the Jesuit and the archbishop, five other diocesan priests and five nuns were assassinated, as well as a seminarian, who was repairing the chapel where he was going to be ordained a priest. Beyond them, there were countless men and women, boys and girls who worked in communities and popular organizations. Sometimes they were killed for having a photo of Rutilio. The paschal mystery irrupted. *The martyrs were a real thing.*

✧ *So far you have spoken of fundamental realities and contexts of what will be your theology, but liberation has not appeared in all of this, and you are known as a liberation theologian. Why this silence?*

What you ask makes sense, and I will try to explain it. It may be surprising, but when we started theology in 1974 in El Salvador, Ellacuría did not talk much about doing "liberation theology," but he talked about doing "Latin American theology," "theology from the Third World." When we began the theology courses in 1974, about which I will soon speak, he wrote a very thoughtful article with the title "Thesis on the Possibility, Necessity, and Meaning of a Latin American Theology." And in June 1975, to a congress held in Mexico that brought together well-known liberation theologians, he sent a text with the title "Laying the Philosophical Foundations of Latin American Theological Method,"[6] which is, by the way, one of his best texts, very useful and much quoted. I was also invited as a young theologian to the congress, and I went. I was not a speaker. They gave me three minutes to speak, and then I published an extensive article: "Theological Knowledge in European and Latin American Theology."

Gustavo Gutiérrez, Leonardo Boff, Carlos Mesters, José Comblin—all known as liberation theologians—were present at the congress. In El Salvador the expression *liberation theology* referred us to these theologians, whom we appreciated. What we were trying to do was to produce a theology, without adding an adjective to it, that would help the establishment of the kingdom of God and the overcoming of the anti-kingdom, taking into account El Salvador. After some time, and certainly when the martyrs began, the theology that we were doing in El Salvador began to be known and be recognized by the great family of liberation theology.

In El Salvador, at least as far as I am concerned, the first people who called me a liberation theologian were people from the oligarchy. Let me explain. A few weeks after the congress in Mexico, a brief article about the liberation theologians appeared in a very right-wing Salvadoran newspaper. It said that the four most important ones had just met in Mexico: Gustavo Gutiérrez, Leonardo Boff, Enrique Dussel, and Jon Sobrino. It

---

[6] See Michael E. Lee, ed., *Ignacio Ellacuría: Essays on History, Liberation, and Salvation* (Maryknoll, NY: Orbis Books, 2013), 63–91.

was the first time someone called me a liberation theologian. It had never occurred to me that I was a liberation theologian, much less that I was one of the important ones. But I understood the intention of the news.

The reason for appearing in the newspaper was not theological interest, obviously, but to denigrate me and the UCA, since liberation theology was considered pernicious, dangerous, and anti-Catholic. Why they included me, I don't really know. But I do know that in El Salvador the right wing soon attacked that theology, Ellacuría, and myself, and later, as if they had lost their minds, Monseñor Romero. They called us communists, Marxists, atheists, Medellinists, liberationists, corrupters of young people, guerrillas. You name it.

And in case I forget to say it later, I would like to remind you that the newspaper *La Opinión,* of the ultra right, once published this news on its front page in big letters: "Monseñor Romero sells his soul to the devil." On another occasion, on the inside pages, it reported that "they will perform an exorcism on Monseñor Romero."

In El Salvador we began to be called liberation theologians, in the global context of persecution that I have already mentioned. Later, at the UCA, we went deeper into the theme of liberation theologically, I think with our own characteristics. As far as I am concerned, I began to participate in congresses on liberation theology, such as the congress "Social Change and Christian Thought in Latin America" (Madrid, 1992) to commemorate the twentieth anniversary of the famous El Escorial congress where Latin American liberation theology became known in Europe. In that congress important new themes emerged to be put in relation to liberation theology. My theme was "From a Theology of Liberation to a Theology of Martyrdom." For me, living in El Salvador, the theme was obvious, but it was a novelty.

✤ *Did the total darkness about God of the St. Louis years disappear?*

To a large extent, yes, but never completely. In El Salvador the *negativity of reality* burst in, something that had not struck me before. It was something different from the well-known *darkness.* It burst in with an impressive force, as had not happened to me in St. Louis or in Germany.

To clarify what I mean, *negativity* refers to objective reality, while *darkness* refers to the subject. Well, then, accepting with gratitude the hint of God, in El Salvador, I had to admit *the horror of negativity*. And although the language is abstract, I think it expresses well the most important issue of the country to this day. Let's say two words to clarify.

In his mature years Ellacuría placed great emphasis on *the negativity of this world*. He did so without any masochism, but with immense honesty and I suppose with subjective horror and regret. He gave a lot of thought to such a central theme. In my opinion he approached it by historicizing evil and its consequences in his time, analyzing how evil can shape the reality of the world as a whole and how, in spite of everything, there can be salvation. All these things are present in his last public speech, in Barcelona, on November 6, 1989, nine days before his assassination. He enunciates the reality of evil in society and announces the possibility of good. In speaking of evil, he adduces historical arguments. And in formulating the possibility of salvation he also appeals to realities. Let us hear him about both.

> What I have called on other occasions *coprohistoric* analysis—the study of the feces of our civilization—demonstrates that this civilization is gravely ill and that, to avoid a fatal and devastating outcome, it is necessary to change it from inside itself. . . . Only by being utopian and hopeful can one believe and have the energy to work with all the poor and oppressed of the world to reverse history, subvert it, and launch it in another direction.

There can be salvation, for which—he adds—it is necessary to develop all kinds of projects to configure a more just economic, political, legal, and religious order.

✧*And how did you and do you handle the darkness, even if it is not as radical as in St. Louis, in the midst of negativity? Specifically, doesn't God distort or vanish again?*

Not as happened in St. Louis. From Rahner's "mystery remains mystery forever" I have remained to this day, in my own words, able to maintain the "chastity of intelligence" in the face of mystery. But, with time, something has also been imposed on me that at first seemed to be contrary to the chastity of "letting God be God." First I will say in my own words what it is. Then I will explain it. It is about *ruminating on God, rummaging in God*.

The terms are abstruse, and I think unusual when referring to what to do with God. I will explain it descriptively and with concrete examples as it has been appearing in my experience.

The term *God* appears in obvious contexts for theology, in scripture, tradition, the councils, the magisterium. These contexts invite us to reflect, to deepen our reflection. But there are other contexts—many more—spiritual, popular, artistic, of other religions, in which *God* is also mentioned. Those contexts, which are not the ones I have called *conventional,* also attract me, and sometimes more than the conventional contexts in which God is mentioned. And I am struck by what they mean by the term *God*.

To understand this, it is usually not enough to relate them to conventional contexts, since these offer norms to direct thought *correctly*. But in nonconventional contexts, when speaking of God, it is not the norm that reigns, but freedom. And then reflection takes the form of *ruminating*, savoring, tasting God, or becoming bitter about God—which can even lead to vomiting God. And it also takes the form of *rummaging:* digging manually, with our hands, not with illustrations or advanced technical machinery, to see what we find of God.

If the reader still has patience, allow me to mention some moments of the Christian tradition. Not the ones I have called conventional, but some that are not often mentioned, but which for me personally do not get old. When it is my turn to explain these texts in class, I have to reflect and argue. But in thinking things through for myself, helplessly, I am led to rummage and ruminate without following methods already accredited by the academy, sometimes even falling into what is called wild exegesis (which Pope Francis is not very fond of), if I may put it that way. I think that *rumination* and *rummaging* can bear fruit if they come from a primordial curiosity to know what God is.

A first text is taken from the third week of the *Spiritual Exercises* of Saint Ignatius, dedicated to the Passion of Christ. Saint Ignatius says that "the divinity is hidden." He does not say that it disappears or fades away. Nor does he wonder if it has ceased to exist. But he invites us to place ourselves before a divine reality that the suffering and death of Jesus may well hide, an unthinkable reality to which we will have to respond and correspond in an unthinkable way.

The words of Saint Ignatius could have been conceptually more radical, but I have always felt sympathy for this Saint Ignatius. And the mere fact of writing like this invites further rumination and rummaging: What will this divinity that hides have to do with the God of the beginning and foundation—who has arranged reality in a certain way—and with the God of contemplation to attain love—who makes himself present in his creation? How can these three dimensions of divinity fit together and relate to one another? In that way "divinity is hidden" can lead one to be and stand more helplessly before God, but perhaps also more honestly and deeply. It will be a being before God, *knowing without knowing.*

The other texts on which I am going to focus are taken from scripture. The first text is from Mark. Ever since I taught Christology, I have been struck by the words of Jesus on the cross as told by Mark the Evangelist: "My God, my God, why have you forsaken me?" Whatever the most correct exegesis, the words overwhelm, and I also feel sympathy with Mark's sincerity, or at least audacity. The text is canonical, but there is nothing conventional about it within the Gospels. And one can be left ruminating and pondering who this God might be. And, by the way, God's resurrection action, as it appears in Mark's account—before the addition of Mark 16:9–20—does not make the question go away.

The second text from scripture is of a different nature; "Jacob wrestled with God," it says in Genesis. To a certain extent the anthropomorphism is understandable, and it is quite possible for us to grasp a wrestling with God or something similar within ourselves. We can say that, in speaking of struggle, we introduce conflict into the subject *God,* but the understanding does not have to calm down. So it happened to me, as I said before. And it became connatural for me to rummage and ruminate. These are modest words. They do not express the assurance of finally "being at peace with God." Nor do they exclude it.

The third text from scripture I do not remember having heard in a public act of the church, and certainly not in any solemn liturgical celebration—obviously I could be wrong. The text is anthropomorphic and legendary, certainly, as are the texts of creation and paradise. It is the account from Genesis 6 onward: "When the Lord saw that man's wickedness was increasing on the earth and that his whole attitude was always evil, he was sorry that he had created man on the earth, and he was heavy-hearted toward him. And he said, 'I will blot out man whom

I have created from the face of the earth; man with the four-footed animals, creeping things, and birds, for I repent that I have made them.'" In El Salvador I have given these words much thought. Later, seeing Noah, God *repents of having repented of creating man.* And he brings salvation.

The text today, here in El Salvador, with ten or fifteen homicides a day, is anything but legendary. For the believer in God it remains to continue to *ruminate on* his word. "But Noah found favor with the Lord. He built an ark and the flood did not completely wipe out human beings." And the question remains: What is God doing today?

And a last reflection on God, no longer on a text in which *God is mentioned,* but in the presence of some refugees, locked up in the basement of a church, without seeing the light for more than a year, with the mattresses pulled up vertically so that there was room to walk. I went to visit them. I stared at a middle-aged woman. I saw in her suffering, beauty, serenity, and dignity. And I said, "I have seen God."

✧ *Is this the new direction that your "wanderings with God" have been taking and the beginnings of the theology that you will be writing?*

In these conversations I have said a lot of things, sometimes with an excessive amount of jumble and getting ahead of myself. I hope the reader will understand.

Yes, what you say is true. In what I have said so far there are perspectives and ways of thinking that have been shaping my theology, and certainly my increasingly close and personal knowledge of Ellacuría. I hope that it will come out more precisely what are the fundamental contents of my theology and what has been the most appropriate way of doing it. I will soon speak concretely. But I would like to make one last preliminary observation.

I must say that from the beginning I was never very interested in method, perhaps because I never really understood what it consists of, nor do I have much capacity to reflect on it. I found myself in medias res, *doing theology,* for better or worse. And I want to say how I feel now before your questions. I said it in a text I wrote fifteen years ago:

In speaking of "the vital" part of my itinerary, I would like to begin by saying that I do not consider myself a professional theologian or a scholar of theology, although I have done several things that, conventionally, belong to "the profession": teaching, writing and publishing, researching (not much in recent years). . . . I say this to clarify the vital environment of my theological work: I have not understood it as a way of entering into a sphere of reality already constituted in itself and called "theology," but as a way of thinking, reflecting, ruminating, if you will, on reality as it has presented itself to me and has affected me.

Reality has given me food for thought, and in conceptualizing it I have mainly used concepts from the Christian tradition. Thus arose, I think, theology. Perhaps this may seem obvious and not worth mentioning. But I do so in order to insist that, for me, fundamentally, doing theology is not the exercise of a profession, certainly, but a way of being; it is not something that has formally arisen for me because I am a Christian, but because I am human (although the human in me has included the Christian from the beginning); it is not, at first, a service to others, to the church, but a necessity for myself. In peace or in crisis, in joy or in desolation, there is the irresistible impulse to ask myself who is Jesus, what is sin, gratitude, God, hope, liberation?

All these "things," expressed in texts, many of them even sacred and revealed, are things that, above all, belong to the realm of reality and not so much to the realm derived from a knowledge called theology. In this sense, and paraphrasing what Zubiri says about the human being, I like to think that the theologian is an "animal of realities," and that the theological task consists in dealing personally with real things. To put it simply: I intend to do theology with a sense of reality.

3

Teaching Theology

Texts and Witness, the Assassination of Rutilio Grande,
Encountering Father Arrupe

✧ *When and how did you start doing theology?*

In 1974, I arrived in El Salvador to stay. Ellacuría was waiting for me to begin overseeing a master's program in theology at the UCA. It was going to be four years of theology, standard in the Society at that time. And since the students arrived with three years of philosophy, taking into account both studies, the UCA could well grant them a master's degree.

For the first time in the province there would be theology studies for Jesuits, and it is important to know why this decision was made. These studies were designed so that the Central American Jesuits would no longer have to leave the country—go to Spain, the United States, Italy, Germany, Belgium—to study the fundamental course of theology. Being absent from the Salvadoran reality at that stage in their formation had the danger of uprooting them. The students would lose contact with the reality of the Third World, which in El Salvador was conflictive, and with the Jesuits who were already in the struggle for justice. The academic standards of the First World—important for other chapters—did not compensate for the evils that could be caused by ignorance of the Central American reality. It would still be necessary to go to the First World universities for doctoral studies, but after the imprint of a Christian faith as lived and thought in the Third World had been established. Along with this important reason, the aim was also to produce theology in the province.

The four-year curriculum, by the way, was formally the same as that of the Gregorian, and there were no problems with the approval. That is how we began, and that is how we continued, albeit with serious difficulties, which I think it is important to mention from the beginning. The atmosphere of persecution against the Jesuits in El Salvador, the rejection of the rich people of Aguilares, where the students lived and worked raising awareness among the peasants, and the assassination of Rutilio Grande on March 12, 1977, prevented us from completing the first master's course at the end of 1977.

In 1979, we started a second master's program with a new group of students, but once again we could not finish it. There were serious threats against Ellacuría, and he had to leave the country and spend three years in his second exile in Madrid. The first, also in Madrid, was from 1977 to 1979. Persecution was very real, certainly in our life outside the classroom, but it was also felt inside. In large part what was being taught was converted in some way into public speech and a praxis of liberation. By its nature this generated conflict and persecution, which in turn verified that the teaching was Christian.

From a strictly academic perspective, persecutions and conflicts automatically became important *contents* of theology, unlike what happened in other renowned faculties within the Society. And to put it simply, everything that historically accompanied persecution also became content: the vision of faith, of sin, and of grace existing in reality. On the other hand, the theology also inspired the necessary fortitude to remain in the midst of persecution as well as the stubbornness to continue. One could not forget that this theology entailed the possibility of martyrdom, that is, of being killed. That possibility was not simply a matter of abstract or pious words.

In 1984, with naturalness, conviction, and without fuss, we began teaching theology for the third time, and, allowing for some changes, we have maintained it until today. The number of professors, students, courses, and publications has steadily grown.

We will talk about all of this at greater length. But to understand what my first steps in theology were like, I now speak of my experience as a professor of theology in El Salvador, in a poor, oppressed, and repressed country, engaging in the first attempts at liberation from below; in a church that took Medellín seriously; in a university that was committed and persecuted. And very soon with Monseñor Romero, who gave a turn to faith, to hope, and to the practice of justice. I think that all this was shaping my theology from the beginning.

❖ *What courses did you offer when you started teaching theology?*

The first year I presented the classic themes of inspiration and revelation, with the notes I brought from Sankt Georgen, without saying anything special. Then I read and incorporated Juan Luis Segundo, who was a great help in understanding and updating these topics. I was especially helped by the chronological and logical relationship between God's revelation and the signs of the times. I was able to distinguish the signs of the times in their *historical version* (what characterizes an epoch, *GS*, no. 4) and in their *theological version* (what expresses the presence or will of God, *GS*, no. 11). With regard to the negative response of human beings to revelation, I was enlightened by how Segundo developed the distinction between atheism and idolatry.

The second year I taught Christology. I had studied and read a lot about it during my years in Germany. Of the contents, I will mention those themes that most attracted my attention, above all, the kingdom of God and the essential relationship between the ultimacy of Jesus and the kingdom, which helped transcend an overemphasis on the intimate relationship of Jesus with the Father, and consequently of our own relationship with Jesus.

In showing how to respond and correspond to the kingdom, I believe that the foundations were laid for important elements of a Christian anthropology. We must respond to the kingdom with historical *hope*, because, as was already accepted in the progressive theology of that time, the kingdom *is coming*. And what we insist on here is that it is necessary to correspond with a *practical* hope, building it—an idea that was not usually taken into account in other theologies. Without intending it, the problematic of grace and the practice of the human being also appeared. The kingdom is given to us. And the kingdom must also be constructed.

The content of the kingdom of God was fundamentally presented as a world of justice for the poor and oppressed—and in such an important matter we were helped by biblical scholars who came from abroad, such as José Luis Sicre and later Xavier Alegre. The goal is that life reaches everyone, and first of all those who do not take life for granted, those who are deprived of life and prevented from having it, those who die before their time, as Gustavo Gutiérrez used to say.

Beginning Christology with the kingdom of God was a great novelty and very beneficial. It caused a great impact. It also had a significant impact on Ellacuría. Once he approached me to make sure that what I was saying in class was well founded. I explained to him what I had learned from Pannenberg, Moltmann, and other notable theologians of those days. Years later, in 1986, Ellacuría was invited to a conference on Abrahamic religions, which, if I remember correctly, took place in Córdoba. Ellacuría gave an important paper entitled "Contribution of Liberation Theology to Abrahamic Religions in Overcoming Individualism and Positivism." Regarding the kingdom of God, he wrote:

> The category of the kingdom of God is not exclusive to the [theology of liberation] either, but certainly in it it takes on a fundamental importance and is, moreover, understood in a special way. It has come to be proposed as the very object of theology, morality, and pastoral care. The very thing that Jesus came to announce and bring about, that is, the kingdom of God, is what must become the unifying object of all Christian theology, as well as of Christian morality and pastoral care: the greatest possible realization of the kingdom of God in history is what the true followers of Jesus must pursue.

From this fundamental thesis Ellacuría emphasized that, in addition, the kingdom of God avoids a whole series of deviations and dangers, such as the dualism of the earthly and the heavenly. He does not accept that the kingdom should be identified with the church, and even less with the institutional aspects of the church, which would imply an evasion of the world and an impoverishment of the Christian message and mission. And he also said something that is not usually taken into account: "The kingdom of God does not allow the name and reality of God to be manipulated in vain, because it proves its invocation in the historical signs of justice, fraternity, freedom, preferential option for the poor, love, mercy, etc."

I have quoted Ellacuría at length because he demonstrates a very good understanding of the importance that the kingdom of God came to have among us and shows a novel theological understanding. He implicitly refers to the theology we did at the UCA. At one point he explicitly referred to it when he affirmed that, among liberation theologians, this servant is the one who has most insisted christologically and theologically on the kingdom of God.

❖ *Were there any other important topics in the Christology course in those years?*

Yes, another very important theme was the passion and the cross of Jesus. Fundamentally, I focused on the thought of some Protestant thinkers, among them Dietrich Bonhoeffer, and also cited some eloquent texts by Martin Luther King Jr. Systematically and at length I expounded upon "the crucified God" of Jürgen Moltmann. Because of the novelty that Moltmann represented and the novelty and scandalousness of the title of his book, *The Crucified God,* a number of auditors attended those classes, including our provincial, Father César Jerez. I remember the silence in the class, whether from reverence or astonishment, when I mentioned Moltmann's title. And something similar happened when I read texts by Bonhoeffer, such as the widely known phrase "only a suffering God can save us."

For the Christology of the cross that we were developing, Ellacuría's specific approach soon became important, although he could not offer it in class, since he thought about it during his second exile. His double question—Why does Jesus die? and Why is he killed?—attracted attention and made a big impact. It is true that other theologians asked somewhat similar questions, but as far as I remember, not in such a radical way. They did not insist so strongly on distinguishing the two questions without confusing them. And above all, they did not do so in the presence of historical crosses and crucified peoples, as we did in El Salvador.

In my opinion, and contrary to other Christologies of the time, Ellacuría tried not to take for granted that *the* most adequate and fundamental *christological question* was the first one: Why does Jesus—the Son of God—die? In other Christologies the story of that death can and often does fade into insignificance. And then the mystery of the death-as-being-killed disappears, which is a greater mystery, regardless of whether the victim is simply a human being or, above all, the Son of God.

Personally, I think that these ideas of Ellacuría had a kinship with the theologies of Bonhoeffer and Moltmann, which had such an impact on me as well as on Ellacuría. But he added specific and novel thinking.

✧ *What other courses did you teach in those first four years?*

Before answering I would like to make a clarification. It may seem simple, but it is important to understand many things that we will be seeing.

El Salvador was, and is, Third World, a world without many resources. In the teaching of theology it was neither possible nor thinkable to have specialized professors for each of the disciplines, as was considered the ideal in the great faculties of the past. This was not the case with us. With some help, Ellacuría and I had to teach what we knew and what we were prepared for—but also, certainly in my case, what we did not know much about.

Thus, I ended up teaching the course on the sacraments. I did know, as I said before, Rahner's notion of sacramentality, and with that I began the course. But on the first day Ellacuría corrected me. It was good to keep Rahner in mind, but using only his concepts; he pointed out that there was no real historical basis to begin the course and to think about the sacraments as a *Latin American theology* should approach them, which is what we wanted to do. In the first class the *real* should appear, the reality to which the sacraments in the country *referred*. To begin simply with concepts, even with those as profound as Rahner's, did not put us on the right path and distracted us from doing theology as we intended to do it in El Salvador.

This little memory also serves to illustrate what we will say later: the importance of all teachers attending all classes. It was a matter of teaching *together*, of taking note of what a teacher said well and correcting what a teacher did not say well or said with limitations.

The spirituality course was given by several of us, although I can't say much about it now. If I remember correctly, Ellacuría dealt with the theme of faith and justice, the commandment of love, and the beatitudes. I dealt with the theme of prayer and celibacy, and I will dwell on the latter. The reason for speaking about celibacy was not to add a possible appendix to the classic course on spirituality but to deal with an important topic in itself. The concrete reason was a request made to me by the head of the young Jesuits of the province. Talking about celibacy in Latin America could help to deal with the obvious difficulties of a celibate life. I wrote a long text that was soon published in Colombia as a booklet: *El celibato cristiano en América Latina* [Christian celibacy in Latin America].

In class I approached it as a matter of spirituality, that is, of *living what is human with a certain spirit,* in short—*christologically speaking*—with love and unconditional dedication to one's neighbor. More specifically and *theologically,* living with radical availability to whatever is the will of God. Nothing can set limits or be an obstacle to the will of God. Speaking of celibacy for the historical reason I have mentioned was also a sign of how *reality* influenced thinking and doing theology.

✧ *What did you do to maintain the teaching of a curriculum that required a good number of professors?*

The need was clear, but so was the conviction that teachers with training and openness to the Third World could come from outside. And so it happened. Those who came from overseas to teach theology at the UCA were not only a great help, but they also offered an important expression of solidarity. I will explain what I mean in a digression that may help in *doing theology.*

In recent decades, the term *solidarity* is fortunately used very frequently, although sometimes not precisely, and it can even conceal somewhat self-interested or superficial intentions. For what concerns us here, *solidarity* has a social connotation and generally refers to the help that groups, institutions, collectives, and peoples (with the means to do so) offer to the poor and to the victims of this world. Dom Pedro Casaldáliga [a prophetic bishop from Brazil] grasped what was happening and captured it with these beautiful words: Solidarity is the tenderness of peoples.

I began to think about what solidarity means in the 1970s, when aid from abroad to the poor of El Salvador was overflowing in the form of monetary funds, food, medicine, and goods of all kinds. Above all, there were many people who came to the country to offer help with varied knowledge and with the mystique of accompaniment, in their intimate presence and the affection and appreciation that they showed. By helping in this way they ran risks, and yet they stayed in the country. And the most important thing to understand about the meaning of solidarity and what is most endearing is that those who came to *give* could say, "We have *received* more than what we have given." They felt loved and appreciated by the people of El Salvador. As for the world of faith, doubting Christians and some agnostics acknowledged having rekindled their faith through their encounters with the simple and suffering people of El Salvador. All this led me to conceptualize the essence of solidarity, not as aid or an alliance of common interests, but as giving to one another and receiving from one another the best that we are and that we have.

I thought this happened in the theology of the UCA. We obviously received from those who came from afar. They enriched us. But they usually expressed the sentiment that they had received from us more than what they gave, referring not just to the knowledge of the local professors, but above all to the Salvadoran reality, to the reality of the poor and the martyrs.

Speaking personally, I learned that to be a thinking human being, a *theologian,* one must also be open to receiving from and giving to fellow thinkers without an air of superiority or false humility.

✧ *Let's go back to your classes. In these conversations you have talked a lot about God, but you have not said whether you had to give a course on God at the beginning.*

Well, no. The truth is that I have never given an explicit course on God or on the Trinity. In formal courses I have spoken about God when giving courses on Christology. In them I have repeated what others have already said well, insisting with some originality on two things that I am going to explain.

I thought of the *first* one very early on. For Jesus, God is a *God of the kingdom,* of life, justice, utopia, and so on. I am not going to dwell on this, but I am going to dwell on the dialectic in the notion of kingdom and therefore in the notion of God. The kingdom is opposed to the anti-kingdom. God is opposed to the idols. These competing divinities are in struggle, and the mediators who invoke them generate opposing mediations: a world of justice, peace, and conciliation, on the one hand, and on the other, a world of injustice, violence, and rejection. The mediators are Jesus of Nazareth, on the one hand, and the high priests and Pilate, on the other. I formulated a *second* novelty in speaking of God later. That in Jesus there was a personal relationship with the ultimate mystery of his existence seems clear to me, and I have commented on it in class when dealing with the prayer of Jesus. Something more original may have been in the way I have systematically treated that relationship. It has two dimensions.

Jesus has a relationship *with a God who is Father* and *with a Father who is God.* In operational terms, I have written that "for Jesus, God is *Father,* in whom he places his trust and in whom he can rest," and hence his language of *Abba,* his confidence in being heard and helped in his own behavior (as such being God), in a way that is non-authoritarian, affable, and affectionate with the little ones and the despised. But "the Father continues to be God, before whom Jesus is totally available, and who does not let him rest," and hence the important changes we can see throughout his life (as such being the Father), especially if we compare how Jesus spoke and acted at the beginning and how he spoke and acted at the end of his public life: his living and not shying away from temptations; his going forward even without knowing the day of God. In short, Jesus of Nazareth refers to a reality, the *God-Father,* the *Father-God,* who possesses an intrinsic dialectic.

Personally, this vision of the God of Jesus, unitary and dual, has been a way for me to understand that *God is mystery.* It has helped me to clarify myself before God and to speak about God, to keep silent before God, and—I hope—to be available before him, to walk toward the mystery. It has meant living "around God" in a different way than before. And although the Father-God of Jesus never completely calms me, what I have just said has given me a fundamental peace of mind.

In that sense I am not very happy about the current tendency to insist *unilaterally* on "our Father God," on "God's infinite goodness and mercy," on "trust in the Father"—along with the overflow of music, song, dance, theater, and displays of jubilation that can and usually accompany the invocation of the Father.

It is legitimate. It can be very good. And it is understandable as a relief in the face of great suffering to which no solution is seen. And it is also understandable, following so many years of preaching in the churches about a severe God, the judge, creator of hell, to whom he could send sinners for all eternity, apparently without being the least bit disturbed. But neither is it enriching—in fact it is rather impoverishing—to ignore Jesus's availability to a Father who is God, who demands availability, and also makes strong demands, which becomes evident and very concrete when Jesus calls others to follow him.

In any case we must never forget who this God is, what he does, and what he says in the death of Jesus on the cross. In speaking in class about these things, I have noticed special attention in the students.

Mark, the oldest account, which is followed by Matthew, puts a psalm of complaint, even despair, in Jesus's mouth, "My God, why have you forsaken me?" to which I alluded earlier. He does not call God Father, *Abba*. Luke puts a psalm of trust in Jesus's mouth, and he does call him Father: "Father, into your hands I commend my spirit." In John's Gospel, Jesus dies majestically: "All things are being consummated." It was difficult to maintain the vision that Mark had of the death of Jesus on the cross, and it is understandable that in the other accounts it was softened and made less scandalous.

It is not possible to know exactly how Jesus died, but, taking the accounts of his death as a whole, Jesus's death was neither a placid death, like that of Socrates, nor a heroic death.

What I want to insist on is that, according to the accounts, as long as Jesus remained conscious, he did not regret having been available, having let God be God. And let me make an obvious spiritual reflection. It is obviously difficult for us to maintain this total availability. But with simplicity and humility, it is good to try. Or in any case, not to ignore it.

✧ *You have not taught courses on God, but evidently the subject has come up in Christology classes, and you have just mentioned two things to which you attach great importance: God is a God of the kingdom against the anti-kingdom, and he is a God-Father, a Father-God. I guess also outside of class you've talked about God from the beginning. How did you do that?*

I have spoken about God often, and it is normal. I am a priest. On Sundays I celebrated the Eucharist and preached on the Gospel of the day until I had a heart attack at the end of 2017. Some people come to talk about God-related matters. But regardless of my *profession* as a priest, so to speak, which leads me to talk about God, I have said before that, in darkness or in clarity, I have never ignored or trivialized the *God issue*. He has always been present. Sometimes, without the occasion requiring it, I have spoken "theologically" about God to some extent.

In 1976 I gave the *Exercises* of Saint Ignatius to the Sisters of the Assumption. Saint Ignatius begins the principle and foundation with "man is created to praise, reverence, and serve God." I did not content myself with reflecting on the creature-creator relationship, or with mentioning God and assuming that everyone, including Saint Ignatius, already knows who God is. To the best of my knowledge, in the context of that text, I "historicized" that God as "God of life." Shortly afterward I wrote a long text, "The Epiphany of the God of Life in Jesus of Nazareth," which was published in 1980 in *The Idols of Death and the God of Life*.[1] In that text I insist that there is a God of life alongside and against divinities of death.

I don't think what I "theo-logized" about God in those days was a big deal, but I mention it to remind me that the "theo-logical" was very real to me, and I was moved to speak about it as best I could.

In September 1979, in Nicaragua, I also spoke about God. The occasion to talk about God was not so obvious, and it was more demanding. In July the Sandinista revolution, with the participation of many Christians, had triumphed. A group of Sandinista Christians organized a theological meeting to think in a Christian way about the revolution and Christianity, and how to act in the future. They invited several theologians who supported or sympathized with Sandinismo. I was invited too, and I was able to go a few weeks after others had spoken.

Soon I noticed a certain motto that was repeated with enthusiasm: *Between Christianity and revolution there is no opposition.* I understood what they were saying, but I commented that something was missing that should not be ignored. One should ask in what way Christianity could be helpful to the revolution, and in what way the revolution could be helpful to Christianity. That is, what is the positive relationship between Christianity and revolution?

When they invited me, they had not asked me to talk about any specific topic. Given the situation I was coming from, the normal thing would be to talk about Monseñor Romero, about the base communities in El Salvador, about liberation theology, focusing it in a way that would help the new Nicaragua. However, without thinking much about it, I decided to talk about God. I titled my talk: "God and the Revolutionary Processes."

It was not easy for me to think about the talk. I did it keeping in mind my thoughts about God and what I thought of the human and the divine that came out in the midst of the Sandinista revolution. I said three things:

---

[1] Jon Sobrino, "The Epiphany of the God of Life in Jesus of Nazareth," in *The Idols of Death and the God of Life*, ed. Pablo Richard, 66–102 (Maryknoll, NY: Orbis Books, 1983).

1. God is *God of life and of the lifeless poor*. What is the fundamental negation of this God? What are the criteria for a Christian interpretation of a revolutionary process and its future?

2. God is *God of history*, the one who has pronounced words throughout history continues to pronounce a word in Nicaraguan history and continues to incarnate himself in that history.

3. In the revolution, the *mysterium liberationis* could well have appeared, but *the mystery of God*, his unmanipulable reality, must not be dwarfed in order to put him on our side. There is always *more to* this God, and he can generate new history.

In order to speak of God with credibility before these revolutionary Christians, before addressing the three points mentioned above, I made a confession of sincerity and honesty. In the introduction I said that in my experience "it may be that God is good for nothing," but "it may be that he is good for everything." And in closing I insisted that the mystery of God remains a mystery, before, during, and after the revolution.

I don't remember how these reflections were received, but for me it was an important moment. Even if it was groping, I tried to offer something Christian, just as they had asked. And so that I would not lose sight of the radical nature of a revolution, I could not think of anything better than to speak from the radical nature of God.

✧ *You have talked about the beginnings of your theology and its contents. Can you tell us about the pedagogy of your teaching?*

There were several elements that made this type of teaching possible and shaped it. I believe that the most important were the following.

1. Professors and students *formed a body*, a responsible and active *corps*.

2. It was taught in the form of *seminars, with the responsibility of all*.

3. It *was soon seriously criticized* by the highest authority of the Society.

4. Students and professors, some more and some less, *suffered persecution*. This atmosphere of tension brought reality closer.

5. It generated *an impulse to produce and publish theology* that took into account what was taught and learned in class.

6. That first master's degree, by its nature, *led to the expansion of the teaching of theology* in various forms and levels.

Personally, a pedagogy with these dimensions helped me to think and do theology.

✧ *What were your seminars like?*

Two days a week met all met together, both students and teachers, for three hours. We all had to prepare the topics, and we were all asked to discuss them. Personally, the seminars helped me to decenter myself. I was one among other students and professors, different in cultural and even ethnic origin, with very different academic backgrounds.

The seminars also helped to some extent in handling the issue of *mediations* in theology, which at that time was almost an obsession. Outside of theology, I only had a background in engineering, but no one, not even myself, understood how that could serve as a mediation for theological knowledge. There was much more insistence on economics as the privileged mediation of theology. And this insistence made sense, since economics can directly illuminate real poverty and wealth, and indirectly Jesus's vision of both.

The fact that theology was taught at the UCA, that is, in a university with multiple areas of expertise and with a Christian historical orientation of faith and justice, was very helpful in handling the issue of mediations. For me, totally ignorant of the world of economics, it was very important to live and work with Luis de Sebastián, a widely known expert in economics who was also imbued with the Christian ideas we were dealing with. It was not that I studied what he wrote on economics, but since we lived together in the same community and he was sufficiently aware of my theology, that fact assured me that I did not ramble on about economics. Simply put, what I was saying about the God of the poor and Jesus of Nazareth could find some equivalent in a human and humanizing economy.

Personally, the greatest fruit of the seminars for me was to be close to Ellacuría's thought—above all, seeing him do theology in practice.

✧ *You mentioned that tensions with the curia of the Jesuits in Rome were an important aspect of your teaching. What happened?*

I have already said that the theology studies at the UCA were approved without difficulty by the curia in Rome, and no problem was foreseen. But at the end of the first year, Father Arrupe, misinformed, wrote us a warning letter to the effect that, if we did not change radically, he would prohibit the continuation of theology studies. The letter was very harsh and dry. Obviously, it was not written by him, but he signed it.

We were accused point by point of having approached wrongly each and every course of the first year. To this I responded, point by point. My response came to twenty-four pages. Others also wrote defending our first year of theology. The most notable response came from Father Ladislao Segura. He was the oldest professor, I think fifteen or twenty years older than me, and he had been a professor of moral theology and canon law for many years in the archdiocesan seminary. In 1974 he joined the UCA theology faculty and participated with the other professors. He responded to Father Arrupe's letter and said that he saw nothing wrong with the contents and our way of teaching theology. He added: "I would have liked to study theology like that." That was the end of the tension with Arrupe. Now I just want to add that the criticism coming from Rome did not cause me any personal tension.

✧ *Was the whole thing just settled?*

Actually yes, although I personally went through what could have been a difficult time soon after, but which, in the end, turned out magnificently. In June 1976, about a year after receiving our responses to the criticisms, I received a call from Rome telling me to come as soon as possible, because Father Arrupe wanted to talk to me. Two things crossed my mind. One was the teaching of theology at the UCA. The other was my first problems with the Congregation for Catholic Education. A few months earlier I had received a letter from Cardinal Gabriel Garrone, its prefect, pointing out errors and dangers in my writings on Christology that needed to be explained and corrected. I went to Rome without knowing exactly what Father Arrupe wanted from me.

I arrived on June 29, Saint Peter's Day, his saint's day. He soon received me. I will explain later why he called me, but it had nothing to do with teaching or my theological orthodoxy. It had to do with deeper and more personal things about Father Arrupe himself. By talking to him about them I got to know him very well.

In a first brief meeting he did mention Cardinal Garrone's letter to me, but he thought that the situation had returned to normal, since he had not received any more complaints about me from that congregation. Anyway, he told me: "If it is all right with you, go and visit the cardinal." Without any malice, of which Arrupe was incapable, but with fine humor, which he showed in abundance, he told me, "They like it when we pay obeisance to them." I went to visit Garrone with Father Cecil McGarry, one of the assistants general. The cardinal received me in one of those immense palaces of the curia, which I had only seen in movies. In a friendly tone on both sides, I told him that my intention was to make Christology comprehensible to people like Central Americans, whose culture was different from Europeans, and above all to present a Christ who lived in favor of the poor and died to defend justice, which was essential to keep in mind when speaking of Christ in El Salvador.

When I finished speaking, Cardinal Garrone took the floor, and, in a paternalistic and condescending tone, said to me, "You young people worry too much." He continued, "I have also lived in many places, but Christology is the same everywhere." And he went on to say that it was enough to explain the Council of Chalcedon.

The phone rang on the other side of the office, and Father McGarry said, "Let's go. He has no interest in talking further." And that was the end of this little episode, with no consequences for our teaching of theology.

I will return later to Father Arrupe, for I spent many hours talking with him. He was a blessing.

✧ *In addition to tensions, you mentioned persecutions during teaching. What do you mean?*

With the persecutions against the Jesuits, other religious, the church, Bishop Rivera, and especially after 1977 Monseñor Romero, persecution became the norm.

Let me explain. It is not that teaching was prevented or physically persecuted by the security forces. But as far as ideas are concerned, liberation theology was considered highly subversive—without the persecutors really knowing what it was. And, as far as people are concerned, I have already mentioned that it was not possible to finish the master's program that began in 1974 or when it resumed in 1979 because of the persecution of professors and students. On May 1, 1977, the young Jesuit Jorge Aranedas was arrested while he was waiting for the bus. The provincial and Monseñor Romero went to the prison to protest. When they brought Father Aranedas before him, Monseñor asked him how he had been treated and offered him the cup of coffee that had been served to him. Tenderness in the midst of persecution.

These persecutions made possible the deepening of the most important contents of theology. And I think they also generated a deep Christian and Salvadoran mysticism.

✧*As far as I know, very early on, along with the classes, you started publishing articles and small books.*

So I did. I have already mentioned that when it was my turn to cover some topics in the spirituality course, I chose the topic of celibacy. That immediately became a small book published in Colombia in 1977. By the way, I think it is the only book I have written that has not been translated or at least republished. Also, the first time I gave the Christology course, I published the booklet *The Prayer of Jesus and the Christian.*

I am going to expand a little on the specific reason why books from my first Christology classes were published so soon. I gave the course for the first time in 1975. It caught the attention of some Mexican Jesuit students who came to El Salvador, and they encouraged me to publish material from the classes. The final text was a conglomerate, with a certain logic, of the class notes and more elaborate articles related to Christology. I do not remember if the title was given by me or by the Mexican Jesuits who were launching their own publishing house, Ediciones CRT. The title remained *Cristología desde América Latina* [Christology from Latin America]. Years later, Juan Luis Segundo criticized the title, because the content of my book, which he did not criticize in itself, was not really Latin American. The first printing was riddled with errors. The second was more careful. The book was 370 pages long. It was translated into English by Orbis Books in 1978,[2] and several other editions were made. From a Jesuit faculty member in Europe—I never knew which one—I received a criticism: I should not rush to publish but should study certain topics in Christology with greater care and precision. He was right.

Ellacuría, for his part, supported all publications, especially those of members of the master's program, which promoted the theological idea

---

[2] *Christology at the Crossroads: A Latin American Approach* (Maryknoll, NY: Orbis Books, 1978).

of liberation in the world of the poor. He also thought that some of my more novel ideas were sound, although he would pick up on what was not sufficiently sound and let me know in a good way. In 1980, based on the above, I published *Jesus en América Latina,* with an approving prologue by Ellacuría.[3] Those were the beginnings. Later I published a more definitive edition. In 1991, *Jesucristo Liberator: Lectura historico-teológica de Jesús de Nazaret.*[4] And in 1999, *La fe en Jesucristo Ensayo desde los víctimas.*[5] These have been translated into the usual languages.

Going back to the beginnings, I published several small books, *La oración de Jesús y del cristiano* [The prayer of Jesus and the Christian] in 1979, and *Theology of Christian Solidarity* with Juan Hernandez Pico.[6] It is important for me to remember that, at the request of Monseñor Romero, I soon published several texts on the martyrs and, more theoretically and conceptually, on martyrdom. Monseñor told me one day: "Father, in my homilies I speak pastorally about the martyrs. I ask you to help us with your theology." Soon I was writing about martyrs. And after his assassination, I published many texts, reflections, and comments on Monseñor Romero, his person, his dedication, his martyrdom. They are my most personal writings.

To finish answering your question, in 1985 I published *Liberación con espíritu;*[7] in 1989, *Monseñor Romero;*[8] in 1992, *El principio misericordia;*[9] in 2003, *Terremoto, terrorismo, barbarie y utopía;*[10] and in 2007, *Fuera*

---

[3] *Jesus in Latin America* (Maryknoll, NY: Orbis Books, 1987).

[4] *Jesus the Liberator: A Historical-Theological View* (Maryknoll, NY: Orbis Books, 1991).

[5] *Christ the Liberator: A View from the Victims* (Maryknoll, NY: Orbis Books, 2001).

[6] Jon Sobrino and Juan Hernández-Pico, *Theology of Christian Solidarity* (Maryknoll, NY: Orbis Books, 1985).

[7] *Spirituality of Liberation: Toward Political Holiness* (Maryknoll, NY: Orbis Books, 1988).

[8] *Archbishop Romero: Memories and Reflections* (Maryknoll, NY: Orbis Books, 1990; rev. ed. 2016).

[9] *The Principle of Mercy: Taking the Crucified People from the Cross* (Maryknoll, NY: Orbis Books, 1994).

[10] *Where Is God? Earthquake, Terrorism, Barbarity, and Hope* (Maryknoll, NY: Orbis Books, 2004).

de los pobres no hay salvación.[11] And other little books whose titles I do not remember now.

Ellacuría and I worked together on *Mysterium liberationis. Conceptos fundamentales de la teología de la liberación* (Madrid, 1990; San Salvador, 1991).[12] I think it was an important work, and it has been translated into several languages. The idea, as almost always, came from Ellacuría. It fell to me to carry it out—to finalize and introduce it after his assassination.

I have answered your question, I think too much. It is clear that I have a tendency to write and that I have been attracted to publishing. Ellacuría used to say that by temperament I am extravagant, and that I have been so by publishing early and in excess.

◇ *You said that the teaching of that first master's program expanded in various ways. What did you mean?*

The idea of the master's program spread across El Salvador and soon became known. But due to its academic requirements few could access it. Several people asked us why we did not offer theology courses accessible to more people. And so it happened.

Soon we began thinking about how to reach out to religious sisters, leaders of the base communities, committed lay people who worked most of the day. At the beginning the professors were the same as those in the master's program, plus some of the more advanced students. I taught several courses. I believe the initiative came from Juan Ramón Moreno, who was in charge of the faculty until his assassination. Then we started the popular pastoral theology program. For people in the communities we offered five hours of classes on Saturdays for three years.

So there has been a great expansion. It has not simply been the fruit of an interest in growing, which is natural in a university, but from a sense of responsibility for helping to liberate the country with the Christian faith, explained as well as possible to the greatest number

---

[11] *No Salvation outside the Poor: Prophetic-Utopian Essays* (Maryknoll, NY: Orbis Books, 2008).

[12] Ignacio Ellacuría and Jon Sobrino, *Mysterium Liberationis: Fundamental Concepts of Liberation Theology* (Maryknoll, NY: Orbis Books, 1993); abridged ed. *Systematic Theology: Perspectives from Latin America* (Readings from *Mysterium Liberationis*) (1996).

of people. And behind all this is the mother idea that gave birth to theology at the UCA: *the liberation of the oppressed with the help of an adequate theology.*

✧ *Looking at all that you have been saying, what do you think has been the impact of those first years of teaching on your theology?*

Perhaps it may be surprising that we did not miss a *liberation theology* environment. We got to know Gustavo Gutiérrez, Leonardo Boff, and others because they were good theologians, not because they were *liberation* theologians. At that time Ellacuría was talking more about doing *Latin American* theology. We UCA theologians were not known abroad, with the exception of Mexico, and obviously we were not considered liberation theologians.

I was not worried, then, about whether liberation theology was taught in the seminaries. The important thing was to discover what we had not discovered before: in Jesus the poor are the recipients of the kingdom of God, and that God, and no other, was the ultimate reality that I was thinking about. It is the God who expressed himself in the words, "I have heard the cry of my people and have come down to set them free" [Ex 3:7–8]. And in the words of Micah: "Listen once and for all to what is good and what the Lord requires of you: that you practice justice, that you love tenderly, and that you walk humbly with your God" [Mi 6:8].

As for my incipient theology, I was forging a path in the midst of historical, community, and academic realities that were very new. These forced me to think, and they made it easier to think. My theological way of thinking was taking shape. And the fundamental thing, I believe, was the *reference to the real.* As I said before, the theologian is an animal of realities. I believe that the first years of teaching helped me with this.

In those years I also learned that there is a *theology of texts* and a *theology of witnesses*—although I do not entirely like that formulation. The theology of texts arises from the ideas and stories of the great thinkers of the Old and New Testament, of Christian thinkers, of the councils, and of the teachings of the popes. The theology of witnesses arises from capturing realities that make these ideas present in real flesh, in the history of real people, obviously sometimes more and sometimes less.

In the first four years, for various reasons, two people helped me to do *witness theology*. The first was Rutilio Grande, because of his life and especially because of his martyrdom. And the second witness, or "text made reality," was Father Arrupe, to whom I became very close for about ten days in June–July 1976.

First, I will recall how Rutilio Grande helped me to do *witness theology*. The repression had already begun, not yet the great massacres or open warfare, but there had already been deaths. What had never happened was the assassination of a priest. On March 12, 1977, Rutilio Grande was assassinated along with two peasants, a young boy and an elderly man, about seventy years old. Priest and peasants died together, and it is important to maintain the significance of that fact.

That day *I encountered Christianity*. In what happened on that day and in what happened immediately afterward, a Christianity *irrupted* that I had never experienced or suspected. The rules had been broken—not only of good but of evil, even if the cruelty against the poor had begun long before. But in Rutilio and in Monseñor Romero, who from that day on became an ex officio defender of the poor, it was also the case that Jesus of Nazareth, though known and studied for years, also became *visible*.

What occurred was an *ôfthê*—from the Greek verb meaning "to see"—which is the form used in the Gospels in speaking of Jesus's apparitions. It means allowing oneself to be seen, a vision that does not depend on the subject who sees, but on the one who is seen.

And an ecclesial body irrupted with conversion to the poor, with the folly of the Beatitudes, the "greater love" that John speaks of, and the emergence of a body united as never before and determined to follow. Many prayed to the heavenly Father. The conviction, the commitment, and the pride of *being Christian* were palpable. For me, that March 12 was a new and more real baptism.

✧ *Did you know Rutilio before that day? What was he like?*

I only have a few memories that I include in the impact of his murder. In his seven years of studies in Burgos, in Spain, in the 1960s, he was a delicate person. When he returned to El Salvador he worked in the seminary and in school. But he did not feel at ease in Jesuit works, which were mostly city apostolates. It bothered him, and I suppose it hurt him, that we Jesuits did not take into account the peasants, the majority of the Salvadoran population. To find new ways in his pastoral work he went to Ecuador. There Bishop Leonidas Proaño, father of the Indigenous people, opened his eyes and encouraged him. Then, in 1972, he began his work as parish priest of Aguilares, a peasant place.

I saw him in person, I think only twice. One time was in August 1976. I went to Aguilares with Ellacuría to be present at the corn festival. The festival was really beautiful. It was a feast of the peasants. Rutilio spoke to them, also beautifully. At one point he saw Ellacuría and me standing in the middle of the crowd. In the middle of his long homily-speech he said with satisfaction, "Today we are visited by the masters of Israel." He was pleased that Ellacuría and I were there with the peasants.

I think I only saw him one more time. The atmosphere in the capital was already very disturbed. There were persecutions and riots. He came to ask me about the relationship with the non-Catholic churches in El Salvador and ecumenism. Years later I saw a half sheet of paper on which Rutilio had written down what we were talking about. He was interested in knowing as much as possible about ecumenism in order to speak at a meeting of the clergy outside of San Salvador in which he was going to participate. From what I learned later, at the meeting Rutilio became irate: "What are we doing here talking about ecumenism when the city is on fire?" That was Rutilio.

A peasant movement was being created in Aguilares. Rutilio encouraged the basic ecclesial communities and trained the Delegates of the Word. Obviously he encountered fierce opposition among the landowners, who saw his pastoral work as a direct attack on their untouchable power. It is probably that they conspired with members of the army and security forces to assassinate him. He also had enemies in the more conservative Catholic Church. With Monseñor Romero, whom he had met many years before, Rutilio always maintained a good friendship until the end.

In his last years he preached impressive homilies, which I published after his death. In his way of speaking he adopted an endearingly peasant style. Rigorous and vigorous in his denunciations, his homilies were comparable to those of Monseñor Romero. In theological intuition they were exquisite.

✧*Do you remember excerpts from those homilies?*

I read them again before talking to you. With texts from those homilies, Father Carranza, his companion in Aguilares, wrote *El Evangelio de Rutilio Grande* [The gospel of Rutilio Grande]. I will quote a few excerpts without commenting much. It is not necessary. In a long paragraph he said programmatically:

> We want to be the voice of those who have no voice to cry out against so many violations of human rights. That justice be done, that so many crimes staining the country, the army, do not go unpunished. That the criminals be recognized and that fair compensation be given to the families who are left helpless.

A month before his death, in Apopa, he gave his most widely known homily. It addresses the most radical human and Christian realities. This is how Rutilio saw God and his plan for us:

> We have a common Father, so we are all children of the same Father, even if we are born from the wombs of different mothers. . . . Jesus spoke a lot about the kingdom of the Father God. And he liked to compare it to a big dinner at a large table with long tablecloths, which reached everyone equally. And that no one was left out, without his own stool.

He clearly denounced the oppressors, especially if they claimed to be Catholic:

> All human beings are clearly brothers and sisters. All equal one to the other! But Cain is . . . a negation of God's Kingdom. Woe to you, hypocrites, who pay lip service and call yourselves catholic, inside, you are nothing but evil filth! You are Cains and you crucify the Lord when he goes by the name of Manuel, the name of Luis, the name of Chabela, the name of the humble field worker![13]

---

[13] Anthony Ferrari, "A Life of Faith and Courage," Ignatian Center for Jesuit Education–Santa Clara University (November 4, 2015).

He preached the Jesus who was *killed*, and who is not usually or not wanted to be remembered:

Many prefer a mute Christ without a mouth to be carried through the streets. This is not the Christ of the Gospel, the young Jesus of thirty-three years of age! The one who risked his life and died for the noblest cause of humanity. I am afraid, brothers, that if Jesus were to return today, coming down from Galilee to Judea, that is, from Chalatenango to San Salvador, I dare say that he would not arrive with his preaching and actions as far as Apopa. They would stop him there, at the height of Guazapa. And [be] hard on him! Until he was silenced or disappeared.

The death of Rutilio had a great impact, and from that impact came Monseñor Romero. "Monseñor Romero was Rutilio's miracle," people used to say. And a dynamism arose that reached the simplest people, the grassroots communities. Also the UCA.

Rutilio's witness was for me an important *text* to understand and deepen other texts about God, the kingdom of God, and Jesus of Nazareth, about sin and grace. And obviously, about persecution and martyrdom as central themes of theology that are often not central.

Romero and the martyrs of the UCA, especially Ellacuría, are undoubtedly spoken of more than Rutilio. But many people remember Rutilio with great affection and gratitude. On March 12 a good number of people usually go to his tomb.

From what I have heard, Rutilio's cause for beatification is in process.[14] This will undoubtedly make Rutilio better known, and I will be happy. But these human and Christian things are not measured in meters or in decibels produced by applause; neither are they weighed in kilos. The dedication, the will for truth, the love for the little ones, the self-forgetfulness of Rutilio, are and remain in the depths of the Salvadoran reality. Circumstances will bring them more or less to the surface. But they are there and always remain as a reserve of truth, faith, and commitment, with a freshness and an invitation that are always within reach.

---

[14] Following this conversation Blessed Rutilio Grande was beatified in 2022.

✧ *You said before that you would come back to Father Arrupe.*

Yes, and I think I am going to go on and on. After his death, on February 9, 1991, in the mass we celebrated in the chapel of the UCA I gave a homily entitled "Father Arrupe, Man of God, Man among Men, and Man of History." On this and other occasions I did not say anything that others had not said. Ellacuría, with his well-known way with words, said, "Father Arrupe has been the John XXIII of religious life."

Now I would like to recall how important Father Arrupe has been for doing *theology as a witness.* I will refer to some moments that I remember well. All of them, in one way or another, led me to think about the *theological* reality of Father Arrupe, which is what makes it possible to do *witness theology.*

In order not to get lost when talking about very different things, I am going to organize them. I have come up with eight points:

1. In 1976, a *visit to the curia* in Rome.

2. A long *personal meeting,* about eleven hours, over a period of two weeks.

3. Arrupe's *turnaround* of the Society from the perspective of the periphery.

4. His defense of *the crucial struggle* of our time, that of faith-justice.

5. His reaction to the *assassination of Rutilio Grande* in 1977.

6. His *visit to a favela* in Brazil.

7. His *relationship with Monseñor Romero.*

8. A *very brief visit* in 1989 in the infirmary.

To put it in rather technical language, in all this I perceived that in Father Arrupe there was *transcendence.* And to put it in human and religious language, in Father Arrupe I perceived that *in everything he was, did, and said, there was something of God.* That is what moves me to speak at length about Father Arrupe, and I hope the reader will understand.

✧ *Let's start. What happened in Rome in 1976?*

I mentioned earlier that Father Arrupe called me to Rome, where I arrived on June 29. As soon as I arrived at the curia, Father Briceño, one of his close collaborators and a good friend of mine, told me, "You Central American Jesuits are causing a lot of trouble at the curia." He said it laughing. I did not understand what he was referring to, so he explained himself. He told me that the assistants general were frightened because something unprecedented had happened. They were preparing a letter from father general in which he communicated that he was elevating what until then had been the vice-province of Central America to a province. Well, in that letter Father Arrupe "wanted to ask forgiveness from the Central American Jesuits." I do not know in what terms he intended to do so, but that was his intention. That is what puzzled his assistants, and they prevented him from doing so.

In August, two months later, Arrupe went to Guatemala, and there he read the letter about establishing the province. I did not go to Guatemala, because I had just been with him in Rome, but I was very interested to see how the letter had turned out. And I found out. In it, Father Arrupe formulated a fundamental thesis: the reality of Central America gave vitality to the mission of the Society, but it also gave rise to the radicalization of different points of view and the sharpening of tensions. And he added these two central paragraphs. The first is supportive and consoling:

> From Rome I have tried to follow this evolution closely, but my hope has never waned, because in the midst of so many difficulties I have always seen in everyone a determined will to follow Christ, to live a radical, pure, and genuinely Ignatian evangelical spirit.

The second paragraph touches on the issue that had caused the bewilderment of the attendees. I quote it below. Even when read almost half a century later, it is still astonishing:

> Looking back over the experiences of these years with regard to the vice-province, I must confess that memories of different kinds come flooding back to me: some very consoling, others painful; but what I personally regret most is the fact that my limitations have sometimes been the cause of misunderstandings, pain, and suffering that a different direction could have avoided.

These words made me understand what Father Briceño had told me as soon as I arrived in Rome, and above all they showed me a Father Arrupe I did not know in such depth: a human being of total honesty, not at all self-centered, and certainly unselfish. And without being able to help it, I felt that Father Arrupe referred me to God. Not to a God explained in concepts and present in words, not even in scripture or in the words of Saint Ignatius. He was communicating a real God.

✧*And the meeting with Father Arrupe?*

What I have just said I also experienced with immense surprise and depth in the long interview I had with him, spread over eleven hours during a week starting on June 30. I want to insist that the most important thing for me was not his actual words, but the *glimpse of God* in his person.

He had called me to Rome because before making a trip to Latin America he wanted to speak with a Latin American theologian who could explain to him the theology of liberation, which was then in vogue.

Arrupe being Arrupe, he asked me a thousand questions: about theology and liberation, about justice and poverty, about community life, about the Trinity, and more. Coming from him, every question was important. He asked with a real interest in knowing. I did not feel nervous or uneasy but at peace. Nor did I feel in any way privileged that Arrupe had called me so that I could clarify some things for him. The air of close transcendence that he conveyed made me breathe purer air. I felt *small*, but not *dwarfed*.

One day he did surprise me beyond the ordinary. I don't quite remember what we were talking about when he suddenly said to me: "Father, you will think I am crazy. I have written a poem to Jesus Christ. May I read it to you?" I was shocked and silent, and then I said yes. I don't remember what he said in the poem. What I do remember to this day is what I felt inside: "This man really loves Jesus Christ." And if I remember correctly, I think this is more or less what a monk of Montserrat said when, in the process of canonization for Saint Ignatius, he was asked what he remembered about that strange man he met in Montserrat, that Iñigo who did crazy things. If I remember correctly, I think he answered, "That pilgrim was a madman for Christ."

Some years later, in a book on the prayer of Father Arrupe, I read the poem he had read to me in Rome. I read it slowly, curious to remember what he had read to me in his office and, above all, interested in knowing better who Jesus Christ was for Father Arrupe.

And I also came to learn about one of his important concerns. Using the language of that time, he was concerned that behind the kingdom of God that had to be announced and initiated, Jesus Christ would be hidden. In the prayer he wrote on the feast of Corpus Christi he says to Christ:

> When the needs of humanity demand of us an apostolate and a service much more dangerous and difficult than before, it seems that we should have more need of an intimate and continuous contact with you in order to win the world for you, but this is precisely the case now, when it would seem that there are many Jesuits who, if not in word, at least in deed, seem to show that they do not need you. Is it true? Are they sincere? Are they not deceiving themselves?

This complaint before the Lord was not, as far as I know, about what was happening in the Central American province, although at one time I would have thought so. It was a general concern. But it seemed important to me to recall it, because he undoubtedly saw a serious problem in the new direction that the mission of the Society was taking, though, on the other hand, it was something he himself was promoting.

For Father Arrupe, the biggest problem could be not so much that the Jesuits, in the skirmishes of the struggle for justice, would allow themselves to be captivated by Marxism—a fear that others had—but that the Jesuits would lose the *sensus Christi*. I have already quoted the letter of March 19, 1977, which he wrote to the whole Society after the assassination of Father Grande. Now I return to the fundamental point: "In order to fulfill this mission—exemplified in that of Rutilio—the Society today must have men and communities filled with the *sensus Christi*."

I end these reflections with some well-known words he pronounced in a television interview when explaining who Jesus Christ was for him. With total spontaneity and enthusiasm he said: "For me Jesus Christ is everything. . . . Take Jesus Christ out of my life and everything collapses, like a body whose skeleton, head, and heart have been removed."

✧ *You said that Father Arrupe worked to turn the Society around, not from power, but from the periphery. What do you mean?*

Arrupe felt that what God wanted him to do was to put the Society of Jesus in tune with God, as God manifested himself to him. I cannot think of a more graphic way of putting it. In that sense, I believe that

Father Arrupe grasped the need for the Society to make a turnaround. And he saw it more and more clearly from the periphery. Reforms were not enough; radical changes were needed.

The turnaround occurred, and its most genuine expression was in the emphasis on faith and justice. It was clear to Arrupe that the Jesuits had to overcome things that seemed important to them. He did not shrink from stepping into the void that this entailed, which was a great contribution. And a greater contribution was to help the Society to establish itself on new, unsuspected, dangerous, and necessary foundations.

Over the centuries there had been important shifts in relation to the original intuition of Saint Ignatius. Ellacuría exemplifies this magnificently: freedom and grace "were overprotected and subjected to law and to institutional structure." In this way the Society shielded the Jesuits from reality instead of opening them to it and pushing them to enter into it, with its conflicts and dangers, and also with its promises and hopes. In this context the turn meant, among other things, entering the world of atheism, as opposed to faith, and dealing with the reality of injustice, destroyer of God's creation.

When Father Arrupe took over the reins of the Society, it was only with difficulty that it had the capacity to humanize an increasingly new world and to guarantee a future for Christianity in that world. I think that this is how Father Arrupe saw it. This obviously did not mean undoing the Society, but neither did it mean introducing only a few changes, even if they were notable. It seems to me more appropriate to speak of remaking the Society, and for this it was necessary to return in earnest to Jesus and in due proportion to Saint Ignatius. In any case, by the time of Father Arrupe's death the Society was a different one. Since the generalate of Father Arrupe, dozens of Jesuits have been killed for the faith and even more clearly for justice in the Third World. This is the clearest—and most exemplary—expression of the turnaround.

At the origin of everything was God, *the ultimate ultimacy*. But in his relationship with God, Father Arrupe introduced another ultimacy, just as Monseñor Romero had done. Speaking of the latter, Ellacuría said, "His hope rested on two pillars: a historical pillar, which was his knowledge of the people, to whom he attributed an inexhaustible capacity to find solutions to the most serious difficulties, and a transcendent pillar, which was his persuasion that ultimately God is a God of life and not of death, that the ultimate reality is good and not evil." Pedro Casaldáliga, when

Benedict XVI insisted on overcoming relativism, provocatively cited *two* ultimates: "Everything is relative, except God and hunger."

I believe that in Father Arrupe we can also find two ultimate pillars. The first pillar is undoubtedly God. The second is more difficult for me to formulate correctly. I think it is human suffering. It certainly affected him. He spoke about this when he first visited slums in Madrid as a student, and when in Lourdes he felt the pain of illness up close. And there is no need to recall the atomic bomb explosion in Hiroshima, where he cared for many badly wounded.[15]

But I believe that he was more and more affected by a specific suffering: the *massive* suffering and death of great majorities in times of war, and the *massive and unjust* suffering resulting from oppression and repression, and death by hunger and disease in times of peace. And Father Arrupe believed that from that suffering arose the great question directed to everyone and very directly to the Society: What part do we have in it, what are we going to do to repair that suffering? And it is no small thing to start thinking about reparation in order to eradicate it and redeem ourselves.

The process of coming to feel the suffering ultimacy of human beings, conceptualizing it and formulating it, seems important to me in order to understand the turnaround that Father Arrupe had to make, and that he made as superior general. And it is equally important, and not mere curiosity, to know in what real place he was capturing the need for the turnaround. In Arrupe's case the question of the place was not so decisive, given his extraordinary ability to be in tune with everything and in depth in any place. But that does not explain everything.

He spent the years of the turnaround of faith and justice in Rome. But Father Arrupe did not find there, in the center of Christianity, in Europe, in the West—that is, in the places of power in its various manifestations—the sap from which the root of things lives or the encouragement to give an impetus to the turnaround. Before that, he had lived for many years on the periphery. It is rightly said of Father Arrupe that he is a "universal man," but I think it is not good to rush into his universalism. *He became universal from the periphery.* His was a "universalism" certified by "partiality." Arrupe propitiated the turnaround of the Society. In that

---

[15] Arrupe's first assignment as a Jesuit was to Japan. On August 6, 1945, he was living on the outskirts of Hiroshima when the first atomic bomb was dropped.

turning around there was his faith in God, but there was also, as I think, the periphery, configuring that faith and that God.

✧ *Before you referred to Arrupe's role in promoting faith-justice as the crucial struggle. Can you explain it a little bit?*

It meant putting an end to a long history of unconsciousness and, to a great extent, of ecclesial sinfulness. This is how Ellacuría explains it. "In the Western church, faith and justice had become, if not divorced—and each in search of another marriage—at least very far apart. Instead of justice, they went the way of almsgiving charity. Arrupe and his congregation wanted to make a decisive turnaround in this truly scandalous situation for the faith." Father Arrupe made faith and justice walk hand in hand again. He saw it clearly as God's will.

As far as justice is concerned, and more specifically in Latin America, the first thing he did was to face reality. Father Arrupe saw reality and listened to it. And Arrupe, appointed general in 1965, shortly before Medellín, grasped very well the word that after centuries was being uttered by reality in Latin America. It was a cry, radical in tone and radical in content. We have already said it: "Misery as a collective fact is an injustice that cries out to heaven." This radicalism in seeing the truth of things always accompanied him, which cannot be said of the church and the Society of Jesus as a whole. For this it was necessary to be at the height of the clamor of the impoverished majorities, as Arrupe, along with others, such as Dom Hélder Câmara, was.[16]

It is good to remember that for Father Arrupe this listening to cries had a history. Studying medicine in Madrid, as a member of the Saint Vincent de Paul Society, he went to visit poor families in the suburbs of the capital. For the first time he was confronted with misery and situations of injustice. He recalls: "That, I confess, was a new world for me. I encountered the terrible pain of misery and abandonment. Widows loaded with children who asked for bread without anyone being able to give it to them; the sick who begged for the charity of medicine without any Samaritan giving it to them . . . and, above all, children, many children, some half abandoned, others mistreated, most of them

---

[16] Dom Hélder Câmara (1909–99) was the prophetic archbishop of Recife, Brazil.

insufficiently clothed and all of them usually hungry." The quotation is beautiful, but it is also illustrative. Father Arrupe recognizes that he *discovered a new world*, and he does so by way of *confession*, as if he should have discovered it before. He also *confessed* that the Jesuits should have discovered it earlier.

The ecclesial, Christian tradition, expert in charity and concern for the poor, often in an evangelical way, had been, with some notable exceptions, practically fasting when it came to justice and liberation of the oppressed. And it is remarkable because this is how God's self-manifestation begins: "The affliction of my people is well seen by me. I have heard the cry of their taskmasters. I know their sufferings and I have come down to deliver them." It is a real enigma that the inaugural entryway of God's revelation, continued by the prophets and brought to fulfillment by Jesus, did not become, with exceptions, the central nucleus of Christian being and doing throughout history. Worse still, those who pointed to it were often ignored and even persecuted.

Father Arrupe, as a person, was remaking his vision of God and justice. But he also had to integrate a fundamental fact: in 1965 he became superior general of an order of thirty-six thousand members. This meant that it was his responsibility to see that the whole Society, not just him, should remake its faith in such a way that it would give important space to justice. Arrupe's most important contribution to faith and justice, greater than what he could do individually, was to move the whole Society in that direction. It was the most important and also the most difficult thing. As superior general he moved in the sphere of the powers of this world, ecclesiastical and civil. That is why bishops and government envoys complained to him when they did not agree with what the Jesuits were doing in favor of justice. It is easy to understand the weight that fell on Father Arrupe's shoulders. It was his great contribution to keep the Society moving in this direction against powerful adversaries and enemies.

His greatest personal contribution consisted, I believe, in speaking of faith and justice *in a unified way*, and in making this *the fundamental aspect of the Society's mission*. This option for faith and justice caused Father Arrupe a thousand headaches, attacks, and distancing. Centuries-old alliances were called into question. And it also meant—at least in principle—the end of a certain complacency that from time to time appears in the tradition of the Society. A conference he gave in 1973 to former students of the Society of Jesus in Spain, in Valencia, became famous:

> Have we Jesuits educated you for justice? If we give to the term *justice* and to the expression *educate for justice* all the depth with which the church has endowed it today, I believe that we must respond with all humility that we Jesuits have not educated you for justice as God requires of us, and I believe that I can also ask you to have the humility to respond that no, you have not been educated for justice and that you need to complete the formation you have received.

These are big words. And Father Arrupe encouraged the filling of these gaps and for the Jesuit schools to respond to the demands of justice. It would not be easy, he warned, but we had to try. Still, his words caused a stir. The president of the Alumni Association resigned.

Arrupe was confronted with two difficult problems that arose in the liberation processes in which some Jesuits were involved. He faced them with honesty and determination. The first was violence. His position on this was very clear: violence in itself is not evangelical and must be avoided, and for this reason he did not agree that religious should take an active part in the armed struggle. The second was Marxist analysis, on which he had a much more nuanced judgment. This is shown by the instruction he wrote on this subject after prior consultation with several Jesuits who were experts in the matter, and which underwent two drafts. On the whole there is neither naive acceptance nor dogmatic rejection of Marxism. He was more critical of strictly political Marxist praxis, especially if it implied "more than a class struggle, a class hatred leading to violence"—something that has very little to do with scientific Marxism. And he tried to prevent "with prudence, but also with firmness" the political affiliation of the Jesuits.

The theme of justice also got him seriously interested in liberation theology. He did not attain sufficient technical knowledge, but he did read some significant works. "His impression was that such theology still had more to do, but he encouraged doing it." That was Ellacuría's judgment. As in the case of Monseñor Romero, Arrupe grasped very well what lay behind this theology and its potential for justice and for faith.

What we have said so far is only intended to show that Father Arrupe took justice and all that it entailed seriously. He remained convinced of its decisive importance to the end, and he creatively confronted the difficulties involved in fighting for justice. The clearest expression of the movement that animated him, and that he animated, is Decree 4 of General Congregation XXXII, the high point and turning point in the life of the Society.[17] To understand it well, many other things must be taken into account: the council, Medellín, the 1971 synod on justice in the world, the advances in exegesis, liberation theology, and also the advances in social thought and popular movements, most of which were shaped by some form of Marxism, the practices of insertion among the poor, solidarity with them. . . . All this, together with persecutions, led up to Decree 4.

Arrupe was deeply convinced about the need to convoke a general congregation to take the last step in a process that had begun, but had not finished, with General Congregation XXXI. It was that congregation, in 1965, which had elected him as general and entrusted him with the renewal of the Society. But the advisability of convening another general congregation was controversial.

On October 4, 1970, the congregation of procurators voted against the convocation, with ninety-one votes against and nine in favor. But a few days later, on October 25, notwithstanding this clear vote against, Father Arrupe, in an open letter to the whole Society, in addition to communicating the result of the aforementioned vote, announced as his own decision the convocation of General Congregation XXXII. And he added what we have already said: it was "the most important decision of his entire generalate." In my opinion, he was right. It was for him the way to make *the necessary turnaround* and to make the *periphery central* in the Society.

Under his guidance and encouragement the congregation asked itself the most radical question Jesuits had asked themselves in a very long time: "What does it mean today to be a companion of Jesus?" And the

---

[17] A critical clause in Decree 4 was this: "The mission of the Society of Jesus today is the service of faith, of which the promotion of justice is an absolute requirement. For reconciliation with God demands the reconciliation of people with one another."

answer, as we have seen, was unprecedented: "To engage under the banner of the cross in the crucial struggle of our time: the struggle for faith and the struggle for the justice that faith itself demands." The Society set to work, with different rhythms and with greater or lesser intensity, on a new path. For Father Arrupe it was a cause of joy to see the birth of a Society more like Jesus, with many martyrs for justice. It was also a source of displeasure within the Society and of conflicts outside it with the powers of this world and with the Vatican. Father Arrupe's "faith and justice" caused him unpleasantness and conflicts with Paul VI. It is debated whether it also caused him conflicts with John Paul I and John Paul II.

It is also debatable what his specific contribution was. His documents and letters are illuminating. But in my opinion, the most important thing was the conviction and credibility with which he communicated the texts of the congregation and urged that they be put into practice. And the root from which everything grew was *listening to the cry of the oppressed*. This man of God could not fail to hear the cries of the poor and react with his whole person and with all the weight of the universal Society. We have already said that few had done this so radically before, whether in the church or in the Society of Jesus. Therefore, while his general directives were important, his most effective contribution was to guide, push, and hold on, to move the Society by going ahead, which is what it means to be a leader, taking on the serious problems this caused him, spreading conviction, commitment, and hope, and not shying away from risks and conflicts. And all this with creative freedom, not as one who reluctantly follows an already established doctrine—a law, in short—but as one who allows himself to be led by the power of the Spirit of God. And always with "his eyes fixed on Jesus," as the Letter to the Hebrews says. For this he risked his peace of mind and his health. And in this, ultimately, his life was at stake.

At the end of his life, Father Arrupe acknowledged that faith and justice were arrived at through a process. "Yes, it developed until it reached Decree 4 of the General Congregation XXXII. Today there are already magnificent studies on the relationship between faith and justice," he told Pedro Lamet in the infirmary. Lamet continued to delve gently into the depths of Father Arrupe's life: "But many have accused them of being Marxists," Lamet said. And he continues: "Arrupe laughed charmingly." And without answering directly, he gave the best answer that explained everything: "Today there are many who have given their lives for this dimension of faith. There are many new Jesuit martyrs, like Rutilio Grande."

❖ *And how did Father Arrupe react to the murders of Jesuits, which had already begun in his time?*

Father Grande was one of the first Jesuits killed in those years, although not the first priest. But given the situation in El Salvador and the actions of the Jesuits—both of which were international news—the assassination of Rutilio had a great impact on him. Moreover, it must have reminded him of the tensions regarding our province. The fact is that, seven days after the assassination of Father Grande, he wrote a letter, famous for its content and for being addressed to the universal Society. In it he wrote:

> These are the Jesuits the world and the church need today. Men moved by the love of Christ, who serve their brothers without distinction of race or class. Men who know how to identify with those who suffer and live with them to the point of giving their lives to help them. Courageous men who know how to defend human rights to the point of sacrificing their lives, if necessary.

Without being foolish in any way, these words cannot hide the intimate joy—equal to that of Monseñor Romero when his priests were murdered—of seeing Jesuits dying to defend the victims, and seeing God in them. Nor can they hide the wisdom of General Congregation XXXII, so dear to Father Arrupe: "We will not work for the promotion of justice without paying a price" (Decree 4, no. 46).

Since the generalate of Father Arrupe, I believe that about sixty Jesuits have been killed for defending justice and, in this way, for being followers of Jesus of Nazareth. From the Central American province, Father Rutilio Grande and the six martyrs of the UCA, plus Father Carlos Pérez Alonso—of whom we seldom speak, a Jesuit "disappeared" in Guatemala in 1981 by the shadowy military of that country. Arrupe saw in them the glory of the Society. And in them, and in so many others like them, he felt the presence of God in our world.

When the Jesuits of the UCA were assassinated in 1989, along with two women, Elba and Celina, mother and daughter, Arrupe lay in the infirmary very diminished. Brother Bandera, his nurse, told him the news. He says that Father Arrupe burst into tears.

❖ *You mentioned a visit to a favela.*

That's right. I found it in the book by Toño García. In Brazil, after visiting a favela where some Jesuits worked, Arrupe wrote a text entitled "That Mass in the Favela." I copy it here, slightly edited and without comments:

In the slum, which was filthy, lived about a hundred thousand people. The mass took place under a kind of dilapidated roof, without a door, with dogs and cats that entered freely.

The Eucharist began with the not very cultivated music of a guitar, and they sang "To love is to give oneself." As the singing progressed, I felt a big lump in my throat. I had to make a real effort to continue the mass.

The moment of the consecration arrived. When I raised the host, I perceived in the midst of the tremendous silence the joy of the Lord, who is among those he loves.

As I gave communion, I noticed that on those dry, hard, sunburned faces there were tears rolling down like pearls. They had just met Jesus, who was their only consolation. My hands were trembling.

The homily was short. It was mostly a dialogue. A little old lady thanked me a million times because "these fathers have taught us to love our enemies." A boy who a week ago had gotten a knife to kill a classmate thanked me because, with the preaching of the little father, "instead of killing that classmate I bought an ice cream and gave it to him."

After mass, a burly man, who looked like a criminal and was almost scary, said to me: "Come to my house. I have a present for you." The house was a half-destroyed barrack, and he invited me to sit on a rickety chair. From my seat I could watch the sunset. The big man said to me: "Look, sir, what a beauty!"

We were silent for a few minutes. The sun disappeared. The man exclaimed, "I didn't know how to thank you for all you do for us.

I have nothing to give you. But I thought you might like to see this sunset. Didn't you like it? Goodbye." And he shook my hand.

To put mass and favela together is to put together two experiences of ultimacy that refer to two ultimate realities. One is God. The other can be many things. In this case, poverty, or dignity, or hope, or justice, or goodness. Or all of them at the same time.

✧ *You also spoke of his relationship with Monseñor Romero.*

They are personal memories that are very dear to me. Ellacuría, a good connoisseur of both and not given to empty rhetoric, considered them truly exceptional persons, from whom one can do a *theology of witnesses.* Although it was in a precise context—the way Father Arrupe exercised authority in an evangelical way—Ellacuría formulated a thesis in solemn words: "I only know of one other remarkable man. He is another martyr, Oscar Arnulfo Romero, so close to Father Arrupe and so comforted by him on his difficult trips to Rome."

Ellacuría saw what was remarkable in both of them, which was ultimately the depth of their faith, so that, as far as it is possible to write about these things, I believe that the very faith of Ellacuría, the deepest part of his person, "was carried by the faith of Monseñor Romero." We will return to this topic later.

Monseñor and Father Arrupe spoke of each other with great appreciation and affection. Romero mentions Father Arrupe several times in his diary. On May 3, 1979, he writes: "I went to lunch at the General Curia of the Jesuit Fathers. And they did me the honor of placing me at the table of Father Arrupe, with whom I talked before lunch about the ecclesial situation in my country. He also told me about various projects of the Society in Latin America."

On June 25, 1978, he ended the account of his long conversation with Father Arrupe with these words: "He is a very holy man, and it is clear that the Spirit of God enlightens him." For his part, Father Arrupe spoke about Monseñor Romero in an interview with Pedro Miguel Lamet in July 1983. At the time he was already suffering difficulties in his speech and other limitations of a seriously ill person, but also with the freedom of one who has consummated his career. Asked about Monseñor Romero, he said: "Yes, he was a very good friend of mine. He was converted thanks to the example of Father Grande." On another occasion he had already said, and I quote from memory, "Monseñor Romero is a saint."

Though different in their temperaments and ministerial responsibilities, they were very similar in their dedication to God and to those who suffer, in their strength and their freedom to confront the powers of this world, and in their joy in seeing the gospel flourish. And what I want to emphasize now is that they were also similar in substance, although obviously different in form, according to their geographical immediacy or remoteness, their way of situating themselves before the Salvadoran reality and its repercussion on both of them. In any case, between the two there was a great spiritual and historical harmony, since both had to deal with similar historical and ecclesiastical problems and drink from the same source of life: the surrender for the love of many. Both Monseñor Romero and Father Arrupe were burdened with an exceptional reality and let themselves be burdened by it. And that enlightened them also in their mission as archbishop and as superior general.

❖ *You've been at ease talking about Father Arrupe. What is your last memory?*

The last time I saw him was in the summer of 1989, when Father Kolvenbach [Arrupe's successor as superior general] gathered the deans and theology directors of the whole Society at the curia. Father Arrupe was retired to a room in the curia, ill and very weak. We were allowed to visit him, two by two, and the visit was to be for a very short time. I went with a Latin American who spoke to him for a minute or two. Arrupe did not move or speak. When my companion finished, I approached him, kissed him on the forehead, and said, "Father Arrupe, we Jesuits of Central America love you very much." He showed no reaction. From the door I looked at him, and it occurred to me to say goodbye with a Basque word from his native Bilbao: *Agur.* Arrupe heard me, saw me, and smiled. With that smile I left him.

4

Inalienable Themes

<hr>

The Crucified People, Jesus of Nazareth, the Church of the Poor, the Civilization of Poverty

✧ *You have commented on your first years of doing theology and the themes that you began to elaborate. Now, several years later, new themes have emerged. Do any of these interest you? And are any among the old themes still absolutely important to you?*

Undoubtedly there are many important new themes: bioethics, ecology, nonbiblical religions (especially those of the East and of the Indigenous worlds), Islam, gender, feminism, and so on.

At my age and with very little energy I no longer spend time thinking about the new topics that theologians deal with. I inform myself only to a minimum of what is said about them. And I remember Segismundo from *Life Is a Dream:* "To do well is what matters."

Having said this, I will mention what for me continue to be inalienable themes. In addressing them, I will frequently quote the words of Monseñor Romero and Ignacio Ellacuría.

✧ *What are these issues?*

There are four of them. I mention the titles and the task each requires of us.

1. *The majorities of this world.* And from there, *never to forget the crucified people.*

2. *Jesus of Nazareth.* And from there, *that we should not be robbed of Jesus of Nazareth.*

3. *Ambiguities of the conciliar church.* And from there, *recovering the Pact of the Catacombs and the church of the poor.*

4. *A new and necessary civilization.* And from there, *to work for the civilization of poverty.*

NEVER FORGET THE CRUCIFIED PEOPLE

Where Did the Expression and Concept of Crucified People Come From?

As far as I know, it was in El Salvador forty years ago. Ellacuría used it for the first time in 1978 in a text he wrote in preparation for Puebla: "The Crucified People: An Essay on Historical Soteriology."[1] In that piece the interest was fundamentally soteriological. In 1981 he elevated it to a sign of the times, with a fundamentally revelatory interest.

Before Ellacuría, Monseñor Romero had already used an equivalent expression in a more prophetic and religious tone. In May 1977 the army had occupied the town of Aguilares, and in a few days they had assassinated dozens of peasants. When the army abandoned the town, on June 19, Monseñor immediately went to Aguilares and celebrated the Eucharist. With deep feeling he said: "That figure representing Christ nailed on the cross and pierced by the lance is the image of all those people who, like Aguilares, have been pierced and violated"; "I will never tire of denouncing the assault on human life by arbitrary arrests, by disappearances, by torture" (June 24, 1979). "The violence, murder, and torture that leave so many dead; the people chopped with machetes and thrown into the sea—all that is the dominion of death" (July 1, 1979). Later, in a Sunday homily, he denounced the forms of crucifixion of the people: "I denounce above all . . . wealth and private property as untouchable absolutes. Woe to those ones who touch that high-tension wire—they'll get burned!" (August 12, 1979). And still later: "The organized sector of our people continues to be massacred merely for going into the streets in an orderly manner to ask for justice and freedom" (January 27, 1980).

---

[1] In Ignacio Ellacuría and Jon Sobrino, *Systematic Theology: Perspectives from Liberation Theology,* 257–88 (Maryknoll, NY: Orbis Books), 1996.

Who Are the Crucified People?

Ellacuría offered a quasi-definition that included the crucifixion of the majorities and the sin of the crucifying minorities:

A crucified people is understood here as that collectivity which, being the majority of humanity, owes its situation of crucifixion to a social order promoted and sustained by a minority that exercises its dominion according to a set of factors, which . . . must be considered as sin.

Are the Crucified People Always *the* Sign *of the* Times?

Ellacuría wrote about this in 1981. He included in the expression *sign* the two connotations that the term has in the texts of Vatican II. In its historical-perceptible version, the crucified people characterizes the reality of the time (*GS*, no. 4). It is a *historical* sign. In its historical-transcendent version, the crucified people is a true sign of the presence or plans of God (*GS*, no. 11). It is a *theological* sign. He explains:

Among the many signs that are always present, some striking and others barely perceptible, there is in every age one that is the principal one, in the light of which the others must be discerned and interpreted. That sign is always the historically crucified people, which joins to its permanence the always different historical form of its crucifixion. That people is the historical continuation of the Servant of Yahweh, whom the powers of the world continue to strip of everything, even life, especially Life.

It could not be said of Ellacuría that he was one of the prophets of doom that John XXIII warned about, and from whom the pope wanted to distance the church. But even less could he ignore "the dramatic bias that often characterizes our world" (*GS*, no. 4)—quite the contrary. And for the church to carry out its mission sensibly, it must know well the world in which it lives (cf. *GS*, no. 4). This is the reason for beginning with the negativity that characterizes the world as a "crucified people."

This Crucified People Is the Suffering People

"The crucified people" is a sign with content. The crucified people are stripped of everything—massively, defenselessly, and innocently—and their lives are taken from them. They are deprived of dignity. Because they are *the* principal sign in the midst of so many others, some visible, others barely perceptible, a hierarchy can be established among the signs of the times. The criterion is the greater or lesser closeness to the crucified people. The crucifixion of the people sometimes reaches an unprecedented magnitude of cruelty and perversion. Metz insists on Auschwitz, on not forgetting it and keeping it as *memoria passionis*. And Dom Pedro Casaldáliga has called Africa "the dungeon of the world," "a continental *Shoah*."

Let's say a word about *crucifying*: nailing human beings to two wooden beams, usually in the shape of a T—sometimes tied hand and foot. Death usually came by asphyxiation after many long hours. The Roman Empire, having apparently borrowed it from the Persians, used the cross for slaves and rioters, to denigrate them and to horrify others who might intend to revolt. For Christians, it is important to remember that Simon Peter was crucified as a Jewish rebel, a member of those who sought liberation from the Roman Empire, while Saul, maintaining his dignity as a Roman citizen, was beheaded. As far as I know, Spartacus, who sought the liberation of the slaves, was crucified in Rome in the year 71, along with hundreds of other slaves. These facts are rarely explored in theological texts, and even less often in homilies where the cross of Jesus is spoken of.

The Crucified People in Analogy with the Crucified Christ

Monseñor Romero said it with great acuity in his homily of October 21, 1979: "We find in Christ the model of the true liberator. So closely did Christ identify with the people that commentators on the Bible cannot tell whether the Servant of Yahweh proclaimed by Isaiah signified the suffering people or Christ who comes to redeem us." Monseñor rejoiced: "How beautiful it is when a liberator identifies so profoundly with the people that it is impossible to distinguish his cause from the people's cause. I am deeply grieved that the organized sector of our people continues to be massacred merely for going into the streets in orderly fashion to ask for justice and freedom." And further on he delved into the relationship between Christ and the people in their suffering.

How well Christ identifies himself with the suffering of our peoples! So many things seem to cry out, so many slums, so many in prisons and suffering, so many hungry for justice and peace. My God! My God! Why have you forsaken me? You have not forsaken us.

The Crucified People in Analogy with the Suffering Servant

Ignacio Ellacuría, in speaking of the crucified people, did not so much use the Persian-Roman metaphor of the crucifixion, but rather the songs of the Suffering Servant of Yahweh from the prophet Isaiah (42:1–9; 49:1–10; 50:4–11; 52:13—53:12). Ever since I heard this for the first time in the 1970s it has struck me. And I have used it several times. In 1981 *Sal Terrae* magazine asked me to write a text for the Lenten issue, and I wrote about one of the massacres in El Salvador, that of the Sumpul River. I began with the words of one of the survivors, Toñita:

We were there when we were attacked. We had the soldiers three hundred meters away, and when I say we, I mean almost five thousand people. We crossed the Sumpul River, what a painful scene! Everyone was throwing themselves in. The children were running down, the old people couldn't resist either, they were drowning. Children, old people, women, all drowned in the river crossing.

And remembering the Suffering Servant, this was my comment: Of the Servant it is said, first of all, that he is a man of sorrows, accustomed to suffering (Isa 53:3). This is the normal condition of the crucified people: hunger, sickness, life in the slums, illiteracy, frustration due to lack of education and work, pain and suffering. And their hardships increase when, like the Servant, they decide to establish justice and law (Isa 42:1–4). Then repression falls upon them, and the verdict is proclaimed: *they are guilty, under sentence of death* (53:7). And they are even more like the Servant: without human semblance, without beauty, without an attractive face (52:14—53:1). To the ugliness of daily poverty are added the tortures, the mutilations, the disfiguring blood. And then, like the Servant, they produce disgust: many were frightened of him, because in his disfigurement he did not look like a man, did not have a human appearance (52:14). And before him people hide their faces, not only because they are disgusted, but also so that nothing will cloud the false happiness of those who have produced the Servant, so that they do not unmask the truth that is hidden in the euphemisms that we invent every day: we call crucified peoples *developing countries, incipient democracies,* and so on.

Like the Servant, the crucified people are rejected (53:3); everything has been taken away from them, even their dignity. And really, what can the world learn from them, what do they offer for its progress, except their raw materials, their beaches, their volcanoes, and their folklore? They are not esteemed, but despised. And contempt is consummated when ideology takes on religious overtones to condemn them in the name of God.

Of the Servant it is said that we consider him to be smitten by God (53:4), numbered among sinners (53:12). And of these people, what is said? While they suffer with patience, they are recognized for a certain kindness, simplicity, and above all for their religiosity. But when they decide to live, to invoke the true God, the one who defends and liberates them, then they are not even recognized as people of God, and the well-known litany is intoned: they are subversives, terrorists, criminals, atheists, Marxists, communists.

Of the Servant it is said that he was buried among the wicked, in a tomb of evildoers (53:9). The crucified people sometimes do not have even that. According to ancient piety nobody should be denied a tomb, but now the disappearances occur, and clandestine cemeteries are built.

Of the Servant it is said that he humbled himself and did not open his mouth, that he suffered and died in total meekness and helplessness (53:7). Today, not all the crucified die like this. Monseñor Romero was able to speak in life, and his death was a great cry that shook many consciences. So are the deaths of priests and prominent people. But who even knows the names of the tens of thousands of people murdered in

El Salvador or Guatemala? What words do the children of Biafra or the 90 percent of illiterate people in Haiti utter? Millions die without uttering a word. Neither the way they live nor the way they die is known. Their names are unknown.

Of the Servant it is said that he was taken away, without defense, without justice, in total impotence (53:7) in the face of arbitrariness and injustice. This does not apply exactly to the crucified people. Many are fighting for their lives, and there is no lack of prophets to defend them. But the repression against their struggle is brutal; and the prophets are first discredited and then coopted by a society that presents them as a sign of freedom and democracy, until the point when they are truly dangerous. Is there a real court that defends the cause of the poor?

The Crucified People Bring Salvation

We return to Ellacuría and to what is most original in speaking of the *crucified people*. According to Isaiah "the crucified people is the victim of the sin of the world and bears that sin." And they are also the ones who "will bring salvation to the world." Of the Servant it is said that he is innocent, there was no deceit in his mouth (53:7), and he had committed no crimes (53:9). Though he was not deserving of such punishment, others have inflicted it on him; it is a product of our hands. He bore the sin of many (53:8). He was pierced for our rebellions, crushed for our crimes (53:3). By his wounds we have been healed. Mysteriously.

At this point Ellacuría confesses that "only in a difficult act of faith could the author of the Servant's Songs come to affirm what goes against all evidence," but he maintains the affirmation against the world that is unwilling to tolerate the salvific potential of the crucified people. That world discards the cornerstone for the construction of history and seeks to build it from power and domination, from the annulment of the vast majority of oppressed humanity. In biblical language Ellacuría says the stone that the builders rejected "became the cornerstone. In this crucified people are the living stones with which the new house will be built.

This Salvation Is Real

There are signs that the poor are evangelizers and saviors. The splendid experience of the base communities as a leaven of renewal in the church and as a factor of political transformation, the not purely occasional example of the "poor in spirit" who organize themselves to fight in solidarity and martyrdom for the good of their brothers and sisters, the humblest and weakest, are already proof of the salvific and liberating potential of the poor.

These are the words of Ellacuría. And in this context he recalled the affirmation of Puebla: "[The poor] have begun to organize themselves for an integral living of their faith and, therefore, to claim their rights" (no. 1137). And he commented, "The faith of the poor is thus constituted as a political force of liberation."

The Crucified People Save with Historical Responsibility

Ellacuría made an important point, and one very much his own. He says that salvation does not only come from the crucifixion and death. Rather, he affirms that "only a people that lives, because it has risen from the death inflicted on it, can save the world." But he maintains the fundamental thesis that historical salvation will not happen *sine efussione sanguinis* [without the shedding of blood], as he said in an ethical-political speech to the presidents of El Salvador and Costa Rica in September 1989. In any case, in the crucified people—and in the diversity of its forms—there is a potential for salvation.

We cannot go into a long analysis of Ellacuría. Suffice it to recall the following. On the positive side, the crucified people (sometimes he speaks of the "people of the poor") bring salvation because (a) they possess human values, not so well known elsewhere, such as a spirit of welcome, simplicity, sharing; (b) with spirit they organize themselves and work for liberation; and (c) above all, they live and survive, they wish to live with one another, and sometimes they live for one another. On the negative side, because they are a product of our hands, they can show us our truth. To make himself understood Ellacuría used two metaphors: (1) The inverted mirror of the carnival—looking at it, we appear deformed, but that way we know ourselves in our truth; and

(2) the coproanalysis—the crucified people are what appear in a stool analysis; the feces show the true health of our world.

What to Do in the Presence of and with the Crucified People

The question is the most important, remembering Ellacuría. In a conference in Valladolid he spoke about the crucified people, and when he was finishing, he said: "And since I am a Jesuit, I am going to ask the three questions that Saint Ignatius asks us to ask in the meditation of sins in the presence of Christ placed on the cross: 'What have I done, what am I doing, and what am I going to do for Christ?'" With a genius that I have not found in other thinkers, he asked that in the presence of the crucified people we ask ourselves, "What have we done to crucify him, what are we doing to take him down from the cross, what are we going to do to raise him up?"

Saint Ignatius ends the colloquy with Christ on the cross with words that have always struck me: "Discuss whatever is offered." These words do not point to anything in particular, but for me they are very effective. They express a fundamental conviction: "In the face of the crucified people, it will occur to us what to do; it will occur to us with what urgency; it will occur to us what risks we may be willing to take."

The Crucified People Are Universal

We have begun with the barbarism at the Sumpul River. Thousands of peasants have walked to rivers like the Sumpul and died there, some drowned, others by army bullets. In this way they have completed a much longer journey—sometimes as long as the days of their lives—in which they have been dying little by little from misery and exploitation. And like the Sumpul massacre, there are many other barbarities: near us, Huehuetenango, in Guatemala, where hundreds of Indigenous people have been massacred; the eastern neighborhoods of Managua bombed by Somoza; or in Haiti. And further away, Biafra, the boats of Vietnamese refugees, the boats of Africans in the Mediterranean.

People are crucified, and the grandiose signs that, according to the gospel stories, accompanied Jesus's death on the cross do not occur.

The tombs are not opened so that the dead may protest, nor is the sky darkened so that God may show his repudiation, nor are the rocks broken—nor is the heart softened—nor is the veil of the Temple torn so that all may not remain the same in the church. Romero says that "this is the empire of hell," and Dom Pedro Casaldáliga reminds us, "Cursed are we of the living God if we ignore the pain of Central America." But doesn't it seem that in substance everything remains the same?

MAY JESUS OF NAZARETH NOT BE STOLEN FROM US

Since my study in Germany, and even more so since I started teaching Christology in El Salvador, two things were imposed on me.

One was to ask myself what was the ultimate for Jesus, and this is what I wrote: "As we begin to analyze the reality of Jesus of Nazareth, the first thing that jumps out is that Jesus did not make himself the center of his preaching and his mission. Jesus knew himself, lived, and worked from something and for something other than himself. Jesus's life was a decentered life, centered around something other than himself. In the Gospels, that which is central to the life of Jesus appears expressed in two terms: 'Kingdom of God' and 'Father.'"

The other thing was that Jesus was the one from Nazareth, the historical Jesus, the earthly Jesus, or whatever you want to call him, the one who was "lower than the angels," as the author of the Letter to the Hebrews says. And that is what I want to dwell on now. Systematically, I wrote many years ago that *Jesus is the way to the Christ.* And more important, and more fundamental for what we are now touching, that *Jesus is the safeguard of the Christ.*

This Jesus was rediscovered after many efforts in the last decades, but I think that interest has been decreasing since then. And the main reason is that this Jesus demands to be followed, often accompanied by persecution, by the cross and death. In any case, the importance of the historical Jesus has been decreasing. Moreover, I think that, consciously or unconsciously, they have wanted to take him away from us because the historical Jesus is too much of a hindrance. That is why, for the last twenty years or so, the desire has been growing in me that Jesus of Nazareth not be diluted. To put it in strong language, that they do not "steal Jesus" from us, which can happen in many ways. Certainly, through concupiscence, but also through orthodoxy and institutional rigidity. And all kinds of Pentecostal and charismatic groups want to snatch him away from us, knowingly or unknowingly. I would like to add, in all honesty, that this situation is changing with Pope Francis.

Let's go back to Jesus. The Jesus who burst into Latin America caused a strong impact. Among various ecclesial sectors and in popular majorities this generated awareness, faith, hope, and commitment, especially in the form of a struggle for justice. Of necessity it caused, as we have seen, a counter-reaction, harsh attacks from the powerful outside the church that produced a cloud of martyrs for justice. But there were also strong attempts to dilute him within the church, whether consciously or not, because an undiluted Jesus continues to pronounce the words of Mark 8:34: "If anyone would follow me, let him deny himself and take up his cross and follow me."

Today things have changed in Latin America and in the church as a whole. I could be wrong, but I think that in many communities and churches, in quite widespread forms of spirituality, in public ecclesiastical expressions, in splendorous liturgies, and sometimes also in theologies, the image of Jesus of Nazareth has been blurred. And the image of Jesus of Nazareth, who burst forth as a faithful and merciful man (Heb 2:17) who is not ashamed to call us brothers (Heb 2:11), and on whom we must keep our eyes fixed so as to walk to the end without losing heart (Heb 12:1–3), is no longer so clearly present in the atmosphere.

Some have said it very clearly that they see that the greatest danger in the church will come from making Jesus disappear or at least become diminished. Accepting the "Christ" in whom one can believe is not the same as accepting the "Jesus" who must be followed. This is what José Antonio Pagola, who knows about ecclesial and curial problems, has said. He sees as the most necessary thing that we mobilize ourselves and join forces urgently to center the church with more truth and fidelity in the person of Jesus and in his project of the kingdom of God. And to make it clear, he adds that many things will have to be done, but none more decisive than this conversion. We are glad that he mentions the word *conversion,* because with this word—much forgotten—the proposed ecclesial task is given serious weight.

In the recent past, in the years after Medellín, there were groups in the church that "behaved well" with Jesus of Nazareth. That is why "going wrong today" means going backward. And that is why "going well" must be in good part a return to Medellín, to Monseñor Romero, to Father Arrupe. . . . And that means, as with the prophets, "returning to fountains of living waters."

Not returning to Jesus is a form of impoverishment, and not wanting to return would be a specific sin of the church. Beyond the phonetic kinship, the expression "to return to Jesus" brings to mind two classic quotations that continue to be illuminating.

The first is by Roger Garaudy[2] of the Marxist era. In a meeting with Christians after the council, he told them: "Men of the Church, give Jesus back to us." It is as if, in an atmosphere of dialogue and friendship, he said to us: "You handle Jesus as if you were his masters. But the worst thing is that you have kidnapped him." We have to return Jesus. But that implies that, first, we Christians have to return *to* him.

The second quotation is more solemn and is usually more widely known among scholars. It is the acid words of the Grand Inquisitor, the Cardinal Archbishop of Seville, from Dostoevsky's *The Brothers Karamazov*. The Inquisitor reproaches Christ, who does not utter a word, for having brought freedom, which he says is a mistake, for what humans really want is security, and that security is precisely what the church offers them. The Inquisitor at first announces to Jesus that he is going to burn him at the stake, but finally he opens the door and lets him go with these words, saying essentially: "Thank you very much for having come here fifteen hundred years ago, but now we no longer need you, and in fact you are a hindrance to us. Go away and don't come back."

Today we do not speak like the Grand Inquisitor. But we must ask ourselves if we do not say to the Jesus who came with Medellín, with Dom Hélder Câmara, Leonidas Proaño [of Ecuador], Monseñor Romero: "Go away, Lord. Do not come back. We will do good things, but do not demand from us a radical option for the poor, a clear and harsh denunciation of the oppressor. Do not demand of us to enter into conflict or to surrender ourselves to the point of martyrdom."

---

[2] Roger Garaudy (d. 2012) was a French Communist who published widely on Christian-Marxist dialogue.

Jesus of Nazareth gets in the way, and it is understandable that we do not want to have him very close. And the worst thing happens when, without saying so, we justify our distance as if we now have better Christs to offer.

However, the Christ who is Jesus of Nazareth, not any other, is the best way to the total Christ and is his best safeguard. I think those of us who have had the good fortune to live with Monseñor Romero and to have been infected, even if only a little, by the Jesus who lived with him, understand this. And we ask God that Jesus not be stolen from us.

❖*Allow me to interrupt. You have spoken a lot about Jesus of Nazareth, but you have not yet said anything about the resurrection of Jesus, although you have written more than two hundred pages about it in your 1999 book* Christ the Liberator. *What do you have to say?*

You are absolutely right. Moreover, I have also often written about hope, whose christological correlate is usually the resurrection of Christ. "Christ is risen as the first fruits of those who have fallen asleep. . . . And if Christ is not risen, our faith is vain," Paul tells the Corinthians. Although I explained earlier that Moltmann relates hope essentially to the love present in Jesus crucified.

Let us say, then, a few words about the resurrection. I do not believe that the reason I have not spoken is due to the obvious difficulties of showing, and even less of proving, its factual reality and of unequivocally determining its cultural meaning. I dealt with it at length in my book, and I refer to it. Now I will only make a more personal reflection.

The reason for not speaking—yet—of the resurrection, that of Jesus and ours, can be understood by the context of our conversations. In fact, the irruption of the poor and the martyrs did not refer me to what we conventionally understand by resurrection. They referred me to *life*, that is, life *in spite of* and *against* the death of the poor. And I suppose that what Ellacuría said in the *Exercises* of 1971 in the meditations on the resurrection of Christ must not have had a special impact on me either.

However, I do remember what I heard him say in the homily during a Eucharist in which two Jesuit novices took their vows. It has stayed with me. It was in August 1972. Ellacuría told them that "it is necessary to live the following of Jesus in history," which did not surprise me. But I was struck by what he added: "We have to live already as risen in history."

Incidentally, one of those two novices is still a companion in work and community, a faithful follower of the faith-justice. The other soon left the Society and joined the guerrillas in El Salvador. He was killed. He is still remembered and loved by the peasants with whom he lived. Of him and two other young Jesuits who joined the guerrillas Ellacuría said, "We have lost them for the Society, but we have gained them for the people." And I remember these facts because reflections like these have also made me think about doing theology.

Returning to living as resurrected in history, I soon thought that, although surprising, the idea itself is traditional. The Corinthian Christians were so convinced that they were already living in fullness that they did not even expect their own resurrection. They saw extraordinary signs everywhere: miracles, the gift of tongues. And Paul's harsh reaction against the fatal error—that one would live more in the world of the resurrection the less one lived in the historical world—is well known.

And without going that far, some will recall that the superiority of celibate religious life over other states of life has been justified by the fact that celibacy, more than others, makes it possible to participate now in the fullness of the risen life. The reason is that the celibate is more detached, in principle, from the material conditions of existence.

Obviously, in this way we do not advance in living the resurrection in history. We do not live more fully by living less in the conditions of historical existence. This is not the way to reflect what is triumphant in the resurrection of Jesus. Paul affirms this programmatically in his confrontation with the Corinthians. He proclaims the supremacy of love. And that love is crucified, like that of Jesus. In short, the way to live with ultimacy in history is in the following of Jesus, which Paul will proclaim by more than words but by his own way of living.

However, I have asked myself what resurrection adds to living in love. In my simple analysis I have come to the conclusion that, in order to be able to express living already as risen in history, that life must have the flavor, so to speak, of *the impossible having become possible*. It must also have the flavor *of triumph*. And both things can appear in two realities, *freedom* and *joy*. To live as risen in history is to live already in freedom and to live already in joy. That is what has occurred to me.

Living in freedom means that nothing has to be an obstacle or to serve as a limit to love. It has nothing to do with licentiousness, of course, but neither does it have to do with getting out of history. It is about freedom to love. This freedom means that nothing has to be an obstacle to doing good. It is the triumph over living in slavery.

Living in joy means that nothing has to be an obstacle to celebrating life. "What opposes joy is sadness, not suffering," said Gustavo Gutiérrez, who has been through a thousand sufferings and has celebrated life a thousand times in his community. It is the triumph over sadness.

To live in this way, without anything being an obstacle to doing good with freedom, to celebrating life with joy, is a historic way of living in fullness, of living the triumph of love and the victory of life. And to this we can add "to be deciders of the truth," triumphing over lies and concealment, even if our life is at stake. When this happens, I think that even today we can see the fullness, triumph, and victory of Jesus's resurrection.

When speaking of how to live as resurrected in history, there is no apodictic argument in its favor. But I think that if there were no experience of fullness, freedom, and joy without limits, it would be vain to repeat that in the resurrection of Jesus there has been fullness and triumph. Words alone, even those of the New Testament, do not introduce us to the reality of what they say.

Hearing about "living as resurrected" can easily induce vertigo, and it is quite possible that one does not find in one's own life, or in one's surroundings, realities that allow one to say with honesty, or at least with meaning, that "the impossible has become possible," that "nothing is an obstacle to serve," that "nothing is an obstacle to celebration."

At this point I have nothing more to say. But it can still be useful to unmask some prejudices: (1) Jesus did not return to our way of being, even though he ate and drank; (2) Jesus was the only human being who could resurrect, resurrected as an elder brother; and (3) in the resurrection there was an awakening from the sleep of death, which is described in various ways (awakening from sleep, rising up, standing upright, being exalted, being elevated, living). Here there is not only analogy, but also a language barrier that does not allow a clear leap from the historical to the transcendent.

In short, to speak of resurrection I can only point to people who for me have lived as resurrected in history: Monseñor Romero, Thomas More, Martin Luther King Jr., Dorothy Day, the four American church women. Just how positive it will be to point to these human beings to decipher the mystery of the resurrection and our living or not living in fullness, only God knows.

RECOVERING THE PACT OF THE CATACOMBS AND THE CHURCH OF THE POOR

Shortly before the Second Vatican Council there reemerged with force an awareness of what, in my opinion, is the fundamental problem of a church that refers back to Jesus of Nazareth: the relationship of the church with the real poor.

Going back to the beginnings of Christianity, it is important to remember that at the Jerusalem meeting Paul defended himself against the Judeo-Christians, who were very suspicious of him and would not leave him alone, with this forceful argument: "At the Jerusalem meeting they only gave us one condition: that we should not forget the poor of Jerusalem." Paul fulfilled this condition to the letter, going around the empire collecting alms and returning to Jerusalem, running great dangers there, to deliver the alms that were for the relief of the poor. From its origins in Jesus and Paul, it is essential for the church to make the poor a central reality. If it ignores them, it is not the church of Jesus.

Half a century ago a group of bishops took up the fundamental issue of the church and the poor. They signed a not very widely known pact, which was called the Pact of the Catacombs, which has come to light again. It was an extraordinary event, not at all normal. With this act they wanted to support Pope John XXIII and encourage one another.

In fact, shortly before the inauguration of Vatican II, John XXIII said in a radio message, calmly but incisively, that the concern of the church for the underdeveloped world is because the church, as it is and as it wishes to be, is "the church of all, and especially the church of the poor."

There were already new ideas and impulses in this direction: the worker priests in France, with the support of Cardinal Suhard; and voices from the Third World, such as that of Archbishop Hélder Câmara in Brazil and Bishop Georges Mercier of the Missionaries of Africa. And it is important to remember that these groups also advocated a break with the civilization of capitalism, with which the Catholic Church had agreed to make a pact.

When the council began, other bishops were going in the same direction. However, on December 6, 1962, two months after the council began, Cardinal Lercaro, Archbishop of Bologna—apparently at the request of the pope himself—spoke along these lines with a certain pathos: "After two months of fatigue and of truly generous, humble, free and fraternal searching, we all feel that the council has lacked something up to now." And he continued with the words of John XXIII: If it is "the church of all, today it is especially 'the church of the poor.'"

On that day a journalist commented that "the great moment of today's session was during Cardinal Lercaro's intervention. One could cut the silence with a knife." At the end of Lercaro's speech, "the conciliar assembly burst into applause."

I learned about all this later, and I was surprised and happy. But my greatest surprise was that the desire of John XXIII did not prosper in the conciliar hall. The times were not ripe for that.

There are those who think that the council did take up the idea of the church of the poor, and they justify this with some texts, especially *Lumen gentium,* no. 8: "Christ was sent by the Father to evangelize the poor and to raise up the oppressed (Lk 4:18), to seek and to save that which was lost (Lk 19:10); so too the Church embraces with her love all those afflicted by human weakness, indeed, she recognizes in the poor and suffering the image of her Founder, poor and patient, strives to remedy their needs, and seeks to serve Christ in them."

These texts are important and beautiful, but I do not think they clearly express the dream of John XXIII in proclaiming the church of the poor. And in any case they do not explain what happened outside the council hall. A good number of bishops who shared John XXIII's inspiration decided to meet confidentially and regularly at the Domus Mariae, on the outskirts of Rome, to discuss the subject. And at the end of the council, practically all of them met in the catacombs of Saint Domitilla, where they signed the document known as the Pact of the Catacombs.

The full text of the pact is in Appendix 1. Here I cite the introductory paragraph, to which I add some reflections.

Pact of the Catacombs

> We, bishops assembled in the Second Vatican Council, are conscious of the deficiencies of our lifestyle in terms of evangelical poverty. Motivated by one another in an initiative in which each of us has tried avoid ambition and presumption, we unite with all our brothers in the episcopacy and rely above all on the grace and strength of Our Lord Jesus Christ and on the prayer of the faithful and the priests in our respective dioceses. Placing ourselves in thought and in prayer before the Trinity, the Church of Christ, and all the priests and faithful of our dioceses, with humility and awareness of our weakness, but also with all the determination and all the strength that God desires to grant us by his grace, we commit ourselves to the following.

The text is magnificent, and several things are striking. It is extensive, which implies a thorough study of the subject, but it is easy to read and does not become tiresome, since its thirteen points are clearly expressed. In short, neither wealth in any degree, nor honors, nor vanities. No further comments are necessary. But I do want to draw attention to the *human mettle* of those who signed the document, as it appears in the introduction.

"We," they begin. And that word is of absolute importance. They speak, then, as bishops, but they do not speak doctrinally, not even only pastorally as bishops, but—a rare thing—they speak personally and existentially. They do not speak to others or of others, but they speak to themselves and of themselves. And by the nature of the matter, to a large extent whether the covenant begins to be fruitful or not will depend on what they do. "We" are "we who are here." It cannot be said more clearly.

"Conscious of the deficiencies of our lifestyle." And they mention here the fundamental weakness in terms of evangelical poverty. And they mention other important attitudes: motivated by one another . . . avoidance of ambition and presumption . . . united . . . humble . . .

depending on the prayer of the faithful . . . aware of our weaknesses . . . strengthened by God's grace.

In thirteen points they oblige themselves to live the real poverty of the majority and to suffer the disparagement that real poverty causes. And they do so not for ascetical reasons, but to incorporate and introduce the real poverty of humanity into the church (pts. 1–5). They call for avoiding favoritism toward the rich (pt. 6) and for striving for justice and charity (pt. 9). They encourage governments to implement laws, structures, and institutions in favor of justice, equality, and harmonious development (pt. 10). Toward the end, they note the fact that "two-thirds of humanity . . . live in physical, cultural, and moral misery." And they point to the speech of Paul VI at the United Nations as an example of witnessing to the gospel and promise to do likewise (pt. 11).

To conclude the introductory paragraph, they write: "We commit ourselves to the following," words of strong and determined people. And at the end of the pact they state: "When we return to our dioceses, we will make these resolutions known to our diocesan priests and ask them to assist us with their comprehension, their collaboration, and their prayers. May God help us to be faithful."

If I may take a leap of half a century, I wish the words of those bishops would be pronounced and put into practice, with the same conviction, by the bishops of today, and by the United Nations, the United States, the Organization of American States, the European Union, and so on.

In 2015 I was in Rome, invited by the Urbaniana University and by members of an institute of political theology in Munich to celebrate the fiftieth anniversary of the signing of the Pact of the Catacombs. I learned that two survivors were there. I was able to speak with one: Don Luigi Betazzi, Auxiliary Bishop of Bologna. I knew him from his trips to El Salvador, when he had come during the war to bring solidarity and work for peace. At more than ninety years old, he is still fiery. He spoke to us in the catacombs, after mass, and asked us to stop talking so much about the signing of the Pact of the Catacombs and to talk more about Pope Francis.

Overall, my stay in Rome during those days helped me to understand the depth of the Pact of the Catacombs.

The Church of the Poor

In El Salvador, as far as I remember, neither Ellacuría nor theologians spoke of the Pact of the Catacombs after the council. But we did talk about the poor and the church. In 1977 Ellacuría published an important article entitled "The Church of the Poor."[3] I now highlight some important insights that from a systematic perspective complete what the Pact of the Catacombs says in a more descriptive way.

Preliminary Reflection: The Institutional and the Profound

Ellacuría accepts that there is room for institutional development in the church. Therefore, there can be changes, even institutional changes, and a church of the poor can represent such changes. But before the institutional there is something deep and essential; that is, the church must be the sacrament of salvation. This is a central reality in Ignacio Ellacuría. In dealing with what can be changed, he insists that it must be changed in the way of Jesus. Historical accommodations in the manner and form of carrying out the task of salvation are possible and necessary, but there is no room for or need for modes and forms that are not a continuation of the modes and forms used by Jesus. He also insists on the danger of the church becoming institutionalized according to the powers used by the world to oppress.

Ellacuría insists on the need for the institutional element in the church, which is necessarily derived from its corporeality, and which distances it from anarchistic idealisms. But he also insists on its danger, that is, that the church be institutionalized according to the powers that the world uses to be powerful.

What Is the Church of the Poor?

Ellacuría explains the fundamentals of his thinking on the church of the poor, which goes beyond what is commonly said when speaking of it:

---

[3] Ignacio Ellacuría, "The Church of the Poor: Historical Sacrament of Liberation" (1977), in *Ignacio Ellacuría: Essays on History, Liberation, and Salvation*, ed. Michael E. Lee, 227–54 (Maryknoll, NY: Orbis Books, 2013).

The church of the poor is not that church that, being wealthy and establishing itself as such, concerns itself with the poor. It is not that church that, standing outside of the world of the poor, generously offers its help to the poor. It is, more properly, a church in which the poor are its principal subject and its principle of internal structuring. The union of God and humanity, as it is evidenced in Jesus Christ, is historically a union of God emptied primarily into the world of the poor. Thus, the church, being itself poor, and, above all, dedicating itself fundamentally to the salvation of the poor, could become that which it is and could fulfill its mission of universal salvation in a Christian way. By incarnating itself among the poor, dedicating its life to them, and dying for them, it could constitute itself in a Christian manner as an efficacious sign of salvation for all humanity.

And Ellacuría adds a sadly necessary explanation, although it should be unnecessary: "The question of who are the poor, in the real situation of the third world, is not a problem that has to be resolved with elaborate scriptural exegesis, sociological analysis, or historical theories." Later he clarifies, "When we speak here of the poor, we are speaking of a relationship between poor and rich (more generally, between dominated and oppressor), in which there are rich people because there are poor."

Some Practical Consequences

Personal and social significance, here and now. "The Christian faith must mean something real and palpable in the life of the poor." This may seem obvious, but it has not always been achieved.

The Christian faith is a force for liberation, an object of persecution and misunderstanding. The Christian faith, far from becoming an opiate—and not only a social opiate—must become what it is: a principle of liberation. There is no liberation unless the human heart is liberated, but the human heart cannot be liberated when its personal totality, which is not merely interiority, is oppressed by collective structures and realities that invade everything. This places the Latin American church in a difficult position. On the one hand, it brings persecution, as it brought persecution to Jesus himself.

We must not fall into a new form of elitism. The very concept of the church of the poor goes beyond the elitism of those who see Christianity as a way of being that only the perfect could enjoy or put into practice. The church of the poor does not close its doors to anyone, nor does it reduce the fullness and universality of its mission, even if this means madness for some and scandal for others.

Nor should it give way to another form of elitism: that which passes from all the people to a more conscientious part of them, and from this more conscientious part to what can be considered their most committed vanguard, and from this committed vanguard to the vertical leaders, who guide from above with preestablished schemes and become dogmatic monopolizers of what the popular needs are and of what is the way and the rhythm to solve them.

These and other texts of Ellacuría seem to me fundamental.

PROMOTING A CIVILIZATION OF POVERTY

As far as I know, this concept is the brainchild of Ignacio Ellacuría. He published four texts on this civilization. And he kept the formulation civilization of poverty until the end.

Now I want to emphasize Ellacuría's *insistence* on speaking about the civilization of poverty in the last years of his life. And he did it practically alone. I will recall some ideas from each of his four texts on the topic.

He first addressed the issue of the civilization of poverty and its fundamentals in an article in 1982.[4] The civilization of poverty is that which has as the engine of history ensuring the basic needs of all and that finds its meaning in solidarity. That civilization is the one that can overcome the civilization of wealth, for which the engine of history consists in the accumulation of capital and its meaning in the enjoyment of what has been accumulated. The latter dehumanizes; the former makes the human flourish. And it can bring salvation to the crucified people.

In 1983 the Jesuits were going to celebrate General Congregation XXXIII. Ellacuría had the idea of writing a text that could eventually serve as the basis for a declaration of the future congregation that would

---

[4] Ignacio Ellacuría, "The Kingdom of God and Unemployment in the Third World," *Concilium* 180 (1982).

reorient the mission of the Society of Jesus.[5] The mission of the Society consists in the defense of faith and the promotion of justice. The purpose of Ellacuría's text was to promote the conversion of the universal Society to the world of the poor, especially to that world of the poor which is the Third World. This conversion would give the whole body of the Society and its members a new apostolic and religious vitality.

To draft the document, Ellacuría invited a small group of Jesuits—among whom I found myself—although the intuition and the fundamental development were his own. In speaking of the resounding no of God the Father to the violence that the powers of this world commit against his most helpless children, depriving them even of their lives, he stated:

> The message of salvation must move the implementation of a civilization of poverty more in tune with the Christian faith and more in tune with the reality of man and the relationship between "world resources-universal well-being."

The Third World, not as subjugated and dominated, but as an objective reality, can become the natural place of the Christian faith, which certainly does not have its place among the richest and most dominant nations of the earth. And from the overcoming of the civilization of wealth, he describes how a true civilization develops among the poor:

> This poverty is what really gives space to the spirit, which will no longer be stifled by the desire to have more than others, by the concupiscent desire to have all kinds of superfluities, when the majority of humanity lacks the necessities. The spirit, the immense spiritual and human wealth of the poor and the peoples of the Third World, today suffocated by misery and by the imposition of cultural models that are more developed in some respects, but not for that reason more fully human, will then be able to flourish.

In October 1988, he gave an important speech in Berlin, "Building a Different Future for Humanity," at the opening of an international congress. Among other things he said:

---

[5] Ignacio Ellacuría, "Misión actual de la Compañía de Jesús," published posthumously by Jon Sobrino in *Revista Latinoamericana de Teología* 29 (1993).

In cultural terms, the civilization of poverty implies the overcoming of the nationalist or bloc division . . . by the unity of humanity, human solidarity, while respecting the diversity of peoples and the richness of their cultures, so often denied by the uniformity demanded for the greatest return on capital.

In 1989 he published his last written text, "Utopia and Prophecy in Latin America."[6] He takes up several ideas, especially utopia and prophetism, and relates the reality of the church and the reality of civilization. He ends with these words:

The signs of the times and the soteriological dynamic of the Christian faith historicized in new human beings insistently demand the prophetic negation of a church as the old heaven of a civilization of wealth and of empire and the utopian affirmation of a church as the new heaven of a civilization of poverty. Although always in the dark, these new human beings continue firmly to proclaim an ever great future, because beyond the successive historical futures is discerned the God who saves, the God who liberates.

Global clarifications. As far as I know, Ellacuría did not define precisely what he understood by *civilization*, but he described it sufficiently in parallel to *a general project of humanity, to an order of values, to a firm state of things.* In any case, he was not referring to a particular area of social reality, such as the economy, religion, or the cultivation of science, but to a totality.

Nor did he define precisely what he meant by *poverty,* insofar as it names a civilization. But it is important to understand what the term implied and what it did not imply.

To those who object to the use of the term *poverty,* he warns that it is not a question of universal pauperization, which should be evident. To understand what *poverty* is, it is necessary to understand it in opposite and dueling relation to the *wealth* of the other civilization. They are

    [6] Ignacio Ellacuría, "Utopia and Prophecy in Latin America," trans. James Brockman, in *Mysterium Liberationis: Fundamental Concepts of the Theology of Liberation,* ed. Ignacio Ellacuría and Jon Sobrino, 289–327 (Maryknoll, NY: Orbis Books, 1993; original Spanish edition, Madrid: Editorial Trotta, 1990).

contrary and in conflict. The fundamental thing is that the civilization of poverty is *overcoming* the civilization of wealth. It brings *healing* to our present *sick civilization*.

Clarifications on the civilization of wealth. Private accumulation of as much capital as possible can occur by individuals, groups, multinationals, states, or groups of states. The judgment on it should not be simplistic, since it has brought goods to humanity that, as such, should be preserved and promoted (scientific and technical development, new modes of collective consciousness, and so on).

But it has brought greater evils: (1) it does not satisfy the basic needs of all; (2) not only does it not generate equity, but it cannot generate it; and (3) it does not generate a humanizing spirit.

- *The first is a crime.* It is the denial of life, the slow death of the human beings or the violent death when human beings rebel and fight for life.
- *The second is usually concealed* by those in power, but without convincing. There are no resources on the planet for the enjoyment that is the product of accumulation to be universal, so, following Kant, the civilization of wealth is unethical because it is not universalizable. The accumulators consume so much in the way of resources, raw materials, and energy that the remainder is not enough for the good living of the rest of the world's population.
- *The third point is the denial of spirit.* All this makes it difficult or impossible for the human spirit to flourish as a dimension of an entire civilization. It is the negation of fraternity and universal dignity, whatever the formulations of the Universal Declaration of Human Rights may be. The civilization of wealth is the civilization of the individual, of the selfish good life.

And the air that the spirit breathes becomes even thinner when the West, which produces this civilization, understands itself not only as the fruit of talent and noble efforts (in part very real), but as the fruit of a kind of predestination, as in the past the chosen peoples understood themselves according to the religions.

This civilization of wealth is not confined by geography. It is in force in the East as well as in the West, and must be called capitalist civilization, whether it is state capitalism or private capitalism. It is established in some regions of the world more than in others. Said with consideration and respect, for Ellacuría the United States was the paradigm of this civilization. And those who are shaped by it act as if it obeyed a manifest destiny.

This spirit dehumanizes. It tends to generate contempt in some and servility or irrationally violent responses in others. In 1989, not judging from his economic, but spiritual possibilities, Ellacuría said that the United States has a bad solution, and added that that is worse than having no solution, as is the case in the Third World. Generalizing, he said that the countries of abundance do not have hope—which does exist in the Third World—but only fear.

Looking at the totality of our world, Ellacuría's and ours, it is hard to see how a world can make sense in which the parable of the Rich Man continues to be, without any doubt, its own parable, the one that best describes the totality of the planet.

Ellacuría's conclusion at the time was that the civilization of wealth suffers a humanistic and moral failure. And passing judgment on its long history, he added that its self-correcting processes do not prove sufficient to reverse its destructive course.

Ellacuría did not reject any contribution to salvation. On the contrary, he demanded the development of economic and political models to save history. But to keep his spirits up he only mentioned the poor and oppressed and those who identify with them. Several times he also mentioned them as a source of hope. Until the end of his days he saw in the Salvadoran poor and martyrs seeds of salvation for the country.

Clarifications on the civilization of poverty. What can heal this world is the civilization of poverty. And this civilization is permeated by important elements of the biblical-Jesuanic tradition. In the case of Ellacuría, the Ignatian tradition of the meditation of the two flags is also operative. This meditation affirms that there are two principles that create two paths that lead to salvation or damnation. One begins with poverty, leads to insults such as those that Jesus suffered, and all this leads by its nature to humility, to integral humanization, as we would say today. And from there to all good things. The other principle begins with wealth and leads by its nature to worldly and vain honors, from there to pride, to integral dehumanization, and from there to all evils. Both principles and both processes are dialectical. The one is against the other.

Hence Ellacuría proposes as a solution the civilization of poverty against the civilization of wealth. We must work for this civilization of poverty. It is not enough to preach it as a prophecy against the civilization of wealth, nor is it enough to announce it as good news for the poor of this world. The solution "cannot lie in leaving this world and making a prophetic sign of protest against it, but in entering it in order to renew it and transform it toward the utopia of the new earth."

To build a civilization of poverty, Ellacuría proposes two fundamental tasks. One, the most understandable and accepted in principle, is to create economic, political, and cultural models that make it possible for "a civilization of work to take the place of the dominant civilization of capital." The other consists in strengthening "shared solidarity . . . in contrast to the closed and competitive individualism of the civilization of wealth."

5

Direct and Personal Questions

The Conversion of Monseñor Romero, Keeping the Faith,
Pope Francis

✧*So far you have answered at length and sought to expose the truth of important theological realities, always keeping in mind the "God issue." And you have also mentioned people who have influenced you to think this way. Now I would like to continue with more direct questions, more varied, and a little more concrete. My first question is this: Romero, in his beginnings as archbishop, was more on the side of the wealthy classes; one could say that he belonged to the conservative church. Was the assassination of Rutilio Grande the turning point in Romero's conversion to the church of the poor?*

The first thing you say about Monseñor Romero is a cliche that has been repeated many times, but it is not correct. It is true that Monseñor Romero wanted to *preserve* a church that he saw in danger of falling into the exaggerations of some followers of Medellín. I also believe that, in the beginning, he failed to understand the great evangelical novelty and historical importance of Medellín's message. That is my opinion.

In that context, at the beginning of the 1970s, and in the presence of progressive priests, it could be said that Romero was conservative, but not that he was on the side of the wealthy classes. As far as I know, Oscar Romero was always close to the poor and cared for them. After he was named Bishop of Santiago María in 1976, there are many testimonies, especially from Father Juan Macho and other Passionist Fathers, of Monseñor's dedication to the poor. And they also recall his denunciations of the rich, even if they were not as strong as they would be later. It is not true, and it does not help much, to maintain the fiction of Romero as a supporter of the rich before he became archbishop.

What *is* certain is that after he was named Archbishop of San Salvador, the rich wanted to win him over, as they usually do. They offered him an episcopal mansion, but Romero did not accept it and went to live in a small room next to the sacristy of the chapel of the little Hospital of Divine Providence. And what is *very* certain is that the assassination of Rutilio was a turning point for Monseñor.

✧*As far as you are concerned, did Rutilio's murder change your life?*

Yes, I have already explained before what Rutilio meant for *witness theology*. Now I want to mention the most fundamental change in my life in connection with Rutilio's assassination: seeing the impressive change in Monseñor. On the occasion of Rutilio's assassination, I discovered Monseñor Romero. This discovery, and the important things that happened around Rutilio's assassination, changed my life and that of many other people. It is still important today that we keep them in mind in order to live in a human and Christian manner.

For me, it all began the day Rutilio was assassinated, on March 12, 1977. I was in the Jesuit community at the UCA. They told us the news by telephone, and we went immediately to Aguilares. When we arrived, there were already several hundred campesinos in front of the three corpses. Monseñor Romero had not yet arrived. The Jesuit provincial thought that the Eucharist should begin so that the campesinos would not get impatient, and he asked me to stay and wait for Monseñor.

I had not had any direct relationship with Monseñor Romero, but the situation between the two of us was tense. On August 6, 1976, the celebration of the Transfiguration of the Divine Savior, the patronal feast of the country, an outstanding speaker was chosen for the homily, and that was Monseñor Romero. He began by mentioning the evils of the country and also of the church. And he insisted that new, rationalistic Christologies were being taught that brought violence. . . . He was referring to me.

These were the memories I had of Monseñor Romero. When he arrived in Aguilares, I greeted him. And at that moment all my previous ideas about him disappeared. That encounter with Monseñor, under such somber circumstances, was for me, and for many, the beginning of important changes.

The celebration of the Eucharist had already begun, and Monseñor Romero looked very upset. After the Eucharist, Monseñor Romero asked all of us who were there to stay. He looked worried, nervous, overwhelmed. Rutilio's murder had touched him deeply, and at that moment it was clear that he needed help. But very soon something surprising also became evident. Another Monseñor Romero was being born. I formulated it then with the word *conversion*. Others—perhaps because *conversion* has been used only to express overcoming *sin*—have preferred to use the expression *radical change*. But the words are the least of it. That same night another Monseñor was truly being born, "the miracle of Rutilio," as people would say. And with him, the archdiocese also began to take new steps, as Rutilio would have wished.

Although it may sound a bit abstract, the first thing that Rutilio's martyrdom produced was a true *ecclesial body*. It did not matter who passed by Monseñor's group, which formed after the Eucharist. Peasants, nuns, priests, lay people, UCA professors—Monseñor Romero asked all to stay. An ecclesial body unknown in the country was being born.

The question, obviously, was *what to do,* and very soon Monseñor Romero said what he was going to do: denounce the assassination and demand an investigation. Before all those present he promised something that at that time was important, that he would not attend any official event until these murders were investigated. It was a solemn promise, and it could be dangerous, because it would be possible to verify whether Monseñor Romero was a man of his word or not. That new Monseñor began to change many, and me as well.

During the following week Monseñor called many meetings at the archbishopric. Many people attended, and the church grew as a body. In order not to condition anyone by his presence, he sat in the first pew, facing forward. In several meetings he appointed me as one of the secretaries, and I sat on the dais, facing the attendees. I mention this because I was able to observe how Monseñor behaved, how he responded to questions, and how he reacted to proposals. Monseñor, for his part, insisted that everyone speak freely. And so it happened.

❖ *Of the meetings you attended, which one had the greatest impact on you?*

There were several important meetings, but one seemed to me to be of crucial importance. A nun, speaking naturally and boldly, proposed that on the following Sunday, at Rutilio's official funeral, a single open-air mass be celebrated in the square in front of the cathedral. During the discussion of this proposal, Monseñor listened with great interest but kept silent. It must have crossed his mind that problems of all kinds would arise from allowing, and even supporting, a single mass, in public and under siege. But Monseñor's reflective silence stemmed from something deeper, from his theology, and ultimately from his vision of God. He did not quite agree with the *one mass,* and he reasoned this out before all of us with honesty, clarity, and humility, saying he was taught that the mass gives glory to God. By this he was saying, although it may seem strange to us today, that the fewer the number of masses, the lesser the glory of God.

That moment of the meeting was very important to me. I was curious to know how the matter of the single mass would end. But I thought above all about Monseñor and what he would say. One does not play with the things of God, and even less would Monseñor Romero do so.

César Jerez, provincial of the Jesuits, asked for the floor and with great respect, spoke along these lines: "If I remember correctly, in the theologate in Frankfurt we were taught that the fathers of the church—he was referring to Saint Irenaeus of Lyon, the great theologian of the second century—said: *Gloria Dei vivens homo* (the glory of God is that the human being should live). I never spoke to Monseñor Romero about the impact these words had on him. But I do remember well what happened. Monseñor approved the single mass.

I am going to take a leap in time. Three years later the University of Louvain awarded Monseñor Romero an honorary doctorate. His inaugural speech was entitled "The Political Dimension of the Faith from the Perspective of the Option for the Poor."[1] The first point was the reality of the poor in the archdiocese. In a second point he spoke of the historicization of faith from the world of the poor. He formulated a brief conclusion with the title "Option for the Poor, Orientation of

---

[1] Oscar Romero, *Voice of the Voiceless: The Four Pastoral Letters and Other Statements* (Maryknoll, NY: Orbis Books, 2020), 193–204.

Our Faith in the Midst of Politics." His last words were these: *Gloria Dei vivens pauper*—the glory of God is that the poor live. In February 1980, Monseñor Romero was closing in Louvain a cycle he had opened three years earlier, in March 1977, with the single mass. He began with "the glory of God, which shines in the *human being* who lives," and he concluded with "the glory of God, which shines in the *poor person* who lives."

✧ *What else struck you about the single mass?*

The announcement of the single mass caused a great commotion, for some a source of rejoicing and for others a source of fear. In the nunciature they were very troubled. Romero wanted to visit the nuncio, and he asked me and three other priests to accompany him. As a courtesy, he wanted to tell the nuncio personally that there would be a single mass. The nuncio was in Guatemala, and we were attended by his secretary. If I remember correctly, he was Lorenzo Baldisseri, a career diplomat priest. He has become a cardinal and is now prefect of the Vatican dicastery of the Synod of Bishops.

From the beginning he showed himself master of the situation—opting to distance himself from the single mass and to reprove it. Those of us who accompanied Monseñor looked for ways to argue in favor of the single mass. I used Christian reason, saying more or less: "A priest has been killed, with a child and an old man. They are the body of Christ. The blood of Christ and the blood of the people has been shed. The people are waiting for a strong and clear word from the church. Something important must be done to denounce the murder and encourage the people."

To my surprise, the secretary replied that he was fine with the theological and pastoral arguments in favor of the single mass. "But," he added triumphantly, "you have forgotten the most important thing: canon law." I could not believe it.

For a few moments the discussion on the subject continued, and Monseñor remained silent. When he thought that the discussion had run its course, he said something like: "The celebration of Sunday Mass depends on my archepiscopal authority. I would be grateful if you would inform the nuncio that I have come to inform him that only one mass will be celebrated on Sunday, and it will be in front of the cathedral."

With that, Monseñor got up, and we left. I had listened incredulously to the secretary, and I was indignant as I have rarely been at the way the secretary had treated Monseñor. On the way out Monseñor came up to me and calmed me down. And with some humor he said to me: "They are like Opus Dei, they don't understand."

I would like to add that in order to give importance to that mass, Monseñor asked that Catholic schools suspend normal academic activities for three days and study Bible passages on justice. I remember that in the UCA printing press we spent several nights looking for and publishing texts of the prophets.

Many other things happened during those days. Many people spoke very well of Monseñor Romero and what was happening. Ellacuría was in Spain, and on April 9 he wrote him a letter that a good friend found years later in the archives of the archbishopric. He sent it to me, I read it, and I spread it as much as I could.[2]

✧ *In that letter, did Ellacuría reconcile himself with Monseñor Romero?*

The tone of the letter was not one of reconciliation but of gratitude, admiration, and joy on the part of Ellacuría. From 1972 to 1977 there had been disagreement between the two. Just one example. At the request of the Episcopal Conference of El Salvador in 1974, Monseñor Romero wrote a critical review of Ellacuría's book *Teología política*.[3] Ellacuría, in turn, was critical of Monseñor Romero, because, although he theoretically accepted Medellín as a document of the hierarchy, he did not feel comfortable with Medellín and showed strong distrust, criticizing the clergy, seminarians, and communities, as well as the UCA and the Society of Jesus, who sought to put it into practice.

Everything changed with the assassination of Rutilio. Romero and Ellacuría increasingly agreed on the vision of Salvadoran society, on what the following of Jesus and the praxis of the church should be. At the base of it all was the understanding of God as the God of life in struggle with the idols of death.

The relationship between the two became very close, I would say endearing. Ellacuría came to have veneration for Monseñor Romero.

---

[2] The letter appears in its entirety in Appendix 2 herein. It is well worth reading.

[3] Ignacio Ellacuría, *Freedom Made Flesh: The Mission of Christ and His Church* (Maryknoll, NY: Orbis Books, 1976).

The letter he sent from Madrid on April 9 was the beginning of this new relationship.

✧ *You have told us how you experienced the circumstances surrounding the assassination of Rutilio and how through this your closeness to Monseñor came about. But what did the assassination of Rutilio mean to you as a real and brutal event and as a gift of life?*

In a recent article I wrote that I truly encountered Christianity on March 12, 1977, the day of Rutilio's assassination. I explicitly chose the word *encountered* because I did not simply "bump into" it; rather, I came face to face with it. And that had never happened to me before. There was much that was surprising, painful, and joyful. It was very real and blessed. For many, the assassination of Rutilio meant an important change. And I have already said that it brought me very close to Monseñor.

In those days things began to happen that were unthinkable before. Threatening pamphlets opened with the slogan, "Be a patriot, kill a priest." In June the White Warrior Union gave all the Jesuits a month to leave the country. Obviously, we thought it was nonsense. Without hesitation, we all stayed.

That is how we lived after Rutilio's assassination. To live or not to live, to be killed or not—we were aware of that possibility. But although it sounds strange to say it, we lived in such a way that, if we had been killed, it would not have seemed extraordinary to us either. We were part of the Salvadoran people, with greater or lesser physical insertion. And that meant being in the country, continuing to work and teach in the same or a similar way. Several times we appeared on death lists. But we didn't think it was a big deal. It seemed quite normal.

✧ *You said that Rutilio and Romero, and a few years later, in 1989, the Jesuits of the UCA, with two companions, were brutally murdered. In the face of so many dead bodies—and even if it were only one—is it not coldhearted to see something positive in those corpses? To put it in the most radical terms, where was God in those corpses?*

My Jesuit companions were coldly murdered. Death triumphed over justice and truth. And you ask if I see something positive in that. My answer is yes. Victimizers do not produce truth or love, certainly. But victims can produce truth, hope, and love. I will try to explain this with what I witnessed in a Salvadoran church after the assassination of Rutilio Grande and his companions.

On May 11, 1977, two months after the assassination of Rutilio and his companions, Father Alfonso Navarro Oviedo was attacked and later died. It is said that when they took him to the hospital, he whispered that he forgave his murderers.

On the day of the funeral there was no room in the church. Romero preached a homily that became famous. It was the homily of the Bedouin:

> There is a story about a caravan that was traveling through the desert with a Bedouin as guide. The travelers had become desperate and thirsty and were searching for water in the mirages of the desert, but their Bedouin guide kept saying, "Not that way, but this way." He had spoken these words so many times that a member of the caravan became frustrated, took out a gun, and shot the guide. As the guide was dying, he extended his hand and said one last time, "Not that way, but this way." He died pointing the way to a well.

This is what Monseñor Romero wanted to prevent with his words: "Let us not follow the path of horror, violence, and injustice. Let us walk on the path of peace and justice."

In the church the atmosphere was one of total emotion. After the initial request for forgiveness, the priest who monitored the Eucharist said: "We are before a corpse, but since we are Christians, we are going to sing the Gloria." So we did, and the church was filled with joy. That is what I felt. As we prayed the Our Father with the people who came from many places, we experienced something ultimate. And without being able to help it, I felt that this last thing was something good. I felt that there had been a lot of love.

That, I believe, is what has remained in me from those first hard years. Good does not make evil disappear. But, if I may use the language, good has—can have—stubbornness to at least float over evil, and not only to float, but to swim against the current. And to swim toward something bigger and better. These are metaphors. I use them now so as not to think that on these occasions the only metaphor is that love is stronger than death. The question always comes back about what is absurd and useless in our lives, but I keep hearing the answer that there is a greater meaning and utility: love.

We often say things like this here, but when one lives what we have lived through in El Salvador, then one sees that this love is *real*. Rutilio, Romero, the Jesuits, the cooks, the market vendors, the organized peasants, the American nuns—they were all people of love. What happened to them? The same thing happened to many of them as happened to Jesus. And the same thing *happened to Jesus as happened to them*. There are human beings who continue on their way.

Your question is not silenced by what I have just said, and I think it will never be silenced. But I think that the answer I have stammered out has a weight that does not disappear easily. And in saying these things, the words of Ellacuría when he affirmed the salvific dimension of the Suffering Servant always come to mind: "Only a hard-won act of faith could enable the singer of the servant to describe in this way what looks like just the opposite in the eyes of history."[4] I do not know if I have gone through that difficult act of faith, but I try to live with that conviction.

✧*And to believe in God in a world that is often one of horror?*

I have already spoken at length about the silence of God and the appearance of God, and I will return to it at the end, integrating the new experience of my advanced age and my very diminished health.

Several times I have asked myself what it means for me to believe in God. The answer has not been easy. In fact, I have referred to Jesus, to how Jesus put himself before God. And I have had the audacity to formulate it thus: With trust in a God who is *Father,* and with availability before a Father who is *God.* I thought it could also be a formulation of what is the structure of our faith.

But your question emphasizes the difficulty of believing in God in a world of *horror,* and it seems very reasonable to me. First of all, horror is not an objective extrapolation of subjective masochism. Earlier I recalled the legendary fables recorded in scripture in Genesis 6. In them we find the horror that God felt at the corruption of humanity, to the point of regretting having created human beings and deciding to eliminate them. Today there are no such legends of horror, but there are realities of horror. These days it is the horror produced by Syria, the dead in

---

[4] Ignacio Ellacuría, in Jon Sobrino, *No Salvation outside the Poor* (Maryknoll, NY: Orbis Books, 2008).

Haiti, the eight thousand corpses of Africans drowned at the bottom of the Mediterranean, the twelve or fifteen daily homicides in El Salvador, although some months the number goes down and others it goes up.

I don't see how it is possible to ignore that horror when the subject of *believing in God* comes up, and honestly speaking, Job is not an absolute answer. But having said that, I also feel that *reality is not only horror;* it is also a force that *keeps pushing us to live.* And many times it *continues pushing us to do good and to get along with one another, even to die for one another.* Then, faced with the question of believing in God in a world of horror and being able to continue speaking—or babbling—of trust and availability, the text of Micah 6 comes to mind, which I have already mentioned.

As I understand it, the central issue of the chapter is the question of human beings when they go to God, sometimes with selfish interests: what is to be done before God to have him favor us? In any case, God answers and says what to do. If I may be allowed to answer from my own experience, perhaps I could simply say: *Pray to him.* Not very well, but something I try to do. *Listen to him, obey him.* Would to God that I did this in some measure. *Thank him, praise him, sing to him.* Fine. But the more judicious response seems to me to be that of the Micah text: "Listen once and for all to what is good and what the Lord requires of you: that you practice justice, that you love tenderly, and that you walk humbly with your God."

Those who understand more mystical language may be able to bring order to these reflections or ravings. For me, *walking* with God means somehow encountering the mystery of God and thus overcoming horror.

✧ *Let us now turn to a subject that seems important to me. When Romero was assassinated, Ellacuría picked up the torch. And I ask myself, who picked up the torch when Ellacuría was assassinated, who became the voice of the people?*

In the Christian tradition, picking up the torch is important, and I would like to recall that Jesus of Nazareth participated in this tradition. He went to the Jordan, was baptized by John, and from there went into the desert. When he heard that John had been taken prisoner, he left the desert, went to Galilee, and began to announce the good news of the nearness of the kingdom of God. And when John was beheaded, Jesus hid himself, and then he marched to Jerusalem, knowing that he was going to be executed. Jesus was picking up John's torch, different in important points, but equivalent in his disposition before the will of God. Some even wondered if Jesus was not John who had returned to earth.

In El Salvador we have lived very clearly this passing the torch. When Rutilio was assassinated, Romero emerged. When Romero was assassinated, Ellacuría emerged. I have heard it said by several people. It is true that Ellacuría was already speaking and denouncing before Rutilio and Romero were assassinated, but he did it with a different type of communication. The important thing is that when Romero was assassinated, the country did not fall silent, and the voice that became increasingly clear was that of Ellacuría, because of his capacity; because of the weight of the UCA, of the Society, and of the church at that time; and because of the group of companions and people from outside in solidarity. But when Ellacuría was assassinated, people began to ask, "Now who?"

I do want to insist that in El Salvador there has always been a magnificent group tradition—dedication and love for the poor, confrontation with oppressors, firmness in the conflict, hope, utopias—which passed from hand to hand. People who come from outside still notice it. Well-known people have belonged to that tradition, and also a vast majority of unknown people in El Mozote, in Sumpul, in Mejicanos, in Soyapango, in Chalatenango, and in other places.

The Jesus of the gospel and the mystery of his God, seen with clear eyes, continue to shine in these traditions, even if today they are not so bright. What the real brightness is I leave to the God who sees what is hidden. What I would like to demand of everyone is not to hide, but to guard carefully *a heritage of Christianity and humanity that we cannot squander.* We owe it to those who built it. And we owe it to the young.

✧ *If there are no torches to be seen, wouldn't you be the right person? From what you say, you don't lack conviction.*

No. The six Jesuits, together with Rodolfo Cardenal, were my entire community. After November 16, it is understandable that my person and that of Rodolfo became a point of reference. But to be a torch I think you need specific qualities. It is one thing to uncover the truth, vilely buried in lies, and another to uncover the truth, trapped by a multitude of interests that are willing to do anything to prevent the truth from coming to light. Continuing with metaphors, for the first it may be enough to be a kind of *lamp.* For the second, it is necessary to be a *torch* that both illuminates and burns to eliminate all that prevents us from seeing.

A torch arises with a person of extreme lucidity in his judgment about how reality is and how it objectively is, how it has to be dealt with, and how it has to be carried. The human debacle of our days has not produced nor does it seem that it will mechanically produce a *torch,* a Rutilio, a Romero, an Ellacuría. This happens when it happens.

Ellacuría was a *torch,* not just a lamp or a light. Ellacuría was an extraordinarily intelligent person and a great intellectual, but that was not what moved me most about him. I appreciated and studied the wise things he said, but what moved me most was that he was a compassionate, merciful person. He wanted to put all his values in favor of the poor, more specifically, the poor of El Salvador.[5]

❖ *The UCA has played a very important role since its beginnings. It has been the place where many Salvadorans have been educated with a critical conscience. What role does it play now?*

First of all, it is important to emphasize what Ellacuría tried to transmit to the university. He was interested in it being an inspiration for serious change. And for a university in El Salvador he saw that the most effective inspiration was Christian inspiration, understood historically and biblically. That inspiration is what moves us to build the kingdom of God that Jesus announced and initiated. And he thought that this inspiration could also organize and grow not only or mainly from religious strongholds within the university but from the whole of it.

In answering your question about the role of the university today, we must avoid simplistic remarks: "After Ellacuría the UCA is not the same," or more critically, "It has taken a downturn." These comments can be used positively, but they can become, pardon the expression, simplistic stupidity. Another thing is to ask oneself how to overcome the limitations of the UCA after the assassination and how to let oneself be guided by the eight crucified to do it now as well as possible.

Undoubtedly the 1989 assassination was a sea change. But on a global level, just the fact of moving on after the assassinations was very

---

[5] On the first anniversary of his assassination I wrote him a letter about these things. That letter appears in Appendix 3 herein.

important and a great contribution to the soul of a horrified country. And both the provincial, José Maria Tojeira, and the rector, Francisco Estrada, rose to the occasion, which was no easy task.

In the UCA the main instrument for defending the poor has been the university word, just as for Monseñor Romero it was the pastoral word. That word expressed, and at the same time was also made possible, by Christian inspiration. "It was present both in its mode of expression—in dialogue with others, with regard for truth and credibility—and in its content: justice, the end of the war, the humanization of the country. And after the assassinations, three words of deep Christian substance immediately appeared in the UCA on which Father Estrada insisted: *truth, justice,* and *forgiveness.*

The Jesuit martyrs were convinced that this inspiration was not an *imposition,* more or less costly for them, but a *good* for the university, and more specifically for a Salvadoran university, in a society of horrors and hopes. From the university they defended the poor by fighting against lies and cover-ups. And very soon they experienced that there is no defense of the poor without risks.

Hopefully today more demands will be placed on the UCA, especially that it act with greater and more decisive Christian inspiration. But we should not underestimate what the UCA does in denouncing human rights violations and in defending the oppressed—in short, in taking seriously the reality of the country.

✧ *Jesuits and bishops have come up in our conversation, but sometimes you also mention cooks and market women. What do you mean?*

Romero, Rutilio, and Ellacuría have had an impact on me, obviously. But the cooks, the cleaning women, the market vendors, and others have also had a great impact on me, sometimes even more than the others. They belong to a very different sphere of life. They do not take life for granted, or health, or education, or rest, or appreciation, or travel, or vacations, or so many other things.

We Jesuits can be persecuted and even killed. But we take the primary aspect of life for granted. Not so the people I have just mentioned. And it has also struck me that these people have almost all the powers of this world aligned against them.

Having said that, I will explain about "the cooks." When the Vatican published the Notification on my theology in 2007, several people wrote to me. In replying to a friend I wrote, more or less, these words: "I'm not too worried about what the Vatican says about me. I am more concerned that the cook in my house thinks of me as a good person."

Apart from what there is of exaggeration and irony in these words, for me they have a lot of truth in them. There is something about people who don't take life for granted. It's like an ultimacy that I don't easily see elsewhere. They can tell me my truth in a special way.

✧ *We have spoken of "torches." But I have to tell you that I have never really liked the expression "to be the voice of the voiceless," because I believe that we all—men and women—have a voice: the poor, women, refugees. What happens is that on many occasions there have been people who have thought and spoken on behalf of these groups, and I don't like that, it doesn't seem fair to me. I think that instead of being the "voice of the voiceless," we should give a voice to those who have been silenced. Now, I understand that in the case of Rutilio and Romero what they were doing in some way was to be loudspeakers for the poor.*

I have heard this same complaint from Gustavo Gutiérrez, and I understand it if it is assumed that it expresses our superiority over the poor in something as delicate as being able to express the truth of reality. But it can be understood in a hopeful and courageous way, in how we proclaim reality. I have looked up how Monseñor Romero formulated similar expressions and with what meaning.

On July 29, 1979, in his homily, he said the following words without presumption and with the utmost dedication: "These homilies seek to be the voice of this people, the voice of those who have no voice. No doubt that's why they find no favor with those who have too much voice. But this poor voice finds an echo, as I said before, in those who love the truth and who truly love 'our dear people.'"

✧ *With all that you have lived through in El Salvador, with the contact with poverty, with injustice, with death on the front line, what has helped you to keep walking and to do it from the faith?*

Seeing real love. There is love of many kinds: friendship, eros, agape, and more. But there is a love that is related to the innocent suffering of the other and indirectly to one's own suffering. The greatest love is when one gives one's life for another in a clear way, as in the case of Maximilian Mary Kolbe, a Polish Franciscan who gave his life in exchange for the life of another prisoner in a Nazi camp. Remembering him is something impressive and moving to this day. And without going to such extremes in the way he gave his life, love was evident in the death of Monseñor Romero. Ellacuría was drier in an affective sense, but he was a man with real love for the Salvadoran people. He was a man with a strong temper, sometimes with an excess of temper. But without love, Ellacuría would not have existed.

✧ *When we follow in the footsteps of Jesus, the consequence is often a death like his. You have spoken a lot about the martyrs. What is it that led them to give their lives? What do you think they bring to us today?*

The first I have already said: they love others in need more than they love themselves. The second may vary. They have given me a *sense of reality* because of the abundance with which they occur, *overcoming the ignorance* I had before coming to El Salvador. I believe that martyrs are something that, perhaps unconsciously, we shy away from, not because we are anti-martyrs, but because martyrs say that in this world there are many pools of blood.

✧ *But why do they kill them?*

Why do they kill them? The one who answered it best was Monseñor Romero. Before he was assassinated, they killed six priests, then six others, and then the six from the UCA. Monseñor had experience. On June 24, 1979, he said in his homily:

Several priests have been assassinated and this leads us to ask the question: why have these priests and so many other Christians who attempt to be faithful to their vocation, why have these persons been assassinated? I believe, and I am proud to say this, the reason is that the Archdiocese of San Salvador does not want to be indifferent or an accomplice of the situation of sin and the structural violence that exists in our country. For several years now the Archdiocese has felt obliged, because of her evangelical mission, to denounce the injustices from a Christian perspective. Doing this has cost the church the loss of some of its very beloved members.

And in his homily on September 23, he stated categorically: "Those who are in the way are killed."

✧ *In that atmosphere of tension, threats, and violence, how could one go on with daily life?*

I will give my opinion. I think it was possible. I used to give Christology classes, and I had no trouble giving them, because the classes clarified what was happening in the country and vice versa, and encouraged us to live in a Salvadoran way. Persecution also became a daily reality, and we could not live a Christian life without participating in it in some way. And above all, martyrdom abounded: "No one has greater love than this, to lay down one's life for one's friends." From this great love emerged a torrent of generosity. And everyday life could be lived.

This generosity even led some to join the guerrillas, and they actively risked their lives. But many did not go to the guerrillas to fight with weapons, but so that this movement, which was in places where there was nothing, would have nurses, teachers, priests, nuns, and so on.

Once again Monseñor Romero comes to mind. In March 1977 they killed Rutilio; in May they killed another priest, Father Navarro; and on May 19 the army entered the town of Aguilares and laid siege to it for a month. Three Jesuits who worked there were expelled from the country in a bad way. Some peasants who knew hidden paths were able to get out and bring news to the capital of what was happening in Aguilares.

When the army left Aguilares, Monseñor Romero did not hesitate for a moment to go there. I went with him and a good number of priests, nuns, and lay people. The peasants were afraid to go near the church because they were terrified by what had happened that month. For this reason the organizers put loudspeakers in the church. Romero understood this and began the mass with loudspeakers.

With total freedom he said in his homily of June 19, "It is my job to gather up the assaults, the bodies." And he prayed: "Let us pray for pardon and also for the needed repentance of those who have made this place a prison and a torture chamber. May the Lord touch their hearts before the dreadful sentence is carried out: 'All who take up the sword will perish by the sword' (Matt 26:52)."

But his hope was greater. At the offertory of the mass Monseñor Romero, along with the bread and wine, offered God four nuns who had volunteered to take care of the parish of Aguilares, which had been left without priests.

And the most important thing is what he said to those who listened to him through the loudspeakers from outside the temple: "You are the image of the Divine One who has been pierced."

With people like Monseñor Romero it is possible to live a Christian life even in the midst of difficulties, tension, and threats.

✧ *To end this part I would like to hear a few words from you about Pope Francis. The first thing I want to ask you is what you felt when he was elected pope.*

I was worried, despite the beautiful gestures and words he had from the beginning. The reason is that many people, serious people, said that Jorge Bergoglio was not always as he is now, and his limitations were quite well publicized. After being ordained a priest, he soon assumed positions of responsibility in the Society, which gave him power over people. He was novice master, rector of the theologate, and provincial. In the 1970s he was known for his excessive possessiveness over his subjects. I was able to verify this when some Argentinean Jesuits came to unburden themselves to me during a visit I made to Buenos Aires and Cordoba a few years ago. I have heard this complaint several times. And Francis himself, now pope, has made it sufficiently clear in recent interviews.

I have heard different and even contrary things about his behavior during the military dictatorship. My conviction is that he managed to save lives, although his performance was not like that of Monseñor Romero. Once he became bishop, his closeness to the clergy and his willingness to help tired or troubled priests is well known.

✧ *And what do you think of his four years of papal performance?*

I was very positively surprised. Francis pushes the cart of history with determination, *semper et ubique,* always and everywhere.

Every day he says mass in Santa Marta with members of a parish in Rome and with other invited guests, and at the end he speaks briefly with those who approach him, who are in the majority. On Wednesdays he receives many visitors in the Paul VI Hall, and on Sundays after the

Angelus he speaks to crowds in St. Peter's Square. During the week he receives countless visitors, some diplomats, illustrious personalities, and a multitude of ordinary people. He is seen with the poor, the disabled, migrants, children. He gives interviews on the ground and on airplanes. He makes unexpected phone calls and writes personal letters.

In November 2016 I was at his mass at Santa Marta. His devotion was heartfelt. We talked for a minute and a half. I handed him a little letter written to him by a UCA colleague with pictures of her children. He blessed it and gave it back to me. We said goodbye with a hug. And he told me: "Write, write." Of greater permanent impact are his two encyclicals, well thought out, I suppose with qualified experts: *The Joy of the Gospel* and *Laudato Si'*. His travels have had a great impact on me. Pope Francis travels very frequently—*semper*—and seems to be everywhere—*ubique*. He travels most especially to places where cruel suffering and victims abound. I will note just a few examples, beginning with his trip to Mexico in 2016.

Mexico City, 2016. Harsh words to rulers and politicians. "Each time we seek the path of privileges or benefits for a few to the detriment of the good of all, sooner or later life of society becomes fertile ground for corruption, drug trade, exclusion of different cultures, violence and also human trafficking, kidnapping and death, bringing suffering and slowing down development."

In one of his longest and harshest allocutions he addressed the bishops. "Be vigilant so that your vision will not be darkened by the gloomy mist of worldliness; do not allow yourselves to be corrupted by trivial materialism or by the seductive illusion of underhanded agreements; do not place your faith in the 'chariots and horses' of today's pharaohs, for our strength is in 'the pillar of fire' which divides the sea in two, without much fanfare (cf. Ex 14:24–25)." And he continued. "We do not need 'princes,' but rather a community of the Lord's witnesses."

In Chiapas, the poorest state in Mexico. Here he visited the tomb of Don Samuel Ruiz,[6] and he authorized the ordination of Indigenous permanent deacons and the use of their languages in liturgies. And

---

[6] Samuel Ruiz (1924–2011) was the Bishop of San Cristobal de las Casas in Chiapas, Mexico. He was a courageous defender of the Indigenous peoples and a prophetic champion of justice.

he asked forgiveness from the peoples of communities that, "in a systematic and organized way, have been misunderstood and excluded from society."

In Ciudad Juarez, on the border with the United States, one of the most conflictive points on the American continent. "What kind of Mexico do you want to leave your children? Do you want to leave them a memory of exploitation, of insufficient pay, of workplace harassment?" The border is "a road laden with terrible injustices: enslaved, kidnapped, extorted. Many of our brothers and sisters are the fruit of the business of human transit." Every year, twelve million immigrants pass through this place where thousands lose their lives. There Francis celebrated the Eucharist and blessed an enormous crucifix called the Cross of the Migrant.

We could cite so many other examples: his first trip out of Rome in 2013 to celebrate mass on the island of Lampedusa, where so many refugees have drowned off the Italian coast. To Israel, Palestine, and Jordan in 2014, where he visited the Yad Vashem Memorial and also gave one of his rare political statements at Ben Gurion airport:

> The right of the State of Israel to exist and to flourish in peace and security within internationally recognized borders must be universally recognized. At the same time, there must also be a recognition of the right of the Palestinian people to a sovereign homeland and their right to live with dignity and with freedom of movement.

In 2016, in the United States, he visited prisoners in Philadelphia, made an act of reparation to the nuns who had not been well treated by Benedict XVI, and confirmed a policy of zero tolerance for pedophilia without falling into arrogance, as if the church did it better than other institutions. He gave a solemn and well-thought-out speech in Congress, where he recalled four great Americans: Abraham Lincoln, liberator of the slaves and martyr; Martin Luther King Jr., defender of African Americans and martyr; Dorothy Day, co-founder of the Catholic Worker movement, inspired by the gospel and moved by her passion for justice and the cause of the oppressed; and Thomas Merton, Trappist monk, man of prayer, thinker who challenged the certainties of his time and opened horizons for human beings and the church.

That same year he traveled to Poland, where he visited Auschwitz, the extermination camp, and prayed outside the hunger block where the Polish priest Maximilian Kolbe offered to die in exchange for the father of a family. After his visit he only wrote in the book of honor: "Lord, pardon for so much cruelty."

Outside Auschwitz he spoke out. He demanded the church to change course. He asked the bishops to stop being princes with palaces. To the priests, to stop being civil servants. And to the more than one million young people attending a prayer vigil in Krakow in 2016 he said:

> But in life there is another, even more dangerous, kind of paralysis . . . the paralysis that comes from confusing happiness with a sofa . . . a sofa that makes us feel comfortable, calm, safe. . . . For many people in fact, it is much easier and better to have drowsy and dull kids who confuse happiness with a sofa. For many people, that is more convenient than having young people who are alert and searching, trying to respond to God's dream and to all the restlessness present in the human heart. . . .
>
> Dear young people, we didn't come into this world to "vegetate," to take it easy, to make our lives a comfortable sofa to fall asleep on. No, we came for another reason: to leave a mark. . . . But when we opt for ease and convenience, for confusing happiness with consumption, then we end up paying a high price indeed: we lose our freedom. We are not free to leave a mark. We lose our freedom. This is the high price we pay. There are so many people who do not want the young to be free; there are so many people who do not wish you well, who want you to be drowsy and dull, and never free! No, this must not be so! We must defend our freedom!

And as he said goodbye to them he asked them to "remember, to have courage and to sow for the future."

✧ *This great number of "doings" and "sayings" is a leap in quality. Francis is doing and saying something profound. Now I am only going to mention a few themes on which Pope Francis insists, and I ask for a brief comment from you.*

Mercy. Francis insists on it constantly. The fundamental thing is compassion, to suffer what others suffer, especially cruelties and horrors, ultimately. What I do not hear enough is that mercy is accompanied by taking risks to defend the victims, and in the best way to disable the victimizers.

The reform of the church. The difficulties have been evident, but the pope's decision to go forward seems clear to me. I do not perceive any fear that would paralyze him and lead him to back down from his initial decision.

Women in the church. The problem is obvious. Under Benedict XVI, American women religious suffered serious misunderstanding and a denial of dialogue. At first, Pope Francis did not fix the issue. Now he has taken some steps. In the Paul VI Hall, before the general superiors of the women's religious orders, he said he would appoint a commission to study the issue of women deacons in the church. The Vatican has already announced the creation of such a commission to study the diaconate of women.

Theology. The pope's theology is traditional in tone, to which he adds the perspectives of Vatican II. It is narrative, without much biblical exegesis or historical criticism. Orthodoxy and the documents of the ecclesial institution are present in his theology. The background, however, is something else. In the end, the evangelical and human aspects prevail.

And a final remark. In Pope Francis, I believe that prior to any theological conceptualization, there is a fundamental conviction. In the midst of the enormous evils of this world, he maintains the persuasion that "God is a God of life and not of death, that the ultimate reality is good and not evil."

❖*A very special topic is the beatification of Monseñor Romero.*[7]

That's right. On the day of Monseñor's assassination, a peasant woman said in tears: "They have killed the saint." Pedro Casaldáliga wrote the poem "Saint Romero of America." Time passed, popes passed, and nothing happened. Pope Francis immediately beatified him, and shortly after he canonized him.

---

[7] Following a Vatican decree acknowledging that he had died as a martyr, Oscar Romero was beatified in a mass in San Salvador in 2015. His canonization followed in a ceremony in Rome in 2018.

✧ *What do you see in common between Monseñor Romero and Pope Francis?*

Very briefly, Pope Francis saw in Monseñor Romero a teacher, and above all he saw a blessing from God.

✧ *Finally, what do you think Pope Francis intends to do?*

There are various opinions. Personally, I think that he wants to push the cart of history and the cart of the church forward.

Pedro Casaldáliga said of Pope Francis that he is a gift of God for the church and for the world. This is also my opinion.

6

The Legacy of the Eight UCA Martyrs

A colleague who is reading the text I am writing told me that it would be good to add a chapter on the legacy of the martyrs.

To make myself understood from the beginning, by legacy I do not mean an inheritance, well or badly acquired, that passes from parents to children, but something of importance that has been given to us. Legacies do not appear at will or calculatedly, but when they appear, without giving the matter much thought, they bring with them the request to put their content into production, and that this in turn should be transmitted. I came to this conviction in 1989 when my Jesuit brothers from the UCA and Elba Ramos and her daughter Celina were killed. I begin, then, with a personal experience, the most personal I have ever had. That is why I will be lengthy in recounting it.

MY EXPERIENCE ON NOVEMBER 16

On November 8, I left for Thailand to give a course on Christology in English to missionaries—in the expression of the time—who were working in the countries of East and Southeast Asia. Once in Thailand, on November 13, I was in Hua Hin, 125 miles from Bangkok, in a retreat house next to a beautiful beach. I learned that war had broken out in San Salvador. My Jesuit companions were still at home, and Ellacuría had returned to the country without any problems.

On November 16—at midnight in Thailand—they woke me up and told me that something very serious had happened in El Salvador. They told me to go to the phone, and they would explain it to me. On the way from my room to the telephone I thought, *They have killed Ellacuría.* Once I was on the phone, a friend from London spoke to me. He asked me if I was sitting down and if I had anything with which to write. And he started, "They have killed Ellacuría." And I didn't write anything. My friend continued, "They have killed Segundo Montes, Nacho Martín-Baro, Amando López, Juan Ramón Moreno, Joaquín López y López." Each name was a hard blow that I received without defense, and I still did not write anything. My friend continued, "They have also killed two UCA workers." The information was not accurate. They had killed Elba, cook in a Jesuit student house, and her daughter Celina. That is what outraged me the most. That they killed Ellacuría was horrible, but it was to be expected. But to kill two simple women was ignominious. I felt empty inside.

That day I had spoken in class about the death on the cross of Jesus of Nazareth, but, although I am affected by the cross of Jesus, at that moment I did not feel nearly the weight of the news that had just been communicated to me. I went down to the beach and started walking. A few feet away, in silence, a companion followed me. Suddenly he asked me, "Jon, why do you think it wasn't your turn? And I thought to myself, *I guess I'm not worthy.*"

After walking for a while I went to bed. The next morning I went to the Eucharist that the group had prepared. I remember that the altar was made with flowers beautifully arranged on the floor. During the Eucharist I said nothing. At the end, with great respect, they asked me if I wanted to say something. And I did. I said exactly these words: "I have bad news to tell you: my whole family has been killed. And I have good news to tell you: I have lived with good people."

Before leaving Thailand I had accepted some engagements in places near Hua Hin, and despite my state of mind, I decided to fulfill them. On the trips to go from one place to another the motorist who drove me was a young native who had recently converted to Catholicism. One day he asked me in an incredulous voice, "And in your country, are there actually baptized Catholics who kill priests?" He would have been more shaken if he had known that those who in 1980 assassinated an archbishop, Monseñor Romero, were also baptized, and that on that night, in the wealthy neighborhood of San Benito, baptized Catholics were toasting with champagne and firing shots into the air with pistols, imitating the joy of the rockets at village festivals.

On my way back to El Salvador I had to pass through San Francisco. At the airport, Steve Prevett, a Jesuit, and Peggy O'Grady, a supporter of El Salvador, were waiting for me with undaunted faces. They took me to the University of Santa Clara. The community welcomed me as a brother, and I spent several weeks there. Without expecting it, when I arrived I found eight crosses planted in front of the campus church. And when one night a fiend ripped them down, Paul Locatelli, a Jesuit and the president of the university, immediately replanted them. I will never forget it.

Once settled in Santa Clara, I began to write down my experience, at length and without haste. I titled the text "Companions of Jesus."[1] In the first part I explain who they were, why they were killed, and who killed them. In a second part I explain what I am now being asked about, that is, their legacy. And I formulated it according to these themes: What did they leave us? What kind of university; what kind of church; what kind of theology? And I ended with this question: *What is their legacy?*

I start with the general question: what do they leave us? And I also answer in general, but with differences depending on the addressee.

To every human being, the martyrs confront us with ourselves without escape, they illuminate the deepest realities of our world, they push us to what must be done, and they dissuade us from what must not be done. We have to confront the idols that demand victims in the Third World, even though their deepest roots are in the First World. And we must work to reverse history and thus save a world that is in its death throes.

For those of us who are Christians, the martyrs show us, better than anything else and without fear of being mistaken, the path to follow in life. They are the ones who most encourage us to follow Jesus of Nazareth and best introduce us to the mystery of their God.

And those of us who are Jesuit companions of theirs—especially those of us who had lived with them for years in community and worked with them at the UCA—are required to maintain the fundamentals of what they were and what they did. As the years go by—there are about thirty now—we are required to be creative in the way we do it. But we are forbidden to disengage from their legacy.

I use the language of *martyrs,* aware that in the world of the good life and the desire to live well, the word *martyr* produces a feeling of

---

[1] Jon Sobrino, "Companions of Jesus," in Jon Sobrino, Ignacio Ellacuría, and Others, *Companions of Jesus: The Jesuit Martyrs of El Salvador* (Maryknoll, NY: Orbis Books, 1990), 3–56; also in Jon Sobrino, *Witnesses to the Kingdom: The Martyrs of El Salvador and the Crucified Peoples* (Maryknoll, NY: Orbis Books, 2003), 58–97.

strangeness, even repulsion. But among us——although it sounds paradoxical—the word *martyr,* after Rutilio, Romero, the four American church women, and many others, also produces light, encouragement, and gratitude. That is why we should not allow the word to lose its global vigor, not even by insisting—and thus in my opinion reducing it—on the fact that they are *witnesses.* Above all, martyrs are killed for a cause. They must remain an irreplaceable Christian and social reference point for humanizing this world. And the first thing they point to is the cross of Jesus. For this reason, I will now speak briefly about each of the eight crucified martyrs of the UCA.

The eight people murdered at the UCA touch the deepest fibers of any honest person. And they are a life-giving reference. This is obviously the case with the six Jesuits. But it is also true of Elba and Celina, although when we speak of them it seems that our tongue sticks to the roof of our mouth and it is difficult for us to speak, so insulting was the iniquity.

ELBA RAMOS AND CELINA, A CRUCIFIED PEOPLE

Two women were killed with the Jesuits: Elba Ramos, forty-two years old, cook in a community of young Jesuits, poor, cheerful, and intuitive, and a lifelong worker. And her daughter Celina, fifteen years old, active, a student, and a catechist. She and her partner planned to become engaged in December 1989. The two women stayed overnight at the Jesuit residence, as they felt safer there. But the criminal order was "not to leave witnesses." The photos show Elba Ramos's gesture of defending her daughter with her own body when the murderers found them in the room where they sought safety. A few days ago I heard this testimony about Elba Ramos from a woman who knew her well:

> I tell you that she was very human, because she felt the pain of others. I lived in her house for some time. She was a very friendly person; she knew how to get along with others. She was thirty-three years old, and I was nineteen. She and I had many things in common. We started working when we were very young. She had worked since she was ten years old in the coffee plantations. . . . She was a very strong woman. She always taught me not to

let myself go, not to be cowed in the face of problems. She was a longsuffering but strong woman. She taught me to be a woman of worth, not to depend on others, but on myself.

There are tens or hundreds of millions of men and women in our world like Elba Ramos. They are an immense majority, perpetuating a history going back for centuries: in the Americas, conquered and plundered by the Spanish in the sixteenth century; in Africa, enslaved as early as the sixteenth century and systematically plundered by Europeans in the nineteenth century; on the planet, which today suffers oppressive globalization under the aegis of the United States. They die the quick death of violence and repression, but more often the slow death of poverty and oppression. Without comparison, they suffer more than anyone else the consequences of our excesses. They suffer in wars and invasions: in Afghanistan, Iraq, Colombia, Honduras, Palestine. They suffer in the management of medicine and the pharmaceutical industry: by malaria, AIDS, COVID-19. They suffer in ecological disasters: floods, desertification, agricultural losses. The vast majority of those who die in earthquakes cannot build houses with sufficient strength; they live on hillsides and riverbanks or along railroad tracks. The same in other natural disasters.

There is more wealth on earth, but there is more injustice. Africa has been called the dungeon of the world, a continental Shoah. Globally, 2.5 billion people survive on less than two dollars a day, and 25,000 people die of hunger every day, according to the FAO. Desertification threatens the lives of 1.2 billion people in a hundred countries. Migrants are denied fraternity, even the soil under their feet. In one year, the number of hungry people has increased by one hundred million, and every five seconds a child dies of hunger, *murdered,* as Jean Ziegler points out, because it is quite possible to eliminate hunger.

THE JESUITS OF THE UCA

As a group, I believe that with Medellín in 1968, and the *Exercises* of 1969, the UCA Jesuits were touched by the suffering of the people, by the injustice, and also by the failures of the Central American vice-province throughout its history. And we can well say that they *converted.* They accepted that to be a Jesuit is to fight, not only to work. To struggle for the faith, and more incisively to struggle for justice, as reality demanded and as General Congregation XXXIII (Decree 2) requested, as we have seen. And their deaths confirmed what the same congregation had lucidly foreseen: "We will not work for the promotion of justice without paying a price" (Decree 4, no. 46).

The martyrs of the UCA lived each according to their talents, temperament, and limitations, and it is good to remember this and insist on it so that *all of us,* whatever our talents, temperament, and limitations, can feel challenged and encouraged by them. And likewise those who follow those of my generation. Although in various ways they have already appeared in this book, allow me to give a brief description of each of the six Jesuits of the UCA with their own characteristics.

Ignacio Ellacuría, fifty-nine years old. I have already spoken a lot about him, and I will specifically speak about him again at the end. He was exceptional, like Romero in the cathedral and Rutilio in the countryside. He was a philosopher and theologian, university rector, and responsible for the formation of young Jesuits. He rethought the university from and for the crucified peoples. He exerted all his intellectual, human, and Christian weight to fight oppression and repression in the country and to achieve a negotiated peace. In his last years he dedicated much time to thinking about how to eliminate sin from spreading all over the world and about a universal human civilization.

Segundo Montes, fifty-six years old. He was the founder of the Institute of Human Rights. He focused on the plight of refugees within the country, and especially those who had to leave it, the migrants who were then fleeing violent repression—now they are fleeing hunger and lack of work. He visited them in the refugee camps in Honduras. He took pastoral responsibility for the parish of Colonia Quezaltepeque.

Ignacio Martín-Baró, forty-four years old. He was pioneer of the psychology of liberation, founder of the Institute of Public Opinion of the UCA, created to make it easier for the truth to be known and to make it more difficult for it to remain oppressed by the cover-up that accompanies injustice. Every weekend he visited suburban and peasant communities with whom he celebrated the Eucharist.

Juan Ramón Moreno, fifty-six years old. He was a professor of theology and master of novices and master of the spirit, accompanier of religious communities. He founded the magazine of spiritual theology *Diakonía.* In Nicaragua he participated in the literacy campaign. And in the UCA of San Salvador he promoted the study of theology in the afternoons for three years for those who could not do it during the day because of their occupations.

Amando López, fifty-three years old. A professor of theology, he was rector of the archdiocesan seminary in San Salvador and of the UCA in Managua during the Sandinista Revolution. In both Nicaragua and El Salvador he defended those persecuted by criminal regimes, sometimes hiding them in his own room. On weekends he celebrated the Eucharist in poor places and for very poor people. His proverbial kindness was in itself an apostolic instrument.

Finally, *Joaquín López y López,* seventy-one years old. A simple man with a popular disposition, he was the only Salvadoran by birth. He worked at the school. He moved to get land to build the UCA. In 1965 he was its first secretary. Later, he founded Fe y Alegría, an institution of popular schools for the poorest.

These six Jesuits had two things in common. On the one hand, founding and maintaining institutional realities, and on the other, pastoral closeness to the poor on weekends. In ability and temperament they were different.

My final perception is that in the fundamentals of their lives they did have something in common. I will focus on four things: (1) following Jesus; (2) in the spirit of Saint Ignatius; (3) living in community; and (4) foreseeing and accepting that living in this way could lead them to persecution and martyrdom, which they accepted with normality.

Followers of Jesus, They Reproduced the Life of Jesus

Their gaze was directed at the real poor, those who live and die under the oppression of injustice, poverty, hunger, contempt, and those who suffer repression through murder, torture, disappearances. They looked at those who do not take their lives for granted, a lack that was often accompanied by great cruelty.

They were moved with compassion and worked miracles, putting all their abilities, knowledge, science, talents, time, work, and rest at the service of truth and justice.

They *expelled demons,* or at least they fought against them. Certainly, against demons from outside, oppressors, oligarchs, governments, armed forces, and sometimes against some demons from within: ecclesiastical and religious hierarchs, also from the Society.

They *defended the poor* from their enemies, not just loving and helping them.

In the Spirit of Saint Ignatius, Different from Today's Excessive Ignatianism

The adjective *Ignatian* is easily used today, and we speak of Ignatian spirituality, Ignatian psychology, Ignatian sociology, Ignatian discernment, Ignatian education, Ignatian retreats, Ignatian administration, and the tendency seems to be increasing, not going down. Sometimes it is done with simplicity, but sometimes this "adjectivization" subjectively connotes an air of superiority that does no good. And objectively it can reduce the vigor, the weight, of real important things of Saint Ignatius, certainly poverty. Something similar, and I think more crudely, used to happen with making an adjective—*Jesuitical*—of the term *Jesuit*.

In my opinion, the six Jesuits took Saint Ignatius seriously and did not fall into the excesses criticized. Three things about Saint Ignatius seem to me to be up to date and can continue to serve as effective Ignatian presuppositions even today.

1. To look at the reality of our world and grasp it as peoples who are crucified. Before them, the fundamental reaction—without the need for discernment—is to make redemption.

2. To be honest with ourselves as Jesuits, and to ask ourselves what we have done to crucify these people and what we are going to do to take them down from the cross?

3. To take seriously the decision to walk in poverty against wealth, perhaps the most difficult and least frequent occurrence.

These three things—the crucified people, the praxis of liberation, and walking in poverty—I think appear most in the Ignatian identity of the martyrs of the UCA and what best explains why they ended up as they did. In the tradition of Saint Ignatius there are certainly many other important things to keep in mind: the *magis,* "the greater glory of God," "in everything to love and serve," "the good, the more universal, the more divine," all of which are mentioned frequently, and I have no doubt that in Saint Ignatius they offer utopias to be realized. But I also think that, in the current environmental explosion of Ignatianism, they are often mentioned without sufficient modesty, as if we Jesuits easily sign up to live, or at least to try to live seriously, these utopias.

They Lived and Died in Community

It might not have been so. As for living, it was made possible by their work at the UCA. As for dying, it was caused by the excess of the criminals, since it would seem to have been enough to kill Ellacuría. It was not so. His life and work had been in community, with all its joys and tensions, its virtues and defects. The community was made up of everyone. It was a body, not a sum of individuals, some of them brilliant, others more modest, all valuable.

In this context of the community, I think it is appropriate to recall a singular fact. I believe that the martyrs of the UCA never discerned whether it was God's will to remain in the country, with risks, threats, and persecutions, or to leave it. At least it never occurred to them to consider seriously the possibility of leaving. I lived it with them.

To find out how much there was that was explicitly Ignatian in this procedure, I think we have to go to the *Exercises,* to the first time of making a choice—Saint Ignatius says that the first time the human being acts "without hesitation or the possibility of hesitation," without doubt or the possibility of doubt (*Exercises* 175). And this happens when "God, our Lord, thus moves and attracts the will."

In the case of the martyrs of the UCA, I am not the one to say how their decision not to leave the country came about, whether it was a personal experience of God, as formulated in the *Exercises,* or because of human experiences that led them to stay in the country "without hesitation or the possibility of hesitation." Thinking of my own experience, these could be reasons for not leaving the country: the suffering of the people to the point of being ashamed to leave them; the enriching memory of Monseñor Romero; of nine priests and four nuns murdered; the cohesive strength of the community; even the fact of having become accustomed to persecution. In my case I would like to add that in teaching Christology, talking about Jesus's way to Jerusalem, his being killed on the cross, and simultaneously remembering his demand to follow him, something had to move me to stay in the country without much discussion. Returning to the Christology classes, I do not see how it is possible to teach Moltmann's *Crucified God* and remember that Bonhoeffer put his own life at stake in fidelity to the Crucified One and not be open to the risks of staying in the country.

Faithful to the End

They died like Jesus and have swelled a cloud of witnesses—Christians, religious, and even some agnostics—who have given their lives for justice. With their martyrdom this community of six Jesuits was integrated into a larger community, into the body of the universal Society. More than sixty Jesuits have died in the Third World, killed in one way or another since General Congregation XXXII. And since this is often forgotten, let us recall examples of Jesuits who are geographically close to us, three Americans: Francis Louis Martiseck, sixty-six years old, born in Export, Pennsylvania, killed by gunshot in Mokame, India, 1979; Raymond Adams, fifty-four years old, born in New York, killed by gunshot in Cape Coast, Ghana, 1989; and Thomas Gafney, sixty-five years old, born in Cleveland, Ohio, killed in Kathmandu, Nepal, 1997. It is not uncommon to recall as glories of the Society the reductions of Paraguay and Mateo Ricci in China. Today these martyrs, some more famous, others less so, are the true glory of the Society. And we do not say this to speak with pride and solemnity of the Society, but because they are above all those who keep the Society alive.

The Jesuit martyrs of the UCA were neither perfect Christians nor perfect Jesuits. But I think they allowed themselves to be drawn and carried strongly by Jesus and by the poor. And I think that is their fundamental legacy.

WHAT THE SIX JESUITS LEAVE US

They Have Left Us a Christian-Inspired University

In El Salvador, a Catholic country, six professors from the same university, Jesuits, priests, intelligent, enlightened, creative, were killed.

I don't know if this has ever happened before. That has made them better known. And since the young readers of these pages no longer have that university experience as their specific legacy, we concentrate on the university they left us: a university of Christian inspiration.

If this is how the six Jesuits ended up, it is because they came to have and put into practice an idea very different from the common idea of a university, which does not generate such animosity. They put into practice an idea of a *Christian university for our times in the Third World*.

They let us know that university knowledge can and must be placed at the service of the poor. And they left us with the proof that, in doing so, the university itself can grow.

Ignacio Ellacuría spoke about this when he received an honorary doctorate from the University of Santa Clara, California, in 1982.[2] I comment briefly on Ellacuría's words with some brief personal reflections. And I go on for a while because this is the first time that the subject of the university has been discussed in depth in these conversations.

1. The first paragraph assumes that we should not assume that we already know adequately *what* a university *is*. Ellacuría was looking for starting points to find out. And his interest was not so much to know what a university *is,* but what a university *should be.* It is understood that it is an institution that has to do with the scientific use of reason, and also with culture, which makes it a specific institution.

But less taken into account—although it is extremely important—is that the university is *a social reality.* Factually, it is a conglomerate of realities: professors, administrators, and students, various traditions, buildings, libraries, sports fields, activities such as fundraising. . . . This set of things shapes itself as a social reality and turns it into a force in society, destined to illuminate the society in which it lives and for which it must live.

2. The second paragraph begins to make concrete what he has just said, expanding on several points. The murdered Jesuits were clearly aware of the fact that the UCA was based in a seriously ill social reality. This illness affected it in a bipolar way. It is dialectical, since it is expressed in the predominance of one of the poles over the other, of evil over good. What predominated was falsehood over truth, injustice over justice, oppression over freedom. . . . At times, the bipolarity of

---

[2] His speech appears in its entirety in Appendix 4 herein.

society was also "dueling": with two sides fighting each other until one could eliminate the other.

Immersed in this reality, the Jesuits wondered what to do at the university. Clearly, it was necessary to accumulate knowledge and wisdom. But above all, they responded with an ethical approach: the university should promote the good and eliminate the bad.

And from this ethical perspective there are other reflections to be made. The first is perhaps surprising, but the Jesuit martyrs were well aware that the university, like everything that is a creature, is threatened by sinfulness. It can reinforce the unjust structures of a society through the professionals it produces, through the socioeconomic models it supports—in short, through its weight and social projection. And the university not only can be and can do all this, but it often is and does this, thus introducing sin into society.

3. The ethical approach suggested by Ellacuría was that the UCA should be inspired by Christian values. This meant that all university activity should be regarded from the illuminating horizon of what a Christian preferential option for the poor means. In the case of the UCA, this had to be clarified, at least minimally, since it used to be assumed that its thinking should be in agreement with the orthodoxy of the Catholic Church. What the UCA recognized was that it must freely accept being inspired by what is Christian. And that the measure of what is Christian is Jesus of Nazareth, compassionate and critical, crucified and resurrected, the kingdom of God, announced and initiated by Jesus, and the option for the poor. And the reason for choosing this as its inspiration was the realization that this is what most helps it fulfill its mission.

This also means something that is not usually taken into account. A university of Christian inspiration has to be open to conversion, which consists of putting all its social weight through its specific instrument, rational knowledge—with research and teaching—in favor of the popular majorities and preventing it from falling into the hands of well-off minorities. That is what the six martyrs tried and did: to opt for the popular majorities in a university and in a Christian way, and to avoid falling into the hands of the well-off minorities.

In this context Ellacuría insists that the university must incarnate itself intellectually among the poor. To explain this bold thought, he paraphrased Monseñor Romero when he related the ecclesial word and the world of the poor. In Romero's homily of July 29, 1979, he said:

"These homilies seek to be the voice of this people, the voice of those who have no voice." Ellacuría, for his part, said that the university should "be the science of those who have no science, the enlightened voice of those who have no voice." It is striking that in seeking a point of contact between university reason and the pastoral word, Ellacuría did not enter into the problematic of theory and praxis, fallibility or infallibility, doubt or certainty, but into the sphere of the defense of the oppressed and the victims. Here Romero's pastoral word and El-lacuría's university word resonate. Ellacuría, without naivety, delved into the precariousness of the people, but recognized that in their very reality they have truth and reason, even if at times in the form of dispossession. What they don't have are academic reasons that justify and legitimize their reason. This is what the university must contribute; that is, to be the science of those who do not have academic science to expose their truth.

4. With sensible humility, recognizing the persecutions to which he had been subjected, Ellacuría acknowledged that the UCA had obtained some results. And he mentions two types of effective instruments for this. The first are the most obvious in a university: research, publications. But he insists above all on a second type of instruments, if they can be called that: men who have left other more brilliant, more worldly, and more lucrative alternatives to devote themselves vocationally to the university liberation of the Salvadoran people. Students and professors have paid very painfully, some with their own lives, others with exile, others with ostracism, for their dedication to the university service of the oppressed majorities.

5. In the end, Ellacuría recalls the threats, attacks, and persecution of the UCA in those years. When the word, university or pastoral, is not light and amorphous, but has weight and edges, it is sharper than a two-edged sword. And then the world that presents itself as tolerant and a fierce defender of freedom of thought and freedom of expression seeks to defend itself against a compassionate university reason and the word of Jesus. Fifty years ago even the CIA sought to defend itself from Medellín and liberation theology, because it was afraid of them. "They endanger our interests," it was said in the Rockefeller Report (1969).

The six Jesuits of the UCA were feared and killed for their university defense of the poor. If there had not been some kind of persecution and death, neither they nor the UCA would have fulfilled their university mission. Even less would they have made their Christian inspiration visible. It was thus for Romero, when he proclaimed that his words were the voice of the voiceless. Romero continued, "No doubt that's why they find no favor with those who have too much voice." The same happened with the UCA.

Before concluding these reflections on the university that the martyrs have left us as a legacy, I would like to say something that may be surprising. It is common to speak of the academic excellence that universities should have, and it is normal that Jesuit universities come to mind. But, thinking about it in depth, university excellence goes beyond academic excellence. This excellence involves producing with excellence the three functions of the university: teaching, research, and social projection. And all of this can be carried out to the greatest possible degree in a university steeped in Christian inspiration.

It is also important to ask ourselves periodically how much persecution a university of Christian inspiration, and specifically the UCA, suffers or does not suffer—on the part of those who suffer it, on the part of those who receive flattery, and how they behave in the face of one thing or another.

We end with Ellacuría. "A university that fights for truth, justice, and freedom cannot but be persecuted." These words seem to me especially important for the reader of the new generations.

They Have Left Us, Learning from Others, a Church of the Poor

The Jesuits lived and worked within the church, but that *within* has a different meaning than how they lived and worked within a university, even if it was of Christian inspiration. The martyrs of the UCA left us a church not built by them, although they helped to build it with others.

1. The murdered Jesuits lived within the church and were an important part of it. At the funeral mass the nuncio called them true sons and members of the church. And he gave them the name of martyrs. They put the council and especially Medellín into practice. In this way we Jesuits became more integrated into the people of God and felt less elitist. They wanted to build *the church of the poor*, of which we have already spoken at length.

2. In that church they lived and found enjoyment, but they also suffered. The church hurt them when it looked more at itself than at the pain of the people, when it incomprehensibly silenced Monseñor Romero, let alone when some bishops even attacked him.

They thought that the church as a whole was going through a period of involution, certainly after the assassination of Monseñor. That is why, with freedom and maturity, they were also critical of the church.

3. Let us recall some stupidity they had to deal with. At one point the expression *church of the poor* began to be used. Incredibly, this church was suspected, and even more so when it was reformulated as a *popular church,* a church that makes the poor of this world central in its mission and configuration. It was taken for granted that *popular church* meant only sociological realities of being church. The popular church was discredited, even condemned by the hierarchy.

Rarely, I believe, has such a stupid and unjust misrepresentation of the word *popular* been made. That church, with its limitations and errors, produced much faith, much hope, much love, and much martyrdom. It was a church from the people and of the people. In this context I remember Father Anisate's comment, with his characteristic humor and irony: "If the popular church is not the true church, what will be the true church? The unpopular one?"

4. Looking at the positive side of the ecclesial legacy they left us, we must remember that they enjoyed the friendship and respect of some of our brother bishops. Certainly they were close friends and collaborators of Monseñor Romero and often collaborated fraternally with Bishop Rivera. Bishops like Pedro Casaldáliga have been in our house and have felt at home there. Catholic bishops and bishops from other Protestant sister churches have visited us at the UCA, and we have fraternally conversed with them as members of the people of God and of the church of Jesus.

Other hierarchs, here and in Rome, considered these Jesuits representatives of a dangerous church—not very obedient, suspicious, perhaps even unbelieving. In their priestly pastoral work they were accepted in the archdiocese, and some of them were invited to give talks and retreats to the priests. But on the whole they were not well regarded by many bishops in El Salvador and elsewhere in Central America. Ignacio Ellacuría, Amando López, and Juan Ramón Moreno—to cite the three who were theologians by profession—were not usually invited to offer their theological reflections in the seminary. Monseñor Aparicio in Puebla said publicly that those responsible for the violence in El Salvador were Father Ellacuría and this servant.

5. I would like these martyrdoms to help us not only to know the legacy, but also to make us reflect on what is the true church of Jesus. Will there not be a true church where, in addition to the communion from below toward the hierarchy, there is communion from above toward the people of God, toward the poor of this world? Will there not be a true church where, in addition to the traditional sacramental and worship practices, there is a determined evangelization of the poor, the communication and implementation of the good news of God for them, and the commitment to solidarity with them to the point of sharing their cross? Will there not be a true church where, in addition to obedience and fidelity to what tradition has handed down to us, there is obedience and primary fidelity to the actual will of God, which leads even to giving one's life?

6. Serving the church, and the hierarchical church, are important for a Christian and for a Jesuit, of course, and the murdered Jesuits, as far as I remember, did so whenever they were asked to do a job. But we must not forget something more fundamental; that is, that the church is the sacrament of something greater than itself, it is the sacrament of the kingdom of God. The ultimate goal cannot be to serve *the church*, but to serve *in* the church, and in the church, to serve God and the poor, because God is greater than the church, and communicating the good news to the poor is the raison d'être of the church.

This is the main thing I wanted to say about what church they leave us. I end with some memories of the relationship between Monseñor Romero and the Jesuit martyrs. In his last Sunday Eucharists, Monseñor asked Ellacuría and Segundo Montes to accompany him to the press conference he had with the journalists after mass. When the questions were about the political situation and violence, he gave the floor to Ellacuría. When the topic was about refugees and migrants, he gave the floor to Segundo Montes. Both Jesuits were always at his complete disposal.

For his part, Monseñor defended the UCA in public. In his homily on March 23, 1980, he said:

Yesterday afternoon the UCA, the Universidad Centroamericana José Simeón Cañas, was attacked for the first time and with no provocation. At one-fifteen in the afternoon a large military force mounted this operation, together with the National Police. They entered the campus and began shooting. A student who at the time was studying mathematics, Manuel Orantes Guillén, was killed. They also tell me that the troops captured and disappeared several students. . . . In the name of God, then, and in the name of this suffering people, whose laments rise up each day more tumultuously toward heaven, I beg you, I beseech you, I order you in the name of God: stop the repression!

I have one last memory that expresses how confident Monseñor Romero and Ellacuría were in each other. There was no chapel at the UCA. I think that for Monseñor Romero the subject was important, and knowing him, I believed that he would talk about it with Ellacuría. And they did talk. I heard Ellacuría tell him about it more than once. Monseñor used to thank Ellacuría for the great effort the UCA made to fight injustice and defend the poor, declaring that what the UCA was doing was very good. But in a different tone of voice, Monseñor continued, "But what about a chapel?" Ellacuría replied, "You see, Monseñor, the problems we have now. But as soon as we can we will build the chapel." And so it was.

WHAT IS LEFT

Above all, the people were left suffering more. The assassinations took place in a week that left around a thousand dead, countless wounded, thousands of poor homes destroyed, and poor people who had to leave their homes and seek refuge elsewhere, a people more terrorized and who now saw their hopes for peace dissipate even further. And a more unprotected people remained. Jesuits who could effectively defend the poor were killed. In this context I see the ultimate malice of the murders of the Jesuits. The poor were left more unprotected.

What, then, is really left of the martyrdom of these six Jesuits? I believe and hope that they continue to be a light in this tunnel of darkness and hope in this country of misfortunes, that their spirit remains, as that of Monseñor Romero has remained in the Salvadoran people, as has that of Rutilio Grande in many peasants, as have the North American church women in Chalatenango and La Libertad, as has Octavio Ortiz in El Despertar, as have the hundreds of peasants martyred in their communities.

The six Jesuits will also live. I would like the Salvadoran people to remember them as witnesses of truth, so that they continue to believe that truth is possible in this country; to remember them as witnesses of justice, and for their love for the popular majorities, so that the Salvadoran people might maintain the belief that it is possible to change the country; that they remember them as faithful witnesses of the God of life, so that the Salvadoran people continue to see in God, in their God, a defender; that they remember them as Jesuits who tried to make a difficult conversion and paid the price for defending faith and justice. This is what I hope these Jesuits leave to the Salvadoran people, and that in that legacy they remain alive, a source of inspiration and encouragement. And in Elba Ramos and Celina, I hope they remember the horror of the victimizers and the innocence of thousands and thousands of poor people.

The price to pay has been great, but there is no other. And it can produce a singular joy. Thus spoke Monseñor Romero in words that to this day send shivers down the spine:

> I rejoice, brothers, that in this country priests have been assassi-
> nated. . . . For it would be very sad that in a country where people
> are being so horribly murdered we do not count priests among the
> victims. It is a sign that the church has become truly incarnated in
> the problems of the people.

In his homily at the funeral of Father Rafael Palacios, June 21, 1979, Monseñor said, "The voice of blood is more eloquent than words." The eight martyrs of the UCA leave us a cry to the whole world.

I already wrote my wish in Santa Clara:

> May Ignacio Ellacuría, Segundo Montes, Ignacio Martín-Baró,
> Amando López, Juan Ramón Moreno, Joaquín López y López,
> companions of Jesus, rest in peace. May Elba Ramos and Celina,
> beloved daughters of God, rest in peace. May their peace transmit
> hope to the living, and may their memory not let us rest in peace.

A Long Epilogue

Walking with Monseñor Romero and Ignacio Ellacuría,
with Jesus of Nazareth and His God,
and with Humility, with Hope, with Gratitude

✧*Jon, as I was reading your reflections on the legacy of the UCA martyrs, I thought you were finishing these conversations. But now I feel you are a bit restless, as if you have something left to say.*

That's right. I started working on this book in January 2014, and for various reasons I have had to interrupt it several times and take long breaks. In mid-May 2018 I set out to finish it quickly, briefly, and simply, and I finished it on July 26. I am now writing the epilogue to the corrected and shortened edition.

I begin by explaining two very important things that have happened since the first edition was published: *the canonization of Monseñor Romero* and *the COVID-19 pandemic*. Then, to explain how I have been doing theology for almost forty years, I will talk about my "walking with . . . ," specifically, "with Monseñor Romero," "with Ignacio Ellacuría," and "with Jesus of Nazareth and his God."

THE CANONIZATION OF MONSEÑOR ROMERO

On the morning of October 14, 2018, in Rome, Pope Francis canonized Monseñor Romero along with Paul VI, two priests, and two nuns. I was not particularly interested in going to Rome, but I was there. And I was glad I went, because I was able to capture and participate in the joy of many people, especially in the afternoon when many Salvadorans gathered, and Pope Francis came to be with us. I have already said the most important things of that day, but I want to explain some things that are not usually known and that have serious consequences, at least for me. In part they are criticisms, but I make them so as not to fall into routine and bureaucracy.

Let's begin. *Canonization* comes from the Latin word *canon,* which means "norm," and in order to canonize, a set of norms must be met. The work is arduous and involves many people. Sometimes it is mixed with worldly interests, whether foreign or from the Roman Curia. Sometimes it is done honestly. The positive thing is to avoid evasions or falsehoods in declaring certain Christians as excellent who have not been so.

Well then. A necessary requirement for canonization is that there be miracles. I am going to speak about this first in general, and then I will mention the miracle attributed to Monseñor Romero.

The number of miracles required is one for beatification and two for canonization. If the Christian died a martyr, and if the church recognizes that person as such, no miracle is needed for beatification, and only one for canonization.

Thinking things through, it is surprising that we humans have decided that we must measure the excellence of deceased persons in order to recognize them as excellent Christians, so that they can be venerated, so that we can affirm that they are already enjoying the vision of God, that through their intercession God can grant some benefit to third persons. And in my opinion, the most remarkable thing is that it is necessary, not only to proclaim, but to prove the excellence of the lives of possible saints and blessed by the fact that they have worked miracles.

Miracle means the occurrence of something that violates the laws of nature. Only an omnipotent God can do this. In the miracles attributed to saints and blesseds, God is still the author, but he decides to act through the intercession of those who will be canonized or beatified.

In miracles, God's power is present, which does not prevent other dimensions of his reality from being present. But without God's power, there is no miracle.

Why not say that the miracle is a sign of God's love, whatever the causes for the occurrence of something that apparently surpasses the laws of nature? We can put this in the form of a question. What is more specific about God's performance in miracles: his power or his love? That's why I'm not a big fan of talking about miracles. It could mean that the last word concerning the good that happens in a miracle is that God's power is confirmed.

Now we can speak of the miracle that was attributed to Monseñor Romero for his canonization. What happened is certainly beautiful. On May 23, 2015, while preparations were being made for the beatification of Monseñor Romero, Señora Cecilia and her husband, Alejandro, were praying for their children, Emiliano and Rebeca, and for the good progress of her pregnancy, which had been classified as high risk because Cecilia had lost other babies in the past. Cecilia was admitted to the hospital on May 1 and delivered her son by a cesarean. She was then transferred to the Social Security Hospital in San Salvador, where everything became more complicated to the point that she was placed in an induced coma to stabilize her kidneys and lungs. Cecilia's condition was so serious that the doctors told her family that there was nothing more they could do for her. But then, surprisingly, she was given a clean bill of health. Cecilia was healed. In the technical words of the Congregation for the Causes of Saints, "a miracle took place." The parents had prayed to Monseñor Romero, and then it was recognized that the miracle had occurred through the intercession of Monseñor Romero. Monseñor could now be canonized. And I believe that Cecilia was in Rome on October 14 at his canonization.

Cecilia's healing has made me very happy. I am happy that good things happen to those who suffer, especially when it seems very unlikely for them to happen. I am convinced that Monseñor Romero has made the lives of many people happy when it did not seem possible. He did it during his lifetime, and in a way that escapes our minds, he can continue to do it now. But I also believe that the people remember him more for his great love than for his power. Whether Cecilia's healing meant overcoming the forces of nature or not, I don't know. For me, it is secondary. The primary thing is that because of God, Cecilia is alive and certain human beings did everything possible for her to live. This has made her and her family very happy.

THE COVID-19 PANDEMIC

The horror is known. The first case took place in Wuhan, China, in December 2019. As of this moment, on May 14, 2021, there were 162.5 million cases of the disease in 255 countries and territories of the world. The number of deaths has exceeded 3 million, specifically 3,372,013.

The consequences have been extremely serious for the ability to work; for schools, colleges, and universities to function; for families to live together, to move, to subsist; and more. The horror is known. Now I am going to concentrate on what God says and does in the pandemic.

A word on context. The UN Secretary General António Guterres, in speeches on March 23 and March 30, 2020, said: "This is, indeed, the most challenging crisis we have faced since the Second World War." And "It is the most vulnerable—women and children, people with disabilities, the marginalized, displaced and refugees—who pay the highest price during conflict and who are most at risk of suffering 'devastating losses' from the disease." And finally, he appealed, "End the sickness of war and fight the disease that is ravaging our world."

For these words to hit home, let us remember that the number of victims of World War II is estimated at 55–60 million. And to grasp how far the horror of a pandemic can go—there is no talk of it happening— let us remember that in 1918–19 the pandemic called the Spanish flu caused at least 50 million deaths and affected nearly 500 million people.

As far as I know, God's relation to the pandemic is not discussed very much or with much seriousness. In speaking now on this subject, readers will perhaps be surprised. But I hope they will understand my decision to do so, hopefully with honesty and lucidity, and certainly with the desire that it will do some good.

A Long Story—Where Is God? What Does God Do? What Doesn't God Do?

Throughout history, in various cultures and religions, God has been thought of in different ways. And the existence of evil has led to thinking about God in specific ways.

The Lisbon earthquake of 1755 produced massive destruction. Yet, in recalling this tragedy, someone has commented, and in my opinion correctly, that the Lisbon earthquake would be just another terrible earthquake were it not for the fact that it had more impact on minds than on bodies. Indeed, that earthquake ultimately caused the triumph of rational thinking over closed dogmatism. This didn't happen automatically, and the Catholic thinkers of the time (almost all of them) followed the ideas of the famous Leibniz. He posited that in fulfilling

God's will, the human being lives in the best of all possible worlds. And if something goes wrong in that world, it will have been God's will, but as a punishment for the evil that human beings have done. Voltaire, among others, opposed this justification of God, this theodicy.

He returned to the dilemma that since ancient times has been attributed to Epicurus. In light of what he observed in the world, he wondered if there is a God who is good, or if God has the power to prevent evil. He came to the following conclusion: "If God is good, he is not all-powerful. And if God is all-powerful, he is not good." With this logic Epicurus was not proving the nonexistence of God, but he was radically calling into question attributes of God held as self-evident for centuries: his omnipotence and his goodness, his love for human beings. Throughout history, great thinkers—such as Thomas Aquinas—have tried to demonstrate the existence of God, even while admitting the evils of this world. And they have specifically endeavored to show that God is not responsible for the evils of this world. Now suffice it to mention this. Reason is, or can be, reassured. Yet it can remain unsettled.

When I had been in El Salvador for some years, in 2002, at the request of the Trotta publishing house in Madrid, I published a small book entitled *Terremoto, terrorismo, barbarie y utopía*, with reflections on the catastrophes that took place among us in those days. In El Salvador on January 13, 2001, there was a strong earthquake. In New York on September 11, 2001, the Twin Towers were destroyed. Afghanistan was going through years of terrorism. To express the hope I was also observing, I added a reflection on utopia.[1]

In countries like El Salvador, both in the serious difficulties of daily life and now in the pandemic, God is often mentioned by the poor and also by priests. God is asked to heal, help, comfort, and console the infected and all those in need. He is also asked to keep those who care for them strong and alive. And to reward them.

Pandemic or no pandemic, I think the issue of faith in God is not usually addressed as something that involves any kind of major problem. In the world of plenty many can live quietly without taking God into account, whether there is a God or not. And if they don't take God into

---

[1] Jon Sobrino, *Where Is God: Earthquake, Terrorism, Barbarity, and Hope* (Maryknoll, NY: Orbis Books, 2004).

account, they don't worry much about showing his nonexistence either. There used to be atheists who wondered about God's responsibility for the evils of this world, and some of them concluded that God's justification is that he does not exist. Now these ironies are no longer heard.

With or without catastrophes, *theodicy*, which literally means "justification of God," is not very important today. Nor do I believe that it is alluded to in the churches, in the classrooms of the seminaries, in the infinity of meetings of church movements.

How to Speak on Good Friday of God's Abandonment of Jesus's Cross

Personally, for years I have not been attracted to liturgies that speak a lot about the power of God and that insist repeatedly and unilaterally on his goodness and mercy. We can hear that God is always with us, that we can always place our hope in him, that God never disappoints.

In the Old Testament texts it is clear that God has *power*. He usually uses it in favor of the chosen people. Sometimes he uses it against them, if they do not behave well. But many times he defeats the enemies of his people Israel, and sometimes he destroys and kills many of them. Also in the Old Testament other ways of God's proceeding appear. The Servant Songs of Isaiah, of which we have already spoken, present a God whose power does not consist in crushing, whose servant brings salvation not by crushing the adversary but by allowing himself to be crushed by him.

For many years I have had the impression that in theology, in liturgy, and perhaps in pastoral ministry, one passes very quickly through Mark's account, and after him that of Matthew, in which Jesus dies with the complaint of Psalm 22 on his lips: "My God, my God, why have you forsaken me?" Luke's account, in which Jesus dies praying Psalm 31, of trust, "Into your hands I commend my spirit," is more easily approached. And the Gospel of John offers even fewer problems. In it Jesus dies with a certain majesty, master of himself, saying "All is accomplished." In fact, Jesus must have died without uttering words, but with a cry due to the asphyxia caused by being on a cross. That cry is mentioned in all the Synoptic Gospels. I also think that it is very easily said by some that the horror of the cross of Jesus expresses the infinite love of God.

The Father gave up his Son, Jesus; he did not spare him. And so we are saved. Then he exalted him and made him Lord for having given himself up to death on a cross.

In the face of the horror of the cross, I am not reassured by these affirmations, nor am I reassured by appealing to the resurrection of Jesus as a kind of happy ending. This may evoke surprise or disgust, but I am more reassured by the words of Moltmann, who wrote a book entitled *The Crucified God.* And whether his argument is convincing or not, he proclaims that *God is affected by suffering.* Omnipotent or not, God is affected by the cross.

Of Dietrich Bonhoeffer I have already spoken. Suffice it to recall now that at Hitler's explicit request he was hanged. In prison, on July 18, 1944, he wrote these verses:

> People go to God when they're in need,
>   plead for help, pray for blessings and bread,
>   for rescue from their sickness, guilt, and death.
>   So do they all, all of them, Christians and
>   heathens.
>
> People go to God when God's in need,
>   find God poor, reviled, without shelter or bread,
>   see God devoured by sin, weakness and death.
>   Christians stand by God in God's own pain.
>
> God goes to all people in their need,
>   fills body and soul with God's own bread,
>   goes for Christians and heathens to Calvary's
>   death
>   and forgives them both.[2]

Many years ago I read these verses in class, and there was a silence like no other I can remember. Not even when I mentioned that God resurrected his Son.

---

[2] Dietrich Bonhoeffer, "Christians and Heathens," in *Letters and Papers from Prison,* Dietrich Bonhoeffer Works 8 (Minneapolis: Fortress Press, 2015), 460–61.

The Martyrs of the Pandemic

The pandemic is not produced by human will, but, as with earth-quakes, by nature (although some hold human beings responsible for the damage they cause to nature). What is clear is that it produces many deaths. Now I think of the human beings, men and women, Christians or not, who take care of those contaminated by the virus and suffer discomfort, exhaustion, problems, sickness, and death. They are usually family members, nurses, doctors, nuns, priests. They are martyrs.

To be precise, I mention only one of the first I read about. In Italy, on March 15, 2020, the news of COVID-19 began to overwhelm the clergy. Many priests began to help those infected in various ways. In two or three weeks about sixty priests died. Personally, I am reminded of Saint Aloysius Gonzaga. Many years ago he was held up to us as an example of a young Jesuit for his virtue, insisting on chastity and modesty. Years later I learned that he died in Rome on June 21, 1591, at the age of twenty-three as a result of taking care of the sick during an outbreak of typhus. All these human beings who die caring for those affected by the COVID-19 virus proclaim what Jesus said: "No one has greater love than this, to lay down one's life for one's friends" (Jn 15:13).

✧ *Do you have any final thoughts for ending this book?*

Yes. And two sentences have come to my mind.

✧ *And what are these two sentences?*

One of them is: *In the end God will be all in all.*

The reader will remember that in my first years as a Jesuit I asked myself seriously about God. Now, when I am eighty-two years old, the question of *what this God is* is coming back to me. And Paul's phrase in 1 Corinthians 15 came to mind: "And in the end God will be all in all." I have talked to scripture scholars about the meaning of this profound sentence, but what they say does not quite satisfy me in answering the question of what this God is.

If "all in all" occurs, it will certainly be at the end, not throughout the story. But what the "all in all" means is once again out of our hands. When we seem to formulate a maximum of knowledge, we are thrown back to not knowing. And here all *chastity of the intellect* (Santayana) is too little.

Nor has it been difficult for me to understand Paul when he affirms that the end is reached through a process, and that for him the end will be something triumphant and victorious. This is Paul's faith. He says it forcefully and following a theo-logical and christological process:

> Then comes the end, when he hands over the kingdom to God the Father, after he has destroyed every ruler and every authority and power. For he must reign until he has put all his enemies under his feet. The last enemy to be destroyed is death. For "God has put all things in subjection under his feet." But when it says, "All things are put in subjection," it is plain that this does not include the one who put all things in subjection under him. When all things are subjected to him, then the Son himself will also be subjected to the one who put all things in subjection under him, so that God may be all in all. (1 Cor 15:24–28)

I'm going to come down from those heights, and I hope you will allow me a personal memory. When my mother died, it was an important end for my family. At home—when we all got together because I had arrived from a trip—we would remember things that our mother used to say. One day my eldest sister, who cared for her until the end, told how my mother was not anxious about death. She would say peacefully, "To die? To see God." This simplicity is not Paul's, but deep down I don't think it detracts much from the solemnity of "so that God may be all in all." In the end, whatever it is, the ultimate end will be a great thing, and we will all be able to live in it.

❖*And the second sentence?*

The other sentence is: *Unity has already been consummated.*

It is of a different order, and it may come as a surprise. When my father died in 1975, Ignacio Ellacuría, who was in Madrid, wrote me a very fraternal letter. I was struck by the way he expressed his condolences. Among Christians, the normal way of consoling the death of a loved one is to say "he is now with God." And with greater depth, and now more frequently, "he has already arrived at the Father's house." In 1975, however, Ellacuría used very different language when he wrote to me, "Unity has already been consummated." I was sincerely grateful for his condolences, but the way he said it caught my attention. After a while it occurred to me why Ellacuría used that language to express his condolences.

Ellacuría did not strike me as a Jesuit of the "pious" type, nor was he given to cloying language. His language of condolence echoed a more philosophical language, if you will, with the flavor of a Plato or Plotinus, without suggesting that Ellacuría was thereby skimping on consolation. After all, many of the Greeks extolled unity, the unification of everything, and in this they found perfection, plenitude. Strange as it may sound, my father would already belong to the real and positive reality of unity, of the One, the Good, the True.

I never spoke of these things with Ellacuría, but as I continued thinking about the formulation of his condolences, the opposite formulation also came to my mind. It is the well-known sentence of the ancients: *ubi peccatum, ibi multitudo,* that is, where there is sin, there is fragmentation. Evil breaks unity, harmony. And conversely, we can say *ubi unitas, ibi bonum* [where there is unity, there is good]. Ellacuría did not think of these things when he wrote me his condolences. He was sincere when he formulated that with the death of my father something positive had happened. I could participate in it.

"WALKING WITH . . . "

✧ *Can you expand a bit on how what you have been saying here relates to the subtitle of this epilogue?*

To relate to God we humans use various languages, languages of closeness, adoration, praise, supplication, petition, also of remoteness, fear, asking for forgiveness. And to make this relationship somehow imaginable we use a variety of verbs that have to do with the senses of the body: to see God, to listen to God, to talk to God, to be before God, to embrace God, and so on. And vice versa, God sees us, talks to us, is with us, embraces us, and so on.

I have come up with—God knows if I've got it right—the language of *walking*. In the Bible, *walking* is important. I am going to look at two passages, one from the Old Testament and the other from the New Testament, at key moments.

Micah. I have already mentioned the text of Micah 6:8. Yahweh pleads with his people. Both speak. Human beings wonder what they will have to do in order for Yahweh to be favorable to them. And Yahweh, now in my language, seems to be fed up with the people coming to him to ask him what they should know by heart. And he reacts with forcefulness: "Listen once and for all to what is good and what the Lord requires of you: that you practice justice, that you love tenderly, and that you walk humbly with your God." Before Micah, Amos had already spoken about justice, Hosea about love, and Isaiah about humility before God.

In the text of Micah, the right relationship of the human being with God is preceded by two demands that refer to the right relationship with human beings: to do justice and to love tenderly. And the relationship with God is marked by a way of being and acting humbly. This being and acting in this way are expressed in a unified way with the term *walk.* Hence, God ends his claims by addressing himself personally to the human being, adding: "that you walk humbly with your God."

Mark. The Gospels insist on following the *way* of Jesus. In Xavier Alegre's book on the Gospel of Mark, the author insists on the centrality of the cross and on Jesus's walk toward the cross. He makes it clear that Jesus—successfully or not—wants others to walk with him.

When speaking of orthopraxis, a typical requirement of Mark, he mentions several times the walk that configures it. Orthopraxis is "to be willing to follow him on the way, not glorious in the eyes of the world, of the cross." In the second healing of the blind man, in Mark 11:19, unlike the previous account of healing a blind man in Mark 8:22–26, he adds that the blind man "followed him on the way." In the form of a thesis, Alegre says: "Mark wants us, above all, to keep in mind that Jesus is, in essence, the Crucified One who invites us to follow him on the way he began." And he notes: "Only the way of the cross is the Christian way!"

To walk in Micah is theo-logically encompassing, and in Mark it is more christologically encompassing. In both cases it is something extremely serious and profoundly human. It is certainly not a matter of strolling, of wandering, of healthy physical exercise, or even of pilgrimage.

These reflections may perhaps suggest how I have tried to do theology and how, ideally and in a very modest way, I do theology now: trying, humbly, to walk with God. The transcendent tenor of that phrase becomes more viable for me by trying to walk with Jesus of Nazareth. And to make it even more concrete—although it is not easy—I will speak of walking with Monseñor Romero and with Ignacio Ellacuría.

WALKING WITH MONSEÑOR ROMERO— "THE GLORY OF GOD IS THAT THE POOR LIVE"

◇ *Let us begin with Monseñor Romero.*

I have already described some encounters I had with Monseñor that had a great impact on me. When he was assassinated, and his corpse was exposed for a week to be visited and venerated, Ellacuría told me not to come from home. He feared that seeing his corpse would have a strong impact on my fragile health. He did, however, encourage me to write about Monseñor Romero, which I did immediately. The first thing I wrote and said after his funeral at the first forum organized by the UCA was that "Monseñor Romero believed in God." This is how I began my talks several times in the first weeks after his assassination. In one of those talks Ellacuría was present, and I again referred to "Monseñor's faith in God." To my surprise, at the end Ellacuría approached me, and as if in passing, to show his agreement with my starting to talk about Monseñor with his faith in God, he pronounced the well-known words of Saint Augustine: "O truth, always ancient and always new!" Ellacuría grasped very well what I was saying, and he understood that I was repeating something very fundamental about Monseñor Romero. I was glad that he was of the same mind.

I will now expand on the impact that Monseñor Romero had on me during his three years as archbishop. Romero reminded me of Jesus of Nazareth. And without much consideration I thought that as far as possible I should walk with Monseñor, and that this would be a good thing. To communicate who Monseñor Romero was for me, I will first quote a peasant and then the words of Monseñor Romero in the last pages of his spiritual diary.

The Words of a Farmer

A campesino was asked who Monseñor Romero was, and without hesitation he answered: "Monseñor Romero told the truth. He defended us, the poor. And that's why they killed him." I loved this. And this is my comment.

"*Monseñor Romero told the truth."* Monseñor was a decider of the truth, he was possessed by it, and he spoke it with pathos. The truth shaped him. When reality was good news for the poor, Monseñor spoke the truth as *gospel,* with exultation and joy. When reality was oppression and repression, cruelty and death, especially for the poor, Monseñor spoke the truth as *bad news,* denouncing and unmasking, and with pain. Steeped in truth, Monseñor was an endearing evangelizer and an incorruptible prophet.

To say that Monseñor Romero was a "decider" of the truth may seem minor in comparison with other things he did. But that is where the peasant began, and I think for good reasons. For Monseñor Romero, *saying* meant being in immediate contact with the external reality in which he lived and with the reality he carried within himself." *To say,* for Monseñor Romero, was *to be* in total depth.

As a "decider of the truth," Monseñor Romero made judgments about reality, all of it, and let "reality take the word" (to use Rahner's expression). And he was consequently honored by making public that word pronounced by reality itself. In my opinion, this is the ultimate root of the impact of Monseñor's word. Given the lamentable state of truth in the country at that time, the impact was immense. As it would be immense today if the United Nations, the OAS, the United States, the European Union, the ecclesiastical and religious institutions would let the reality of our world take the floor and speak its truth.

In the biblical tradition telling the truth is a longstanding imperative. And there is also longstanding awareness that truth moves in a dangerous sphere. The Evil One is a murderer and a liar, says the Gospel of John (8:44). First he kills, and then he covers it up. Monseñor Romero was aware of this. And in consonance with what Puebla says about the action of God (no. 1142), he understood that the ultimate purpose of telling the truth consists in *defending the poor.*

From these convictions Monseñor Romero spoke the truth in a way never known in the country, neither before nor since. He said it *vigorously:*

"Nothing is as important as human life and the human person, above all the poor and oppressed" (March 16, 1980). He spoke the truth *at length, in* order to be able to tell the whole truth. And he spoke it *publicly,* from the rooftops, as Jesus asked, in the cathedral and through YSAX radio. He spoke the truth *popularly,* learning many things from the people, so that, without knowing it, the poor and the peasants were partly co-authors of his homilies and pastoral letters: "For you and I together create this homily" (September 16, 1979), to the point of formulating the thesis: "I feel that the people are my prophet" (July 8, 1979). And he was also *popular* in a double sense. He respected and appreciated the "reason," the speech of the people, of the simple people.

At peak moments he *solemnly* spoke the truth. He issued denunciations. "This is the empire of death" (July 1, 1979). He gave hope: "Over these ruins of ours the glory of the Lord will shine" (January 7, 1979). He pleaded: "In the name of God, then, and in the name of this suffering people, whose laments rise up each day more tumultuously toward heaven, I beg you, I beseech you, I order you in the name of God: stop the repression!" (March 23, 1980).

This word of Monseñor was something absolutely unexpected, both for friends and enemies. But it was something absolutely real, without anyone being able to ignore it or refute it. His way of telling the truth led him to be a pioneer of what is now called historical memory. It came to Monseñor naturally. He spoke with scrupulous precision, with Pascal's best *esprit de géometrie,* mentioning each and every one of the names of the victims, of their abandoned relatives, of the victimizers, of the place, time, and circumstances. And he did so with total delicacy and full of pain:

> Last Sunday I informed you, in the light of Christ the King, about the disappearance of José Justo Mejía in Dulce Nombre de María. This week I was horrified when I met with his wife and nine small children. She came to tell me that they found him dead and with signs of torture. Now she and those children are alone and unprotected. I believe that anyone who commits a crime of that nature has an obligation to make restitution. Assistance must be given to all the homes like this one that have been left destitute. The criminals who leave families in this desperate situation are obliged in conscience to help sustain these families. (November 20, 1977)

It is the *esprit de finesse.*

And he also made historical memory a reality, by remembering the goodness, dedication, hope, and trust in God of many of the martyrs. He was not worried that the Vatican, in the case of possible beatifications and canonizations, would fail to take into account the goodness of so many good people. Monseñor was grateful for their life and death. And so, he kept them alive.

In speaking the truth like Jesus, Monseñor spoke "as one who has authority, not like the learned"; "the people were astonished by his doctrine." As with Jesus, his authority did not come to him from his origins: "Can anything good come out of Nazareth"—from Ciudad Barrios? Nor from his status as a bishop. To Monseñor, authority did not come from conventional additions—titles, hierarchical authority—but from real things: his authenticity and conviction, expressed in his honesty with what was real and in the coherence between what he said and what he did. Monseñor grew and overflowed in his doing justice and in his love for the people. And he grew more and more in taking risks to defend them, well aware of what could happen to him. And it happened.

Telling the truth also meant in a very important way unmasking what is covered up, condemning the cosmetics with which the violation of the commandments of God's law are hypocritically disguised: do not plunder, do not hoard, and do not kill. And Monseñor also kept alive the total requirement, sine qua non, of the eighth commandment: not to lie. And in speaking the truth, Monseñor made present "the wrath of God [who] is revealed against all ungodly and unjust men who imprison the truth in their unrighteousness" (Rom 1:18).

Monseñor wiped off the makeup and unmasked wealth: "I denounce above all, the absolutization of wealth. This is the great evil of El Salvador: wealth and private property as untouchable absolutes. Woe to them who touch that high-tension wire—they'll get burned" (August 12, 1979). He unmasked the violation of the seventh commandment, the original sin.

His greatest diatribes were against unjust and cruel death: "I will never tire of denouncing the assault on human life by arbitrary arrests, disappearances, by torture" (June 24, 1979). "The violence, murder, and torture that leave so many dead; the people chopped with machetes and thrown into the sea—all that is the dominion of death. Those who bring about death are in league with the devil" (July 1, 1979).

He cried out against the media and official speeches: "Truth is what is lacking in our situation" (April 12, 1979); "there are plenty of people whose pens are for hire and whose words are sold cheap, but that is not the truth" (February 18, 1979); "in the midst of a world of lies, where no one believes any longer in anything" (March 19, 1979).

In telling the truth Monseñor went about doing good—as Jesus did. It should be obvious that telling the truth is doing good. But the reality can become such that telling the truth can be doing the *greatest* and *most necessary* good. That is what happened on March 23, 1980, the eve of his assassination. Let the reader judge whether, in telling the truth, Monseñor Romero did not do the greatest good:

> I would like to make an appeal especially to the men of the army, and concretely to the National Guard, the police, and the troops. Brothers, you are of part of our own people. You are killing your own brother and sister campesinos, and against any order a man may give to kill, God's law must prevail: "You shall not kill!" (Ex 20:13). No soldier is obliged to obey an order against the law of God. No one has to observe an immoral law. It is time now for you to reclaim your conscience and to obey your conscience rather than the command to sin. The church defends the rights of God, the law of God, and the dignity of the human person and therefore cannot remain silent before such great abominations. We want the government to understand well that the reforms are worth nothing if they are stained with so much blood. In the name of God, then, and in the name of this suffering people, whose laments rise up each day more tumultuously toward heaven, I beg you, I beseech you, I order you in the name of God: stop the repression!

At the beginning of the Eucharist, with horror at the reality of the country and with clear premonitions about his own assassination, he explained to the world how he was preparing Sunday's homily: "As I listen all during the week to the cries of the people and behold so much horrible crime and such shameful violence, I ask the Lord to give me appropriate words for consoling, for denouncing, and for calling to repentance. Though I continue to be a voice crying out in the desert, I know that the church is trying hard to fulfill its mission" (March 23, 1980).

Monseñor told the truth, because he was moved to tears. And in doing so he put his whole life at stake. This was for Monseñor a very important way of doing good.

"He defended us, the poor." These words are not often used when speaking of Monseñor Romero, but they are important. This is how Puebla speaks of God, as we have seen. I don't think the peasant had Puebla in mind, but he got it right. The option for the poor is usually remembered from Puebla, but not with the nuance that the peasant put on what Monseñor Romero did: to defend the poor.

I have nothing to add to this solemn sentence of the peasant. Nor to the language he used: "He defended us, the poor." I will only recall how Monseñor defended the poor and oppressed of the country, and not only made an option for them.

Monseñor supported the popular organization to defend the rights of the peasants. He supported the Legal Aid to defend the rights of the victims. When the repression increased, he opened the doors of the seminary of San José de la Montaña to welcome the peasants fleeing from Chalatenango, which surprised and displeased many hierarchs. And week after week he defended the poor and the victims by telling the truth.

This is clear, but we must also be clear about the implication of *defending*. To defend means to confront and, when necessary, to fight against those who attack, impoverish, oppress, and repress. In defending the poor, Monseñor confronted those who lie and murder, whether individuals, institutions, or structures. And his was a primordial defense, which went beyond what is conventionally understood as defending and winning a case.

This is the context of his famous denunciation to the Supreme Court of Justice. The Supreme Court had publicly summoned him to name "the judges who sell out," whom Monseñor had denounced in his Sunday homily. Monseñor's advisers were frightened and did not know how he was going to respond to such a summons.

Monseñor did not get upset. In the homily following the summons, he clarified first of all that he had not said "judges who sell out" but "venal judges." But he did not dwell on whether he said this or that; rather, he went to the heart of the matter:

> I ask you, sisters and brothers, in view of these injustices that are seen all around us, even in the First Court and many other

tribunals, not to mention judges who sell themselves: what is the Supreme Court of Justice doing? What is the function of this power, so transcendent in a democracy, which should be above every power and which should demand justice of everyone? I believe that the key to a great part of the malaise of our country is in the president of the Supreme Court of Justice and all his collaborators. They should show greater integrity in demanding of the legislature, of the tribunals, of the judges, of all the administrators of that sacrosanct word "justice," that they be truly agents of justice. (April 30, 1978)

I believe that Monseñor was a defender of the poor with everything he was and had. Five days before he was assassinated, to a foreign journalist who asked him how to be in solidarity with the Salvadoran people, he answered: "Those who cannot do anything else, pray." They should do what they could, he was saying; whatever it was, they should do it. And he added the reason for doing it: "And do not forget that we are human beings. And that here they are suffering, dying, fleeing, taking refuge in the mountains."

"*And that's why they killed him.*" These final words of the farmer follow logically from what he said earlier and need no comment.

Monseñor's Last Retreat

A month before his assassination, Monseñor Romero made a retreat with a small group of priests. When Father Azkue, his confessor, came to visit him, Monseñor spoke to him about the three things that were most bothering him. They were two fears and a problem.

The first fear, due rather to his tendency to be scrupulous, was whether he was leading his spiritual life well. Father Azkue reassured him.

Of the *problems* that caused him much suffering, we have already mentioned his great difficulty in working with his brother bishops. In his homily of July 30, 1978, he complained about the malicious intention of the newspapers to discredit him while displaying photographs of other bishops in cordial communion with the supreme government. His enemies took advantage of Monseñor's tension with the bishops to discredit him.

Another shameful fact is what happened when Monseñor Romero wrote and signed, together with Bishop Rivera, the pastoral letter "The Church and Popular Political Organizations."[3] The other bishops of the Episcopal Conference published practically at the same time another letter condemning the popular organizations. Romero was hurt that the bishops were giving an example of serious disunity. And he was greatly shocked by the harm it caused to the people. He even referred to the words of Jesus so that the people could situate themselves well in the midst of the division of their hierarchs. This is what he said in his homily of September 3, 1978:

> I am sorry for this poor witness and ask pardon since I am in solidarity with the hierarchy of El Salvador. I earnestly beseech my beloved priests and the communities of the archdiocese to judge with mature criteria what good there is in both statements and not to encourage commentaries that deepen our divisions. The people have a great instinct given to them by the Holy Spirit. That's what Christ says with these beautiful words: "The sheep know the voice of the shepherd who loves them and is willing to give his life for them." (John 10:14–15)

Personally, I was very shocked that Monseñor complained more about the bad example set by the Episcopal Conference than about the actual attacks against him by the majority of the bishops.

The second *fear* of which he spoke to Father Azkue is the one we are now interested in recalling: the fear of a violent death. In fact, Monseñor lived through three years of death foretold. Bombs exploded in churches, in the seminary, in the residences of religious men and women, in Catholic schools, in the UCA. There were attacks on important workplaces of the archdiocese, such as the printing press and the YSAX radio station. The assassinations of six priests, one Jesuit and five diocesan priests, had to be especially painful and premonitory. Their death was *foretold*.

For three years he also had to live with the hatred of the powerful. They did not forgive him, and they did not repent either for the harm they did to the poor or for the hatred they had for Monseñor. Forty

---

[3] See Oscar Romero, *Voice of the Voiceless: The Four Pastoral Letters and Other Statements* (Maryknoll, NY: Orbis Books, 2020), 93–124.

years after his death I do not know how many have asked his forgiveness, though some have. In a Christian outburst Monseñor said: "If Jesus Christ were the archbishop of San Salvador at this time, they would rain down on him many more insults and calumnies than they do on me" (December 5, 1977).

Monsignor Ricardo Urioste, his vicar general, who recently passed away, used to say of Monseñor: "It is clear that he was the most loved one who brought joy and dignity to the people. And it is clear that he was hated by many here and in Rome."

But Monseñor did not return evil for evil, and he never hated those who hated him. The reason was not the practice of asceticism, but that he could not be otherwise. Very shortly before his death, in his homily on March 16, 1980, he said: "I feel more sorrow than anger when people insult me and malign me. . . . They should know that I feel no rancor or resentment."

Three Very Personal Paragraphs

I end with three paragraphs that show Oscar Romero from the bottom of his heart. The *first* is from the homily of September 10, 1978:

> That's why I say to you, dear sisters and brothers, "Be converted!" I say this especially to you, my dear sisters and brothers who hate me; I say it to you, my dear sisters and brothers who think that I'm preaching violence and slander me even though you know it's not true; I say it to you who have your hands stained with crime, torture, assault, injustice. I tell you all, "Be converted!" I love you dearly, and I feel sorry for you because you are traveling the paths of perdition.

In the *second* paragraph are the words he wrote in his last spiritual retreat. After meditating on the kingdom of God and the following of Christ, he uses the words of Saint Ignatius, saying:

> Eternal Lord of all things, I make my oblation with your favor and help before your infinite goodness and before your glorious Mother and all the saints of the heavenly court; that I want and desire and

that it is my deliberate determination, only to be of greater service and praise to you, to imitate you in suffering all injuries, all blame and all poverty, be it material or spiritual, wishing to choose your most blessed majesty and to receive it in such life and condition.

Monseñor then continues in his own words. If possible, these words are even more personal. The ending, which I have highlighted, is endearing:

Thus do I express my consecration to the heart of Jesus, who was ever a source of inspiration and joy in my life. Thus I also place my whole life under his loving providence and accept my death, however difficult it may be, with faith in him. Nor do I want to give him an intention as I would for the peace of my country and for the flourishing of our church . . . because the Heart of Christ will know how to give him the destiny he desires. It is enough for me to be happy and confident to know with certainty that in him is my life and my death, that, in spite of my sins, I have placed my trust in him and I will not be confused *and others will continue with more wisdom and holiness the work of the church and of the country.*

In the *third* paragraph are a few words he said on November 29, 1978. The day before, Father Ernesto Barrera (called Neto) had been murdered, along with three workers. The government's version was that he died in a confrontation with the security forces. Monseñor Romero found out what had happened. Father Barrera was captured, tortured, and murdered. Then, once he was dead, a frame-up was made by placing a gun in his hand. The only witness who could clarify the circumstances of his death was killed the following day.

On November 29, a Eucharist was celebrated in memory of Father Neto. In his homily, Monseñor Romero said:

Neto felt happy in his priesthood. I had the pleasure of bringing him personally to the parish of San Sebastián. With him I took part in some meetings with young people who questioned me about some of the concerns Christians have these days. I can assure you that this man, consecrated through priestly ordination, remained in communion with his fellow priests and with his bishop, and that is what made his ministry authentic and legitimate.

Some advised Monseñor Romero to send a representative to preside at the funeral of Ernesto Barrera, because they feared that the government would persecute Monseñor even more if he were to officiate at the Eucharist. I remember that Ignacio Ellacuría was aware of this danger: "Monseñor will be very much attacked if he presides at the funeral." But he did not advise him not to go. To those who advised him not to go to Neto's funeral, Monseñor responded with a question: "Where is Neto's mother? She is next to her son's corpse, so I must also be with her." And Monseñor officiated the mass.

Regarding the risks that Monseñor took in general, which seemed imprudent to some, I heard Ellacuría make a categorical statement: "It is what he must do."

I conclude with these brief words of Monseñor himself: "We must be converted, dear sisters and brothers, myself first of all" (November 11, 1979). "How wonderful it is to be Christian! Truly, it means embracing the Word of God incarnate, making ours the power of salvation, keeping hope alive even when everything seems lost!" (July 16, 1978). "My voice will disappear, but my words, which are Christ, will remain in the hearts of those who will have embraced them" (December 17, 1978).

Such was the Monseñor who encouraged us to walk, and with whom, although from afar, we have tried to walk.

WALKING WITH IGNACIO ELLACURÍA—"WITH MONSEÑOR ROMERO, GOD PASSED THROUGH EL SALVADOR"

I have already spoken about Ellacuría several times in this paper. Now I want to talk about *walking with* Ignacio Ellacuría. I will say three things.

Ellacuría Was Converted

I am going to distinguish three moments of a process that was not linear. And as far as I know, this is not often talked about.

Ellacuría's conversion process began, in his first period, with a change in temperament. He once told me about how, as a Jesuit student in the early 1960s, he had strong arguments with his superiors, with the rector of the theologate in Innsbruck. Victor Codina, his Jesuit companion in Innsbruck, remembered him as the Sun King. I have also been told, perhaps by Ellacuría himself, that while in Madrid preparing for his doctorate, a Jesuit with authority said to him: "Have you not thought of leaving the Society of Jesus?" Ellacuría answered: "No, I haven't. Have you?" He could be blunt. He could be stern. And sometimes he could be so firm in his convictions and decisions that he was hard and overbearing. But as the years went by, the excesses and edges, especially the harshness and arrogance, were ironed out.

When I speak now of conversion, I am referring to the change that took place in him during the time he lived and worked in El Salvador, between the late 1960s and the late 1980s. I think he changed in two moments that shaped two other periods, the second being of greater personal depth.

In the first period, from 1968 to 1977, Ellacuría, as a human being, a Christian, and a Jesuit, made an option for the poor, a radical option for justice, and a commitment to struggle against injustice.

At the level of his interior life, the *Exercises* of Saint Ignatius that he gave in 1969 and 1971 are signs of *conversion*. In this Ellacuría was not unique, since a good number of Jesuits of our province and others in Latin America also accepted the change and converted.

In 1977, with the assassination of Rutilio Grande and the immediate reaction of Monseñor Romero, Ellacuría entered a second period in which the change became more radical. Personally, from that moment on, I like to use the term *conversion* when speaking of Ellacuría, as I did when speaking of Monseñor Romero. This began to be noticed in that Ellacuría spoke of Monseñor and of God in a different way, and from the God he envisioned with Monseñor he deepened and radicalized his option for the people and for justice.

By this I mean that it is not enough to consider Ellacuría, even with his limitations and defects, simply as a great person, tremendously intelligent, audacious, and exceptional. Of course he was all these things, but it can be reductionistic if we do not take into account that Ellacuría, living the reality of El Salvador with the poor, the victims, and martyrs, and with Monseñor Romero, underwent a conversion.

Ellacuría Relates Monseñor Romero to the Reality of God

Ellacuría once wrote that it is difficult to speak of Monseñor Romero without being forced to speak of the people, and in 1981 he wrote an article for the magazine *ECA* entitled "The True People of God according to Monseñor Romero." Following the logic of that formulation, we now affirm that, for Ellacuría, it was "difficult to speak of Monseñor Romero without being forced to speak of God."

I have found three texts in which Ellacuría explicitly relates Monseñor Romero to the reality of God. The first is from the beginning of Monseñor's ministry as archbishop. It is in Ellacuría's letter to Monseñor Romero on April 9, 1977.[4] The second is in an article requested by the magazine *Razón y Fe* a few months after his assassination. The third, and most radical, contains the words he spoke in the homily at the funeral mass of Monseñor Romero at the UCA.

In each of these texts the relationship between Monseñor Romero and God appears in a brief and lapidary theological affirmation. Let us look at these three texts.

"I have seen in your action the finger of God." "From this distant exile I want to show you my admiration and respect, because I have seen in your action the finger of God," he writes to Monseñor Romero from his exile in Madrid. He adds three reasons so that the expression "would not be reduced to literary accompaniment." The following is the essence of these reflections:

> The first aspect that impressed me is your evangelical spirit. . . . You immediately perceived the clear meaning of Father Grande's death, the meaning of religious persecution, and you backed that meaning with all your might. . . .
>
> This brings me to see a second aspect: *a clear Christian discernment.* . . . You were able to listen to everyone, but ended up deciding on that which seemed most risky to prudent eyes.
>
> I see the third aspect as a conclusion from the previous ones and as their confirmation. On this occasion, and supported by the martyrdom of Father Grande, you have built a church and you have built unity in the church. You know how difficult it is to do these two

---

[4] The letter appears in Appendix 2 herein.

things in San Salvador today. I think that, as long as you continue in this line and have as your primary criterion the spirit of Christ lived in a martyrial way, the best part of the church in San Salvador will be with you and those who need to pull away will do it.

Ellacuría saw how Monseñor Romero was a follower of Jesus. And that led him to say that in Monseñor he had seen "the finger of God." I do not know why he used these last words, when he could have used others. What strikes me is that Monseñor Romero made Ellacuría feel forced to speak of God.

"Monseñor Romero was sent by God to save his people." The theological affirmation is "Monseñor Romero, an envoy of God." The explanatory texts insist on three things. One, evident given the circumstances, is the martyrdom of Monseñor Romero. The second is that Monseñor Romero was and brought salvation. The third is that Monseñor Romero has been a grace for the people.

Ellacuría describes the martyrdom of Monseñor Romero with appreciation and admiration:

> It has been eight months—since March 24—that Archbishop Romero was killed on the altar while saying Mass. It took only one bullet to the heart to end his mortal life. Even though he had been threatened for months, Romero never sought out the least bit of protection. He drove his car himself and lived in a small apartment adjacent to the chapel in which he was assassinated. Those who killed him are the same ones who kill the people, the same ones who in this year of Romero's martyrdom have exterminated almost 10,000 persons. The majority of these persons are young peasants, workers, and students, but also elderly women and children, who are taken from their homes and appear shortly thereafter: tortured, destroyed, and often unrecognizable.
>
> It is not important to determine who shot Romero. It was evil; it was sin; it was the anti-Christ. However, it was a historical evil, a historical sin, and a historical anti-Christ, which have been incarnated in unjust structures and in those who have chosen to take on the role of Cain. Romero had only three years of public life as archbishop of San Salvador. They were enough to sow the seeds of God's word and to make present the countenance of Jesus to his

people. This was too much for those who cannot tolerate the light of truth and the fire of love.[5]

These words need no comment. They are pure Ellacuría—Romero's affinity with Jesus of Nazareth, his solidarity with the crucified people, and his three years of life from the perspective of the cross. He then wonders what Romero had done in his life, and in a concentrated formulation he says, "What Monseñor did was to bring salvation to his people. . . . He did not bring salvation as a political leader, nor as an intellectual, nor as a great orator."

And following is a last paragraph that is one of the texts that have had the greatest impact on me in recent years:

> The wise and prudent of this world, ecclesiastical, civil, and military, the wealthy and powerful of this world felt this and said this. But the people of God, those who hunger and thirst for justice, the pure of heart, the poor of spirit knew that all of this was false; they knew and felt that the word of Monseñor Romero was pure gospel. They had never felt God so close, the Spirit so operative, Christianity so true, so full of meaning, so full of grace and truth. . . . This evangelical incarnation permitted him to contend with very real political projects without the easy escape of principles, as if the Christian prophet need only announce abstract generalities. That incarnation gained him the love of the oppressed people and the hatred of the oppressors. It earned him persecution, the same persecution that the people suffered. That is how he died, and that is why they killed him. That is why, likewise, he became an exceptional example of how the power of the gospel can become a historical power of transformation.[6]

"They had never felt God so close." It can't be said better.

"With Monseñor Romero, God passed through El Salvador." Ellacuría's thoughts on Monseñor reached their climax in his well-known words: "With Monseñor Romero, God passed through El Salvador." He pro-

---

[5] "Monseñor Romero: One Sent to Save His People" (1980), in Michael E. Lee, *Ignacio Ellacuría,* 286. This article originally appeared in *Razón y Fe.*
[6] Ibid., 290, 292.

nounced them in his homily at Romero's funeral mass at the UCA. This phrase is our third theological text.

In these words there is genius of thought, and I know of no pastors, theologians, philosophers, or politicians who conceptualize and formulate realities with such radicality.

Ellacuría saw in the history of Monseñor an ultimacy and a radicality that he did not find, to the same degree, in any other person of the past, no matter how venerable he might have been. The passage of God in Monseñor produced goods, personal and social, that were difficult to obtain and difficult to maintain.

To Ellacuría, Monseñor spoke, on the one hand, of a God of the poor and martyrs, who was certainly liberating, demanding, prophetic, and utopian. In a word, he spoke to him of what in God is a "more here." But he also spoke to him of what in God is ineffable, not adequately historicized, of what in God there is of "beyond," of unfathomable and blessed mystery.

Ellacuría Was Carried by the Faith of Monseñor Romero

With the assassination of Rutilio Grande on March 12, 1977, the conversion of Monseñor Romero occurred. When Ellacuría was forty-seven years old and had been working in the UCA for ten years, Monseñor Romero "appeared"—*ôfthê*—to him. I consciously use the Greek term for "to appear," language in which the apparitions of the Risen One are narrated, to express with all the analogies of the case what was unexpected and intense, in an event both unsettling and blessed.

His impact on Ellacuría was specific. Certainly he was affected, like many others, by Monseñor's prophecy and denunciation, his compassion and hope, his closeness to the poor and his struggle for justice, his willingness to have his life taken from him and to remain faithful to the end without letting himself be diverted by any risk or threat.

But I think that the most novel and powerful impact was produced by the faith of Monseñor Romero. Romero said in a homily on February 10, 1980:

We do not know ourselves until we have encountered God. . . .
My great desire, dear sisters and brothers, is that, as the fruit of

this preaching today, each of us will have a true encounter with God and will experience the joy of our majesty and our smallness!

In the face of these words I think that Ellacuría felt that in Monseñor Romero there was something different, superior, not only quantitatively, but qualitatively. It did not diminish him, but it helped him to know himself and to situate himself better as a human being. We can reformulate it, with simplicity and some audacity, by saying that in the matter of faith, Ellacuría was a disciple of Monseñor Romero. And I think we should go a step further: Ellacuría was carried in the faith and by the faith of Monseñor. I would like to offer some reflections on this in order to better understand what it means to *walk with* Ignacio Ellacuría.

I have already said it how, in 1969, in a meeting in Madrid, I heard him say in a small group, "Rahner bears his doubts about faith with great elegance," by which he was saying, so I took it, that for him, as well, faith was not something obvious. His words did not surprise me, because those were hard years for faith, my own and that of other colleagues and even professors.

The open and serious contact with modern philosophers, most of them unbelievers; the emergence of critical theology, including that of the death of God (this was the prevailing atmosphere in the years in which Ellacuría reached his intellectual maturity); his own honest and critical disposition, which was not at all prone to credulity and unconvincing arguments with apologetic overtones; and the great questioning of God that is the misery and scandal of the Latin American continent . . . none of this, for Ignacio Ellacuría, made faith in God simple or obvious.

Like many others, I think Ellacuría wrestled with God. In the words of scripture, I think he wrestled with God, like Jacob. My conviction is that years later he allowed himself to be overcome by God. In simple words, what I think happened was that Monseñor Romero pushed him and enabled him to actively place himself, and keep himself, before the ultimate mystery of reality.

He was deeply impressed by how Monseñor referred to God, not only in his reflection and preaching, but also in the reality of his life. God was for Monseñor absolutely *real*. And Ellacuría saw that, with this God, Monseñor humanized people and brought salvation to history.

In his exile in Madrid (1980–83), with more time, and in his last years in El Salvador (1983–89), even with multiple occupations of utmost urgency and responsibility, he always found time to write theo-logical texts, especially on church and ecclesiology, and some of them more specifically theo-logical. In them he addressed directly or indirectly the reality of God.

Ellacuría naturally mentioned God to give force to an idea, even when he did not have to. In a harsh criticism he wrote: "The most important thing is really listening to the voice of God, who . . . is heard in the sufferings and in the liberation struggles of the people." And beyond concrete themes, referring to the thoughts and feelings of Monseñor Romero, Ellacuría spoke quite naturally of *transcendence*. We quote a text, significant because it includes many important themes, which culminates with the transcendence of God:

> Monseñor Romero never tired of repeating that political processes, as pure and idealistic they may be, can never be enough to bring integral liberation to men and women. He understood perfectly that saying of Saint Augustine that to be human one must be "more" than human. For Romero, history that was only human, that only attempted to be human, would promptly cease to be so. Neither humanity nor history is self-sufficient. For that reason he never stopped appealing to transcendence. This theme emerged in almost all of his homilies: the word of God, the action of God breaking through human limits.[7]

Romero came to be for Ellacuría like the face of the mystery that appears in our world, a mystery that is ultimately more *fascinans* than *tremendum*.

In 1983, after returning from his second exile, Ellacuría entered the last six years of his life. The fundamental task to which he dedicated his best energies, time, and health was to put an end to the war through a dialogue that would lead to negotiation. And for this he had to listen to criticism from both sides—more from the right than from the left—as

---

[7] Jon Sobrino, *Archbishop Romero: Memories and Reflections,* rev. ed. (Maryknoll, NY: Orbis Books, 2016).

each side wanted to defeat the other. And with sound reasons or self-delusions they each hoped that victory was possible.

Although he passed through periods of darkness, I never felt that he fell into despair, because he could always think of ways to continue working. Yet, I could sense his dis-ease. Things were not going well for the country, and Ellacuría did not seem to feel a secure handhold for his efforts to promote dialogue. Once he said to me, as if in passing: "All that remains is aesthetics." And another time he told me, also in passing, something that most readers will not understand. For those born in Vizcaya, Athletic de Bilbao, the local football club, is very precious. Every Sunday Ellacuría faithfully followed the results of the club's matches on the radio. Well, one day he told me, "Yeah, not even the Athletic." I understood him perfectly. The expectation of something good happening was slipping from our hands.

Like Monseñor, he too took seriously the possibility of a violent death. He didn't talk about it and certainly didn't want to make a big deal of it. But he was very aware of that possibility. Months before his death he told me, "Now that I work for dialogue and negotiation, my life is in greater danger than when I was considered a leftist and revolutionary." And with great peace he also told me, "I have been told that the pain of a gunshot only lasts twenty seconds."

In 1989 he wrote:

It is in this sense that the church of the poor becomes the new heaven, which as such is needed to supersede the civilization of wealth and build the civilization of poverty, the new earth where the new human being will live in a friendly and not in a degraded home. Here there will be a great encounter between the Christian message without disfiguring glosses and the present degraded situation in the greater part of the world—certainly in Latin America, still for the most part a depository of the Christian faith. That faith has nevertheless little served to make this region a new earth so far, in spite of its having originally been presented as the new world. The signs of the times and soteriological dynamic of the Christian faith historicized in new human beings insistently demand the prophetic negation of a church as the old heaven of a civilization of wealth and of empire and utopian affirmation of a church as the new heaven of a civilization of poverty. Although always in the dark, these new human beings continue firmly to proclaim an ever greater future, because beyond the successive historical futures is discerned the God who saves, the God who liberates.[8]

The prophetic negation of a church as the old heaven of a civilization of wealth and empire and the utopian affirmation of a church as the new heaven of a civilization of poverty is an irrecusable claim of the signs of the times and of the soteriological dynamics of the Christian faith historicized in new human beings.

Although always in the dark, these new human beings continue to announce firmly, an ever greater future, because, beyond the successive historical futures, the saving God, the liberating God, is in sight.[9]

WALKING WITH JESUS OF NAZARETH AND HIS GOD— THE GOOD NEWS

On Christology, Jesus of Nazareth, the Christ, the Son of God, I have published several books and articles, and I refer to them. I believe that I have also spoken sufficiently about Jesus in these conversations. Now, following the logic of those we can *walk with,* I will focus and concentrate on one dimension of his reality: *Jesus of Nazareth, good news.* I will draw substantially from what I wrote in 1999 in *Christ the Liberator.*[10]

That Jesus of Nazareth announces the kingdom of God as good news to the poor and that his death and resurrection are presented as *euaggelion* [good tidings] is evident if one takes the New Testament as a whole. But that Jesus of Nazareth is himself good news may be novel. And I think it is important to keep this in mind.

---

[8] Ignacio Ellacuría, "Utopia and Prophecy in Latin America," trans. James R. Brockman, in *Mysterium Liberationis: Fundamental Concepts of Liberation Theology,* ed. Ignacio Ellacuría and Jon Sobrino, 289–328 (Maryknoll, NY: Orbis Books, 1993); abridged ed, *Systematic Theology: Perspectives from Latin America* (Readings from *Mysterium Liberationis*) (1996), 327–28, slightly edited. This, his last article, was originally published in 1989 in *Revista Latinoamericana de Teología.*

[9] Ibid.

[10] Jon Sobrino, *Christ the Liberator: A View from the Victims* (Maryknoll, NY: Orbis Books, 2001).

Accepting that Jesus is God and man, Lord and Messiah, is not the same as accepting something as simple as the fact that Jesus is "a good person," someone who "is well liked," who "is a pleasure to see and know." It is not the same to adore, pray, obey Christ and worship him, let alone organize crusades to do his holy will, as it is to rejoice in the God who has manifested himself in him. Well, this is precisely what we want to do with these brief lines.

Put in conceptual language, to the double perspective of *orthodoxy* and *orthopraxis* in our relationship with Jesus Christ I want to add a third one, which, for lack of a better expression, we could call *orthopathos—orthopathy,* that is, the correct way of allowing ourselves to be affected by the reality of Christ. And in this letting ourselves be affected, the joy that Christ is Jesus of Nazareth and not another must be centrally present. By this I want to emphasize that it is essential to Christ—as essential, we could say, as his being human and divine—to be good news, and that this must be made clear. Just as the believer must accept his truth and pursue his praxis in order to correspond to its reality, so the Christ who is good news must be corresponded to with pleasure and joy. This is what I am next going to analyze, following some clarifications.

The first clarification is about its *pastoral significance.* Although it may seem purely theoretical and only pertinent to Christology, the topic leads by its nature to a broader fundamental question; that is, whether or not in today's world there is even the expectation that there can be *euaggelion* in the church and in reality, although the future of the church and the contribution of Christian faith to humanity may be at stake in this question. So let us say a brief word about each of these things.

As far as the life of the church is concerned, perhaps some in the First World might say that in the wake of secularization, Christians will have enough to do asking people to accept the truth of the faith without asking them also to welcome it joyfully in its dimension as good news. I believe, however, that without this our faith will become vain and irrelevant, as is already evident, certainly in the First World. As E. Schillebeeckx has written: "The main reason why our churches are emptying out seems to lie in the fact that we Christians are losing the capacity to present the gospel to our contemporaries . . . as good news." Asking ourselves what is good news in the faith is essential to giving the right direction to evangelization.

As far as the *reality of our world is concerned,* we live in a world in which the news is not good, certainly not for the poor and the victims, and in which goodness is not usually news. Much more is said about politics, economics, art, sports, armies, and religion and its protagonists than about goodness and good people. In the First World the best theology has concentrated on showing the *truth* of faith, but not so much its dimension as *good news.* We may ask whether in the era of postmodernity the very expectation of the existence of good news has disappeared. We accept our disenchantment. So, no utopias or good news.

Despite this, I believe it still remains urgent to ask for good news. This is certainly so for the world of the South, permitting it to keep hoping that *life is possible*—in this context, the best of news. And it is also the case for the world of the North, so that it can achieve that *quality of life* that it seeks in a thousand ways, though constantly on the wrong path. This, then, is the pastoral and social context of our reflection.

The second clarification is about *the meaning of good news.* In the Synoptic Gospels, especially in Luke, following Isaiah, *euaggelion* is the good news of the kingdom of God (Lk 4:43), the good that God wants for his creation, and to evangelize is to bring the good news to the poor. The content of the good news, then, is the nearness of the kingdom of God, and its primary addressee is the poor. In today's words, the good news is the utopia of a just and dignified life, and its addressees are the majorities of this world, for whom life is their most urgent task and premature death their most probable destiny. We have already spoken of these things at length in dealing with the *crucified people.* Indirectly, the recipients of good news are also those who are in solidarity with the crucified people.

The third clarification is about *how a person can be good news.* If the above is true, we must ask ourselves whether and in what sense the person of Jesus himself, not only his message and his destiny, is also good news. And we must ask ourselves about the subjective possibility of personal appropriation of Jesus on our part insofar as he is formally good news. The first is more of a *doctrinal* problem. The second is more of an *existential* problem. It demands a *mystagogy,* that is, a way that introduces us to the existential grasp of a Jesus who is *euaggelion.* This is what we want to analyze.

Jesus Was a Good Mediator and a Mediator of Good

The above expression may sound strange, but I will try to explain it. One can be a mediator in various ways. In the New Testament, Paul, referring to the person of Jesus, especially in relation to his cross and resurrection, says that he is *euaggelion.* Here, however, we are not going to analyze the good news of the paschal mystery, but the good news of the person of Jesus *in relation to the kingdom of God.* This means, in language we have used elsewhere, that there is *God's mediation:* the kingdom of God, the world renewed in justice and fraternity according to God's will. And *there is God's mediator:* the person of Jesus.

That the first is good news is evident by definition. Whether and in what way the latter is good news will depend in particular on how Jesus was the mediator of the kingdom, with what spirit he carried out his mission, if and how he won the love and trust of the addressees, the weak, what credibility he had before them. The proclamation of the kingdom can be made in many ways: from above, with power, in an authoritarian and even distant manner, fighting the sin of the world, yes, but only from the outside. Or, it can be made from below, incarnate in the weak and participating in their destiny, bearing the sin of the world in order to eradicate it.

Perhaps this language is strange, but we use it to overcome the routine and to make people realize that one can be a mediator in various ways. What we want to establish is that in the *way* that Jesus was a mediator he was already good news for the poor. This is what Peter's beautiful words about Jesus seem to reflect: "He went about doing good" (Acts 10:38). In other words, Jesus also attracted by the way he was a mediator. In the simplest of language, in El Salvador today we would say of Jesus that he was "good people," and that the poor love to meet such people.

We want to insist that understanding Jesus as good news by *relating* him to the kingdom of God—which is what we are trying to do here—is not the same as *identifying* him with it, as if Jesus were already the kingdom of God in person, the *autobasilea tou Theou,* in Origen's words. When this happens, there is a tendency to devalue the kingdom of God, *the mediation,* in favor of Jesus, *the mediator,* which can lead to serious consequences, as if God could be absolutely happy with the appearance of the mediator on earth, because he was faithful to him, regardless of what happens to his creation. In strong words, that could be as if for God it were no longer absolutely decisive what happens to his creation—whether Auschwitz and Hiroshima, the current recent horrors of El Mozote and El Sumpul, or earthquakes and pandemics—because, after all, the Son has been a perfect work. In language that was meant to be shocking, Ellacuría said that "God the Father has produced or turned out many poor children." And he concluded that "this is a primary and massive fact that cannot be overlooked by anyone who wants to talk about God."

The New Testament says that in Jesus "the kindness of God and his love for men appeared" (Tit 3:4), and that Jesus was not only a man, but also a merciful brother (Heb 2:11, 17). The important thing here is not so much the precise analysis of what is kindness, closeness, brotherhood, mercy, but the fact of having to put into words that an essential thing about Jesus, in addition to his "ontological" reality, in addition to his doctrine and praxis, is that he had such a disposition and was possessed of such a spirit that it produced joy. The people of his time, the poor and the weak, did not say it, of course, with the words we are going to use now, but objectively this is what they were saying: "Not only is the *mediation* (the kingdom of God) good, but it is also *good that the mediator is like this.*"

It is known that the Synoptic Gospels theologize Jesus, but unlike other New Testament writings, they do so by *historicizing* him, that is, by showing him in action, and that is where it is existentially determinable whether Jesus was good news for his listeners. And let us remember that the attitude of the recipient is essential, not just optional, in determining whether a piece of news is good or not. Let us look at it.

What really attracted the attention of the poor and simple people to Jesus? Undoubtedly, the message of hope that he brought and his liberating practices—miracles, expulsions of demons, welcoming the marginalized, confrontations with the powerful—but also his disposition, his way of being and acting. They saw in him someone who spoke with authority because he was convinced of what he was saying, unlike others who spoke like fanatics or paid civil servants. In their tribulations the poor came to him, and when they asked him for a solution to their problems, they did so with what, it seems, was always the greatest argument for motivating Jesus: "Lord, have mercy on me." The children were not afraid of him, and the women also followed him. People flocked to him from everywhere, and at the end of his life those people are at first the ones who move to defend him, and in the people he finds his greatest protection. One woman could not contain her enthusiasm and expressed it with the greatest vivacity: "Blessed is the womb that bore you!"

We cannot now go through the gospel narratives detailing the impact that Jesus had on the simple people. Suffice it to recall that he did have a great impact, and for precise reasons. Those who are poor and simple, the oppressed and marginalized, find in Jesus someone who defends and loves them, and who tries to save them simply because they are in need. This, yesterday as today, is rare and is indeed good news. Paraphrasing the oft-quoted text of Micah 6:8, we could say that Jesus, the good mediator, passed through this world practicing justice, and he did so, as a good mediator, with tender love for the weak and the little ones.

If we try to systematize from our time and in our conceptualization the impact that Jesus could have caused then and can cause now as good news to the poor and to those who are in solidarity with them, we can say, as I understand things from El Salvador, the following:

- Jesus's *mercy and the primacy he gives to it* are striking: there is nothing beyond it, and from it Jesus defines the truth of God and of the human being. It is good news, then, that Jesus's heart is moved by mercy and that he configures his life and his mission from it.

- Jesus's *honesty with reality and his desire for truth* are striking, in his judgment of the situation of the oppressed majorities as well as the oppressive minorities, and in his reaction to this reality: defense of the weak and denunciation and unmasking of the oppressors. It is good news, then, that Jesus is the voice of the voiceless and the voice against those who have too much voice.

- Jesus's *faithfulness in maintaining* honesty and mercy to the end, in the face of internal crises and external persecutions, is striking. It is good news, then, that Jesus is faithful and maintains mercy, wherever it leads him.

- Jesus's *freedom* to bless and to curse, to go to the synagogue on the Sabbath and to violate it, his freedom, in short, to do good, is striking. It is good news, then, that for Jesus freedom is not only or mainly bourgeois freedom, not even existential freedom, but a freedom that consists in the fact that nothing can be an obstacle to doing good.

- It is striking that Jesus wants an *end to the misfortunes of the poor*, and that he wants the good, happiness, and joy of his followers, and from there he formulates the beatitudes. It is good news, then, that for Jesus there is a path that leads to true happiness.
- It is striking that Jesus *welcomes sinners and the marginalized*, that he sits at table and celebrates with them, and that he rejoices that God reveals himself to them. It is good news, then, that Jesus celebrates life and celebrates God.
- Finally, it is striking that Jesus *trusts in a good and absolutely close God, whom he calls Father, and that he is absolutely available to that Father, who continues to be God*, an absolute and unmanipulable mystery. It is good news, then, that Jesus is our brother also on this strictly theological level.

To see each of these things—honesty and truth, mercy and fidelity, freedom, joy and celebration, trust in the Father, and availability before God—made real in one person is always a breath of fresh air in our history; to see people like this is truly good news. But it is also striking, and perhaps even more so than the above, that in one and the same person things that are difficult to reconcile in history appear united and reconciled. And that is what appears in Jesus. He shows himself to us at the same time as a man of mercy ("I pity the crowd") and a man of prophetic denunciation ("woe to you who are rich"), a man of hardiness ("whoever will come after me, let him take up his cross and follow me") and a man of gentleness ("your faith has saved you"), a man of trust in God ("Abba, Father") and a man of solitude before God ("My God, why have you forsaken me?").

And so on and so forth. The important thing is that the Gospels present us with a Jesus incarnated in all that is human, and all that is most human. That is what makes him not only a *good mediator*, but a *mediator of good*. Jesus, in himself, and not only because of the news he brings, is himself good news for human beings, at least for the poor and simple.

That is what struck us about the person of Jesus, and we could concentrate it in the following words: it is not easy to find people in history who truly love the poor, but it is much more difficult to find people who love only them and not anything else above them, whether the Temple, the Sabbath, the law (the party, the organization, the church . . .), and who are willing to run every personal and institutional risk for the sake of that great love.

Ignacio Ellacuría—intellectual, political analyst, philosopher, and theologian—was struck by Jesus's way of being. A present witness tells that in an open theology course Ellacuría was analyzing the life of Jesus, and suddenly he lost his rationality and his heart overflowed. He said, "Jesus had the justice to go to the bottom and at the same time he had the eyes and bowels of mercy to understand human beings." For a moment Ellacuría stood silent, and then he concluded, "Faith, a great man."

Jesus is good news because he takes us to what is most ours and most originally human. He is ultimately good news because he expresses love and only love.

We have tried to find in the gospel accounts the Jesus who was good news for the poor and weak of his time. But if we are asked why we have been able to find these traits in Jesus, indeed, why we have even looked for them and asked ourselves the question of the good news that is Jesus, the answer is simple. Here in El Salvador it has happened that the poor—and some with them—are still waiting fervently for the good news and believe that it is possible for it to become a reality, because they have seen, heard, and touched it in large or small processes. And it has happened that they have also grasped it as something real in people like Rutilio Grande and Monseñor Romero, who have announced good news to them and who, by the way they have done it, have themselves become good news.

Monseñor Romero, Father of the Poor

Thinking about how to conclude the good news, I end with Monseñor Romero. And to do so I find nothing better than the account in a book by María López Vigil, based on testimonies of people who saw, heard, and touched Monseñor. She concludes her book with the following testimony by Regina García:

Years have gone by. The plaques of gratitude are piling up around the tomb of Monseñor Romero—on the walls and over the tombstone.

There are little plaques of varnished wood giving thanks for the miraculous healing of eyes, varicose veins, or the soul. There are marble plaques in square or rectangular shapes, and plastic ones in the shape of a heart or a diamond, giving thanks to the archbishop for a child who was found or for a mother who was healed. They ask for peace. Above all, they ask for peace and for an end to the war. And they name loved ones. There are also little pieces of paper where the thanks are in the form of stories, half-finished novels, letters—even poems and songs. And there are pieces of decorated cardboard, pieces of cloth—embroidered, white, or multi-colored. . . . Everything that has caused pain is here and everything that's brought back happiness, too. Nothing is lost. It all comes back to the arms of Monseñor.

One morning in rainy season when the skies were heavy with the day's rain, a man in rags, with a shirt full of holes and dust-covered hair, was cleaning the tomb carefully with one of his rags. The sun had just come up, but he was active and awake. And even though the rag was dirty with grease and time, it left the tombstone clean and shiny.

When he was done, he smiled with satisfaction. At that hour in the morning, he hadn't seen anyone, and no one had seen him. Except for me. I saw him.

When he left to go out, I felt like I needed to talk to him.

"Why do you do that?"

"Do what?"

"Clean Monseñor's tomb."

"Because he was my father."

"What do you mean . . . ?"

"It's this way. I'm just a poor man, you know? Sometimes I make some money carrying things for people in the market in a little cart. Other times I beg for alms. And sometimes I spend it all on liquor and end up lying hungover on the streets. . . . But I never get too discouraged. I had a father! I did! He made me feel like a person. Because he loved people like me, and he didn't act like we made him sick. He talked to us, he touched us, he asked us questions. He had confidence in us. You could see in his eyes that he cared about me. Like parents love their children. That is why I clean off his tomb, because that's what children do."[11]

---

[11] María López Vigil, *Monseñor Romero: Memories in Mosaic* (Maryknoll, NY: Orbis Books, 2013), 302–3.

Since 2014, when I started writing these conversations, several things have happened that point to a new era in my life. In a few months I will be eighty-two years old. My health has clearly been going downhill. A few years ago I had a pacemaker put in to control arrhythmia, and in 2017 I suffered a heart attack. I had stents put in, and my heart has responded well. The type-1 diabetes I have had since 1973 is still active; it usually causes only minor discomfort and dizziness, but increasingly it is causing me major and more serious confusion and forgetfulness. There has been an increase in fatigue, anxiety, and nightmares. I hardly teach theology anymore, although I do give interviews and write short texts. Obviously, that is not the case with this book. All this has influenced my "walking with . . . ."

It is still very real to me that Jesus is good news and that walking with him is a good thing. And "walking with your God"?

What is very clear to me is that, in order to walk with the God of Jesus, one must walk with Jesus, with Monseñor, with Ellacuría, with men and women who are good human beings.

And to express the transcendent dimension of this walk with God, I have come up with three things that point to something more. The first is *with humility,* without fuss, without worrying too much about ourselves as if we were the ultimate thing. The second is *with hope,* especially for others, the poor and oppressed. The third is *with gratitude*: to so many good people who have come out in these conversations; to Jesus, because he is not ashamed to be lesser than the angels and to call us brothers and sisters; and to God, who carries us mysteriously, like everything God does.

And it is good to walk with Charo Mármol. I am very grateful for her drive, her patience, and her friendship.

—I finished writing this text on May 26, 2021

Appendix 1

Pact of the Catacombs, a Poor Servant Church

We, bishops assembled in the Second Vatican Council, are conscious of the deficiencies of our lifestyle in terms of evangelical poverty. Motivated by one another in an initiative in which each of us has tried avoid ambition and presumption, we unite with all our brothers in the episcopacy and rely above all on the grace and strength of Our Lord Jesus Christ and on the prayer of the faithful and the priests in our respective dioceses. Placing ourselves in thought and in prayer before the Trinity, the Church of Christ, and all the priests and faithful of our dioceses, with humility and awareness of our weakness, but also with all the determination and all the strength that God desires to grant us by his grace, we commit ourselves to the following:

- We will try to live according to the ordinary manner of our people in all that concerns housing, food, means of transport, and related matters. See Matthew 5:3; 6:33ff.; 8:20.
- We renounce forever the appearance and the substance of wealth, especially in clothing (rich vestments, loud colors) and symbols made of precious metals (these signs should certainly be evangelical). See Mark 6:9; Matthew 10:9–10; Acts 3:6 (Neither silver nor gold).
- We will not possess in our own names any properties or other goods, nor will we have bank accounts or the like. If it is necessary to possess something, we will place everything in the name of the diocese or of social or charitable works. See Matthew 6:19–21; Luke 12:33–34.
- As far as possible we will entrust the financial and material running of our diocese to a commission of competent lay persons who are aware of their apostolic role, so that we can be less administrators and more pastors and apostles. See Matthew 10:8; Acts 6:1–7.

- We do not want to be addressed verbally or in writing with names and titles that express prominence and power (such as Eminence, Excellency, Lordship). We prefer to be called by the evangelical name of "Father." See Matthew 20:25–28; 23:6–11; John 13:12–15.

- In our communications and social relations we will avoid everything that may appear as a concession of privilege, prominence, or even preference to the wealthy and the powerful (for example, in religious services or by way of banquet invitations offered or accepted). See Luke 13:12–14; 1 Corinthians 9:14–19.

- Likewise we will avoid favoring or fostering the vanity of anyone at the moment of seeking or acknowledging aid or for any other reason. We will invite our faithful to consider their donations as a normal way of participating in worship, in the apostolate, and in social action. See Matthew 6:2–4; Luke 15:9–13; 2 Corinthians 12:4.

- We will give whatever is needed in terms of our time, our reflection, our heart, our means, etc., to the apostolic and pastoral service of workers and labor groups and to those who are economically weak and disadvantaged, without allowing that to detract from the welfare of other persons or groups of the diocese. We will support lay people, religious, deacons, and priests whom the Lord calls to evangelize the poor and the workers by sharing their lives and their labors. See Luke 4:18–19; Mark 6:4; Matthew 11:4–5; Acts 18:3–4; 20:33–35; 1 Corinthians 4:12; 9:1–27.

- Conscious of the requirements of justice and charity and of their mutual relatedness, we will seek to transform our works of welfare into social works based on charity and justice, so that they take all persons into account, as a humble service to the responsible public agencies. See Matthew 25:31–46; Luke 13:12–14; 3:33–34.

- We will do everything possible so that those responsible for our governments and our public services establish and enforce the laws, social structures, and institutions that are necessary for justice, equality, and the integral, harmonious development of the whole person and of all persons, and thus for the advent of a new social order, worthy of the children of God. See Acts 2:44–45; 4:32–35; 5:4; 2 Corinthians 8 and 9; 1 Timothy 5:16.

- Since the collegiality of the bishops finds its supreme evangelical realization in jointly serving the two-thirds of humanity who live in physical, cultural, and moral misery, we commit ourselves: a) to support as far as possible the most urgent projects of the episcopacies of the poor nations; and b) to request jointly, at the level of international organisms, the adoption of economic and cultural structures which, instead of producing poor nations in an ever richer world, make it possible for the poor majorities to free themselves from their wretchedness. We will do all this even as we bear witness to the gospel, after the example of Pope Paul VI at the United Nations.

- We commit ourselves to sharing our lives in pastoral charity with our brothers and sisters in Christ, priests, religious, and laity, so that our ministry constitutes a true service. Accordingly, we will make an effort to "review our lives" with them; we will seek collaborators in ministry so that we can be animators according to the Spirit rather than dominators according to the world; we will try to make ourselves as humanly present and welcoming as possible; and we will show ourselves to be open to all, no matter what their beliefs. See Mark 8:34–35; Acts 6:1–7; 1 Timothy 3:8–10.

- When we return to our dioceses, we will make these resolutions known to our diocesan priests and ask them to assist us with their comprehension, their collaboration, and their prayers.

May God help us to be faithful.[1]

---

[1] The pact was signed by forty-two bishops; later, over five hundred added their names to the pact (*Vatican News*, "A Group of Synod Fathers Renews the 'Pact of the Catacombs'" [October 20, 2019]).

Appendix 2

Ignacio Ellacuría's Letter to Monseñor Romero

Madrid, April 9, 1977

Dear Monseñor:

I have been able to follow very closely and with abundant information the glorious events—death and resurrection—that have occurred especially in the month of March in El Salvador, and very singularly in the archdiocese. Thus I have learned of your interventions as Archbishop of San Salvador. God has wanted to place you at the very beginning of your ministry in an extremely difficult, extremely Christian trance, because, if in it crime has abounded, grace has even more abounded. I must tell you, from my modest condition as a Christian and priest of your archdiocese, that I am proud of your performance as a pastor. From this distant exile I want to show you my admiration and respect, because I have seen in your action the finger of God. I cannot deny that your behavior has surpassed all my expectations, and this has given me a deep joy, which I want to communicate to you on this Saturday of glory.

Allow me, as a theological scholar, to explain to you the reasons for my pride, admiration, and respect. I believe that the martyrdom of Father Grande and the other Christians has merited for El Salvador a singular and exemplary status for the whole Latin American church. I do not know anywhere else where the priests and their pastors have been at such a high level.

The first aspect that impressed me is your evangelical spirit. I knew it from the very first moment from the communication of Father Arrupe. There are many pastors who boast of an evangelical spirit, but when put to the test of fire—and we have seen it in San Salvador itself—they show that there is no such spirit. You immediately perceived the clear meaning

206

of Father Grande's death, the meaning of religious persecution, and you backed that meaning with all your might. That shows your sincere faith and your Christian discernment. It also shows your evangelical courage and prudence in the face of clear cowardice and worldly prudence. It is very difficult for the Gospel to be on the side of the Government in cases like this; you saw it clearly, and with independence and firmness you drew your conclusions and made your decisions.

This brings me to see a second aspect: *a clear Christian discernment.* You, who are familiar with the *Exercises* of Saint Ignatius, know how difficult it is to discern and make decisions according to the spirit of Christ and not according to the spirit of the world, which can present itself *sub angelo lucis,* as an angel of light. You were able to listen to everyone, but ended up deciding on that which seemed most risky to prudent eyes. When it came to the single Mass, to the cancellation of all activities in the schools, to your keeping clear distance from all official acts, etc., you discovered how to discern where the will of God was and how to follow the example and the spirit of Jesus of Nazareth. This has given me great hope that your ministry, which must be very difficult, can continue to be fully Christian in such a difficult time in Latin America when the true life of the church, more than ever, is called to be a life of witness and martyrdom.

I see the third aspect as a conclusion from the previous ones and as their confirmation. On this occasion, and supported by the martyrdom of Father Grande, you have built a church and you have built unity in the church. You know how difficult it is to do these two things in San Salvador today. But the Mass in the Cathedral and the almost complete and unanimous participation of the entire clergy, of religious, and of so many people of God show that on this occasion you have succeeded. You could not have started off on a better foot to build a church and to build unity in the church within the archdiocese. It will not have escaped you that this is hard to do. And you have succeeded. And you have achieved this not by taking the paths of flattery or cunning, but by the path of the Gospel: being faithful to it and being courageous on it. I think that, as long as you continue in this line and have as your primary criterion the spirit of Christ lived in a martyrial way, the best part of the church in San Salvador will be with you and those who need to pull away will do it.

In this hour of trial we can see who are the faithful children of the church, which continues the life and mission of Jesus, and who are those who want to serve her. It seems to me that in this we have an example in the closing years of Father Grande's life, far removed from the extremism of the Left, but much more distant from the oppression and the blandishments of unjust wealth, as Saint Luke says.

Finally, I believe that this painful and joyful occasion will have given you the opportunity to rediscover the true Society of Jesus, from which interested people have wanted to separate you. As I have been able to hear and read, you have given yourself to the Society and the Society has given itself to you. You will have seen that the Society in El Salvador wants to be faithful to Christ and to the church, and it wants to be faithful to the ultimate consequences. It is not always easy and it will not always be right. The Society is by vocation on the frontier, on the edge, where the dangers of all kinds are greater. In this field it is not always easy to get it right, neither in ideas nor in actions. But I think that there is enough spirit in it to recognize its mistakes and not to give up on its efforts. You must have seen in this difficult hour how many truly spiritual and truly capable people the Society has at the service of Christ and the church in El Salvador.

I pray to God that all these things continue for the good of all. It has only been the beginning, but it has been an extraordinary beginning. The Lord has given you an extraordinarily Christian beginning in your new ministry. May He grant you to go forward amidst such exceptional difficulties. If you succeed in maintaining the unity of your clergy through your utmost fidelity to the Gospel of Jesus, everything will be possible.

This is the heart's desire of this member of the archdiocese, now so far away, though against his will, as I think about proclaiming the Gospel. I reiterate my admiration and gratitude for your first steps—knowing them well in their complexity—as Archbishop of San Salvador.

In Christ, Ignacio Ellacuría

Appendix 3

Letter from Jon Sobrino to Ignacio Ellacuría

On the First Anniversary of the Assassination, October 1990

Dear Ellacu:

For years I have thought about what I would say at the Mass for your martyrdom. As in the case of Archbishop Romero, I never wanted to accept that this would come to pass. But your death was very likely, and the thought of this day has sent me in circles many times. These are the two things that most impressed me about you.

The first is that your intelligence and your creativity had a large impact on me, obviously, yet nonetheless I always thought this was not your most salient characteristic. It is true that these things were very important for you, but you did not orient your life to become a famous intellectual, or a lauded university president. To cite an example, I remember that while you were in exile in Spain you wrote a manuscript that would have made you famous in the world of philosophy. And yet you did not give it much importance, and you did not finish it when you came to El Salvador because you always had other more important things to do: from helping resolve some national problem, to attending to the personal problems of someone who asked for your help. The conclusion for me is very clear: service was more important to you than the cultivation of your intelligence and the recognition that it could bring you.

But whom to serve and why? You served at the UCA, but you did not finally serve the UCA itself. You served in the church, but you did not finally serve the church itself. You served in the Society of Jesus, but you did not finally serve the Society of Jesus itself. The more I got to know you, the more I became convinced that you served the poor of

209

this country, and of all the Third World, and that this service is what gave finality to your life.

You were a faithful disciple of Zubiri, a liberation philosopher and theologian, and a theorist regarding community-based political movements, but you did not fight for those theories as if they were "dogmas." Rather, you changed your points of view, you the inflexible one. And when you would do that, it was always one thing that made you change your mind: the tragedy of the poor. That is why I believe that if you had any fixed "dogma," it was only this: the pain of the crucified peoples.

This brought me to the conclusion that first and foremost you were a man of compassion and mercy, and that what was deepest in you, your guts and your heart, was moved by the immense pain of this people. This never left you in peace. It drove your creativity and your service. And your life, then, was not only service. Rather, it was the specific service of "taking crucified peoples down from the cross," very much your words, the kind of words that are invented not only with great intelligence, but with an intelligence moved by compassion.

This is the first thing I wanted to mention. The second thing I remember about you, and this is very personal, is your faith in God. I will explain what I mean. Faith in God was not made easy by your contact with modem philosophers, most of them nonbelievers, with the exception of your beloved Xavier Zubiri; or the atmosphere of secularization including even the death of God that predominated in the era when you achieved intellectual maturity; or your own critical and honest intelligence, not at all given to easy belief; or finally the great question about God posed by the unjust poverty of Latin America. I remember one day in 1969 you told me something I never forgot: that your great teacher Karl Rahner bore his doubts with great elegance. This brought you to say that faith was not something obvious for you either, but rather a victory.

Yet, nonetheless, I am convinced that you were a great believer, and to me, you certainly communicated faith. You did it one day in 1983 when, upon returning from your second exile in Spain, you spoke to us at the mass of the "Heavenly Father." And I thought to myself that if Ellacu, the thinker, the critic, the honest intellectual, used those words, then it was not just sentimentalism. If you spoke of the Heavenly Father, it was because you believed in him. You communicated faith to me many other times when you spoke or wrote of Archbishop Romero and his God, and when you spoke simply of the religiosity of the poor. And you communicated it to me through your way of speaking and writing about Jesus of Nazareth. In your writings you express your faith that what we human beings truly are has been revealed in Jesus. But there you also gratefully express your faith that Jesus displayed that "more" that surrounds everyone, that ultimate mystery and utopia, which attracts everything to itself. I don't know how much you struggled with God, like Jacob, Job, and Jesus. But I believe that God won you over, and that the Father of Jesus oriented what was deepest in your life.

Ellacu, this is what you have left us, for me at least. Your exceptional abilities can dazzle, and your limitations and defects can leave one in the dark. I believe, Ellacu, that neither has the one dazzled, nor the other obscured, the fundamental thing you have left me: that nothing is more essential than the practice of compassion for a crucified people, and that nothing is more human and humanizing than faith.

These things have come to mind over these years. Today one year after your martyrdom, I say them with pain and with joy, but above all with gratitude. Thank you, Ellacu, for your compassion and your faith.

—Translated by Robert Lassalle-Klein

Appendix 4

The Task of a Christian University

Commencement Address of Ignacio Ellacuría, SJ,
Santa Clara University, June 1982

It is a great honor for me, and a gesture of solidarity and support for the Universidad Centroamerica José Simeon Cañas, that Santa Clara University has decided to confer upon me this honorary degree.

I am sure you intend primarily, not to single out my intellectual activity, but to commend the academic and social work which our university has conducted for more than 17 years. Our university's work is oriented, obviously, on behalf of our Salvadoran culture, but above all, on behalf of a people who, oppressed by structural injustices, struggle for their self-determination—people often without liberty or human rights.

At present, as you know, the United States represents the major political force in Central America—and certainly in El Salvador. The social and political destiny of El Salvador, whether we like it or not, depends to a large extent on the United States government. It is therefore of the utmost importance that the United States carry out a foreign policy in Central America which is both informed and just. It must take into consideration the real interests of the American people. But more important for us it must respond according to the principles of political ethics, to the needs of a people who suffer misery and oppression, not because of their own fault or indolence, but because of a chain of historical events for which they cannot be held responsible.

Some North American congressmen are looking for just solutions for the Salvadoran problems though such solutions are, admittedly, difficult and risky. Some churches and religious groups, such as the Catholic Bishops of the United States, have exerted themselves on our behalf. They have pressed the present administration not to intensify our conflicts through military reinforcement, but to facilitate a just, negotiated solution.

But American universities also have an important part to play in order to insure that the unavoidable presence of the United States in Central America be sensitive and just, especially those universities—like Santa Clara—which are inspired by the desire to make present among us all the Kingdom of God.

In this task, our University, also, is engaged. We bear the name of a Salvadoran priest, José Simeon Cañas, who as a congressman in the Constitutional Assembly in 1824, moved and obtained the abolition of slavery in Central America. These are the words he addressed to the assembly: "I come crawling; and if I were dying, dying I would come to make a request for humanity. I beg before anything else that our slaves he declared free citizens. For this is the order of justice: that the deprived be restored to the possession of their goods, and there is no good more valuable than liberty. We all know that our brothers have been violently deprived of their freedom, that they grieve in servitude, sighing for a hand to break the iron chains of slavery. This nation has declared itself free; so, then, must all its people be free."

In 1863, Abraham Lincoln signed the Emancipation Proclamation, forty years after José Simeon Cañas, who was a priest, a scholar and a politician, obtained emancipation for the slaves of Central America.

In that same spirit of liberation our University works today. Let me say a word about how we understand ourselves so that you can comprehend and support us more responsibly.

There are two aspects to every university. The first and most evident is that it deals with culture, with knowledge, the use of the intellect. The second, and not so evident, is that it must be concerned with the social reality—precisely because a university is inescapably a social force: it must transform and enlighten the society in which it lives. But how does it do that? How does a university transform the social reality of which it is so much a part?

There is no abstract and consistent answer here. A university cannot always and in every place be the same. We must constantly look at our own peculiar historical reality. For us in El Salvador, the historical reality is that we are a part of the Third World which is itself the major portion of humankind. Unfortunately, the Third World is characterized more by oppression than by liberty, more by a terrible, grinding poverty than by abundance.

It may be difficult for you to understand our situation, because you are such a privileged nation but a minority of the human race. We, in contrast, have daily experience of this reality, and unremitting suffering which attest to it.

What then does a university do, immersed in this reality? Transform it? Yes. Do everything possible so that liberty is victorious over oppression, justice over injustice, love over hate? Yes. Without this overall commitment, we would not be a university, and even less so would we be a Catholic university.

But how is this done? The university must carry out this general commitment with the means uniquely at its disposal: we as an intellectual community must analyze causes; use imagination and creativity together to discover the remedies to our problems; communicate to our constituencies a consciousness that inspires the freedom of self-determination; educate professionals with a conscience, who will be the immediate instruments of such a transformation; and constantly hone an educational institution that is both academically excellent and ethically oriented.

But how can a university so shape itself, or come to understand itself and its social obligations? Perhaps, just a word.

Liberation theology has emphasized what the preferential option for the poor means in authentic Christianity. Such an option constitutes an essential part of Christian life—but it is also an historic obligation. For the poor embody Christ in a special way; they mirror for us his message of revelation, salvation and conversion. And they are also a universal social reality.

Reason and faith merge, therefore, in confronting the reality of the poor. Reason must open its eyes to their suffering; faith—which is sometimes scandalous to those without it—sees in the weak of this world the triumph of God, for we see in the poor what salvation must mean and the conversion to which we are called.

A Christian university must take into account the gospel preference for the poor. This does not mean that only the poor will study at the university; it does not mean that the university should abdicate its mission of academic excellence—excellence which is needed in order to solve complex social issues of our time. What it does mean is that the university should be present intellectually where it is needed: to provide science for those without science; to provide skills for those without skills; to be a voice for those without voices; to give intellectual support for those who do not possess the academic qualifications to make their rights legitimate.

We have attempted to do this. In a modest way, we have made a contribution through our research and publications, and a few men have left far more lucrative positions to work in the University for the people.

We've been thanked and supported in our efforts. We also have been severely persecuted. From 1976 to 1980, our campus was bombed ten times: we have been blocked and raided by military groups and threatened with the termination of all aid. Dozens of students and teachers have had to flee the country in exile; one of our students was shot to death by police who entered the campus. Our history has been that of our nation.

But we also have been encouraged by the words of Archbishop Romero—himself so soon to be murdered. It was he who said, while we were burying an assassinated priest, that something would be terribly wrong in our Church if no priest lay next to so many of his assassinated brothers and sisters. If the University had not suffered, we would not have performed our duty. In a world where injustice reigns, a university that fights for justice must necessarily be persecuted.

I would like to think—and this is the meaning I give to this honorary degree—that you understand our efforts, our mission, something of the tragic reality that is El Salvador.

And how do you help us? That is not for me to say. Only open your human heart, your Christian heart, and ask yourselves the three questions Ignatius of Loyola put to himself as he stood in front of the crucified world: What have I done for Christ in this world? What am I doing now? And above all, what should I do? The answers lie both in your academic responsibility and in your personal responsibility.

I wish to thank again your Board of Trustees and your President Father William Rewak, for giving me the opportunity to present to you my testimony on behalf of a suffering, struggling, wonderful people. In the name of the Universidad José Simeon Cañas, I wish to thank you for the distinction you have given it through its president. I thank you for the solidarity and support this represents. I thank you also for the personal honor.

Not many of us doubt the generosity of the real American people. After this occasion, I do not doubt it at all.

Index